Samuel Rutherford, Andrew Alexander Bonar

Quaint sermons of Samuel Rutherford

Hitherto unpublished

Samuel Rutherford, Andrew Alexander Bonar

Quaint sermons of Samuel Rutherford
Hitherto unpublished

ISBN/EAN: 9783337264758

Printed in Europe, USA, Canada, Australia, Japan

Cover: Foto ©Lupo / pixelio.de

More available books at **www.hansebooks.com**

QUAINT SERMONS

OF

SAMUEL RUTHERFORD

HITHERTO UNPUBLISHED

WITH A PREFACE

BY THE REV.

ANDREW A. BONAR, D.D

𝕷𝖔𝖓𝖉𝖔𝖓
HODDER AND STOUGHTON
27 PATERNOSTER ROW
MDCCCLXXXV

Preface.

AMUEL RUTHERFORD'S "Letters" are known in the churches everywhere; and here are notes of his preaching. These sermons, as quaint as his "Letters" in some respects, have never till now appeared in print. They form part of a manuscript volume in which are included other sermons of the same author that have already been published. They are carefully and neatly written in the old style of handwriting. Who it was who took down the notes of these sermons at the time, and who it was that gathered all together into the volume, we do not know. One thing is certain, viz., he was a most attentive hearer and a faithful attender on the minister's preaching; for at p. 232 he notes that he had the misfortune to miss one sermon in the course by absence. It is something of a guarantee for the authenticity of the whole to find, as we do on a close examination, that the first half of the MS. collection contains the discourses that have already been published, but in a much more archaic spelling, and with Scotch words that must have been modernised in the printed copies. Besides, the character of the somewhat peculiar penmanship suggests that it is quite possible the writer was

a cotemporary of Rutherford, and not a mere transcriber of original notes.

This MS. volume of which we speak has been a sort of heirloom in the family of one who knew its value, viz., the Rev. David Russell, for fifty-seven years an earnest minister of Christ, first in Hawick and then at Errol, in Perthshire, in connection with the "Relief" and "United Presbyterian" Church. About six years ago his son, James Eccles Russell, Esq., London, was led to tell me of the manuscript volume, and to let me examine it. Other friends also became interested in it, and the result was that Mr. Russell kindly agreed, at the suggestion of these friends, that the portion of it which as yet had not appeared in print should be published. A greatly esteemed brother in the ministry, Mr. J. H. Thomson, of the Free Church, Hightae, skilled above many in deciphering such documents, and in fullest sympathy with the spirit of the author, was not loath to spend time and labour in preparing the work for the press.

The Discourses are throughout characteristic of the man. Try, for example, the lecture on John xx. 1-9. Christian reader, you may glean many a sheaf of the finest of the wheat in these fields. Samuel Rutherford never fails to set Christ on high, for truly he had—

"A thirst no earthly stream could satisfy—
A hunger that *must feed on Christ*, or die."

ANDREW A. BONAR, D.D.

GLASGOW, *April*, 1885.

Note.

N transcribing the sermons from the manuscript volume, a faithful reproduction has been the great aim. The proof sheets have also been carefully compared with the manuscript volume. In transcribing, it has not been thought necessary to reproduce the original spelling, which is plainly that of the first half of the seventeenth century, such as "behooved" for "behoved," "bot" for "but," "considder" for "consider," "heir" for "here," "lyke" for "like," "noblie" for "nobly," "sall" for "shall," "sould" for "should," "sweit" for "sweet," "whilk" for "which," "wold" for "would," &c.; but the Scotch, or Northern English words, amounting to about 400, have been carefully retained. Notes explanatory of their meaning are printed at the foot of each page.[1]

Perhaps the most remarkable feature about the following sermons is the apparent correctness with which they have been taken down from the lips of Rutherford. The

---

[1] A few notes relating to the proper names in the text, and to the allusions occasionally made by Rutherford to contemporary events, have also been added.

proper names, and the one or two Latin phrases that occur, are always correctly given, so that their writer must have been an educated man, and, from the skill with which he has caught the line of thought, in full sympathy with the preacher. There is no sign of abridgment throughout their pages. The student of Rutherford's letters and his other works will recognize in them a full transcript of what he must have said.

Dr. Bonar has kindly read my transcription, sheet by sheet, as it was made, and he has again read the proofs with me. Our common aim has been to reproduce the sermons in a form that will not in any way do discredit to their author, Samuel Rutherford.

J. H. T.

HIGHTAE, LOCKERBIE, N.B.

Contents.

	PAGE
I.	
"Fear not, thou worm Jacob." (No. 1.)—ISA. xli. 14–16	1
II.	
"Fear not, thou worm Jacob." (No. 2.)—ISA. xli. 14–16	27
III.	
A Charge to the Lord's Prophet.—HOSEA viii. 1–3	43
IV.	
The Weeping Mary at the Sepulchre.—JOHN xx. 9–18	66
V.	
The Spouse's Longing for Christ.—SONG OF SOLOMON v. 3–6	84
VI.	
The Church Seeking her Lord.—SONG OF SOLOMON v. 7–10	116
VII.	
The Deliverance of the Kirk of God.—JER. l. 4, 5	152
VIII.	
The Kirk's Holy Resolution.—JER. l. 4, 5	178
IX.	
The Forlorn Son.—LUKE xv. 11–12	197
X.	
The Forlorn Son seeks away from his Father.—LUKE xv. 11–18	217

CONTENTS.

XI.

The Forlorn Son—The Grounds why he came Home, and his Prayer.—LUKE xv. 14-19 233

XII.

The Forlorn Son—The Father's Welcome.—LUKE xv. 20-1 . 249

XIII.

The Forlorn Son—The Father's Expressed Welcome.—LUKE xv. 22-23 268

XIV.

The Forlorn Son—He was Lost and is Found.—LUKE xv. 24-28 285

XV.

The Forlorn Son.—LUKE xv. 29-32 . . 303

XVI.

The Worth and Excellence of the Gospel.—2 COR. x. 4-5 . 323

XVII.

The Apostle's Choice. (No. 1.)—PHIL. iii. 7-8 . . . 348

XVIII.

The Apostle's Choice. (No. 2.)—PHIL. iii. 8 368

Fear not, thou worm Jacob.

No. I.

"*Fear not, thou worm Jacob, and ye men of Israel; I will help thee, saith the Lord, and thy Redeemer, the Holy One of Israel. Behold, I will make thee a new sharp threshing instrument having teeth: thou shalt thresh the mountains, and beat them small, and shalt make the hills as chaff. Thou shalt fan them, and the wind shall carry them away, and the whirlwind shall scatter them; and thou shalt rejoice in the Lord, and shalt glory in the Holy One of Israel.*"—ISAIAH xli. 14-16.[1]

HE Lord, beloved in Him, in this chapter is looking upon the case of a captive people, looking upon the case of a people that were both weak, few, poor, and were also amongst the midst of their enemies. And the Lord knows well what are the thoughts of His children when they are in such a case. He knows well enough what is in the heart of these who are strangers unto Him. And He knows also the heart and thoughts of His people

[1] In MS., "For preparation to a fast, August 22, 1640." The Scotch army of from 20,000 to 30,000 men had crossed the English border two days before, August 20, 1640. The sermon is full of allusions to the army. This and following sermon on the same text, and the sermons on Hosea viii. 1-3, and John xx. 8, were all preached at this period. The fast day had been appointed by the General Assembly which commenced its proceedings at Aberdeen on the 28th of the preceding month of July. Rutherford was present at this meeting of the Assembly, and took part in the discussions that arose in regard to disorders said to have taken place at night meetings for prayer and reading the Scriptures, &c. Rutherford defended these meetings. See Stevenson's "History of the Church and State of Scotland," Book III., chap. 5, p. 893.

when they are in captivity. And for that reason, to hold up their head above the water, which now might have swallowed them up, and put them in peril of losing for ever the promise that the Lord had made, in the words that now are read there is an encouragement given unto the captive Kirk, unto a base, miserable, weak, and destitute people, amongst the midst of their enemies. And in the words there be thir[1] particulars remarkable.

First of all there is an encouragement, "Fear not." (2) A description of the party to whom the Lord speaks this: "Worm Jacob" and the "Men of Israel." And (3) There is a warrant why the Lord speaks this, and why He comforts "Worm Jacob." "Fear not, says the Lord thy Redeemer, the Holy One of Israel." (4) There is a reason of this taken from a promise of God, and the promise it is set down two ways in the words: first, in general terms on God's part, "I will help thee;" second, more particularly on the people's part, what they shall be, "I will make thee a new sharp threshing instrument having teeth: thou shalt thresh the mountains, and beat them small, and shalt make the hills as caff."[2] All the powers in the world that are against thee, albeit they be grown, and high above the rest, as indeed the enemies of the Kirk of Christ, they are swelled pieces of clay, and yet the Lord says that the Kirk shall get strength from Him to thrash these mountains, and to beat the hills, &c. And, lastly, by whose strength is this done, and who shall get the thanks of it? "Thou shalt rejoice in the Lord, and glory in the Holy

[1] These. [2] Chaff.

One of Israel." That is, thou shalt thank Me for doing of this, and not thyself and thy power.

Now, if ye will consider to whom it is that the Lord speaks this, and gives this encouragement—to a worm and to Jacob, a worm! He says to them, "Fear not." It would teach us this meikle,[1] that a distressed Kirk and people they have cause to rejoice upon luck's head,[2] long before the deliverance come. And the reasons wherefore a distressed Kirk and people may rejoice on luck's head,[2] even before the deliverance come, they are very good.

First, if ye will look to God, who bids them rejoice, He knows very well what will be the end of all the troubles of the Kirk, and He knows very well what will be the end of these who are troublers of them; for His Kirk and people He knows that they shall laugh, and in the end shall rejoice in His salvation. He knows there the rod of the wicked shall not always rest upon the lot of the righteous. The Lord's Kirk maun[3] laugh and rejoice when He calls them to it. And there is none who has right to be merry and to rejoice but the Kirk and people of God, and so He knows that their time is coming. And He knows also what shall be the end of the wicked who are troublers of them (Psa. xxxvii. 13); it is said of them that the Lord laughs at them, for He sees their day afar off. He sees them when they are in all their mirth and joviality, and knows there is a black hour coming upon them, albeit they see it not themselves; and therefore He laughs at them.

And then a second reason wherefore the Kirk may

---

[1] Much. [2] In the chance of winning. [3] Must.

rejoice upon luck's head[1] before the deliverance come, is because the Kirk of God they see this also, what is to come, and so may rejoice beforehand, they know how all shall be in the end. And that is the difference between the Kirk's enemies and the Kirk. The enemy knows not what will be the night-year,[2] and what the end of things will be, and therefore they are led to hell blindlings.[3] They know not what is at the foot of the stair where they are coming down. But where faith is, it has the gift of prophesying and foresight there, albeit hand should join in hand, and all armies by sea and land should gather against them, yet it shall be well with them in despite of them all, as it is, Isa. iii. 10: "Say ye to the righteous, it shall be well with him, for they shall eat the fruit of their doings. Woe unto the wicked! it shall be ill with him, for the fruit of his doings shall be upon him." Faith tells these news beforehand.

A third reason whereupon they may rejoice beforehand is this—if we will look unto God's dispensation, His people under trouble may rejoice upon luck's head[1] before their deliverance come; I say, if we look unto His dispensation of justice and mercy, albeit the people of God be worms and despised ones in the eyes of the world, they need not to cast away their confidence for all that, because there is mercy in God, and it maun[4] out to His people. Let them mourn and weep before noon; yet in God's wise dispensation they maun[4] laugh afternoon. Let them be sorry and afflicted, and borne down

---

[1] In the chance of winning. [3] With the eyes closed.
[2] What will occur a year after this, "this night-year." [4] Must.

this year, yet there is light sown for the righteous and joy for the upright in heart. And if ye will look upon the other side, to the wicked, and to those who trouble the Kirk, there is justice in God, and so they may not win away with it. They maun[1] in the dispensation of God's justice be taen[2] order with. They may not aye[3] be in prosperity and laugh. They maun[1] of necessity mourn at last, and the righteous shall rejoice. Their shell of the balance shall go down, and the godless shall go up. When the short heaven of the wicked is expired, they maun[1] sorrow then, for there are righteousness and justice in God, and it is a righteous thing with God, that He recompense to them who trouble the Kirk vexation and sorrow, and to them who are troubled joy and peace.

Whom to is it that the Lord speaks thus? To "*Worm Jacob,*" and to the men of Israel, or to "*the few men* of Israel." This is sweeter nor[4] if the Lord had said "My people," and it is liker God nor if He had called them "My sons," or "His spouse and married people with whom I am in covenant, by all the people of the earth." It says this meikle[5] to us that the Kirk of God is never so miserable, nor so desolate and forsaken, but they have a Lord that pities them, One who sees their misery, and takes notice of it with a pitiful eye. That is an eye, indeed, that is spoken of, Exod. iii. 7: "I have seen, I have seen the affliction of My people, and their groaning which are in Egypt." There is a Father's eye in heaven that is lifted up towards the Kirk when they are in trouble, and He pities their case. See what a style[6] the Kirk

[1] Must.   [2] Taken.   [3] Always.   [4] Than.   [5] Much.   [6] Title.

gets from God, Isa. liv. 11 : " O thou afflicted, tossed with tempest, and not comforted, behold, I will lay thy stones with fair colours," &c. Even such another style as that which is given to the Kirk, Ezek. xxxvii. 4 : " Prophesy upon these bones, and say unto them, O ye dry bones, hear the word of the Lord," &c.

Why would not the Lord say to them, " My beloved people," " My people with whom I am in covenant," &c., but " Worm Jacob " ? This is a word of pity, and it sets [1] our Lord very well to show pity. The *use* of this is, let us learn to make use of all these styles that the Lord gives unto His Kirk and His children in this world. Isa. lii. : Zion, wallowing in the dust, is comforted with many sweet promises and encouragements. And fra [2] our Lord casts comforts into our hand that way, let us put out our hand and to take a grip of them. Fra [2] the Lord is pleased to make many fair promises to His Kirk, when it is black in the West, let us take them unto us when we are under trouble, let us learn to take all our crosses from our [Lord] as it becomes us to do, and spill [3] not our crosses by taking them from any other cause than the hand of God. If we could learn to put all our crosses over into our Lord's hand to be disposed of by Him, and take them all from Him, we would get a better gate [4] of them nor [5] for the most part we do. But it is well wared [6] that thy cross and trouble be thy death, when thou wilt not put it over upon thy Lord, that puts not a crazed estate or the cross of an ill husband, or an ill wife, or wicked children, or fears

---

[1] Becomes.   [2] Since.   [3] Mar, destroy.
[4] Way.   [5] Than.   [6] Well expended.

for the cause of God, that it go not well, that puts not all over upon the Lord. If all these things could be put over upon the Lord Himself by us, there is no doubt but He who is a giving and a pitying Lord, who sees our sufferings and our crosses, He would no doubt send a sure deliverance to such who, in faith and patience, commit themselves and all things that come upon them unto Him.

Again, "*Worm Jacob, and men of Israel.*" This is as base [1] a style as can be given to any—*a worm.* Where met they His married people and the people in the world whom He thought most of, and why should He not [have] given them a more honourable name? The Lord is now speaking of them as they are in the eyes of the world, and not as He thinks of them; for His people are never the most in multitude, nor are they the strongest to look to, nor the wisest, nor the richest, &c. No; for the most part they are the basest bodies. Jerusalem is a forsaken woman; and (Lam. ii.) when all go by Jerusalem and see it so sore sacked they say, "Thou city which men call the perfection of beauty and the joy of the whole earth, all the enemies opened their mouth against her to devour her." And yet ye will get the Lord's Kirk no better (Mic. iv. 6), ye will get the Lord's Kirk there, a halting cripple woman, that has but one leg to gang [2] upon. Aye (1 Cor. i. 27), His Kirk there is called the nothings of the world, those that are not worth the uptaking, the kinless things of the world, the ignoble, base, contemptible ones, the refuse of men! and (chap. iv.) "the off-scourings of the world." Are

---

[1] Mean. [2] Go.

the Lord's people so, indeed? No. They are not so, indeed; for (Mal. iii. 17) they are called the Lord's jewels, His beloved people. Is Ephraim my dear son? Is he a pleasant child? (Jer. xxxi. 20.) How comes it to pass, then, that God speaks so of His Kirk? *Answer:* The Lord speaks so of His Kirk and people as men speak of them and according to their outward estate in the world, for the world sees not the Kirk's best side. The world knows not our Father, nor they know not our joy nor our inheritance; they see not our day of rejoicing. That which makes the Kirk glorious is hid from the eyes of the world (Prov. xiv.). A stranger meddles not with the joys of the Kirk. They know not our joy, for it is hid up with God in Christ. All our best things are hid from the eyes of the world; they only see our worst.

The thing that we have to learn from this is, if the Kirk of Christ seem to be thus in the eyes of men, and then if the Lord, upon the other hand, count so highly of them, then let us not despise them, bourd [1] not with them, albeit they be baselike in the eyes of the world; [2] for rise against the Kirk who will, because they think her strength not to be great, for, as weak as she is, they shall be broken in pieces whoever they be who draw a sword against the Kirk of Christ, or rashes [3] hard heads with it. Look there! they had not an arm to put up their sword again. See there! they be not all broken in pieces. What a cursed word is spoken of these who are enemies to the Kirk and haters of Zion! Psa. cxxix. 6: "They shall be as grass upon the housetop,

---

[1] Jest not, mock not at them. French, *bourder*, to humbug, from the old French *behourde*, to joist with lances.

[2] Regarded as obscure.

[3] Dashes against it.

which withereth before it groweth up: wherewith the mower filleth not his hand; nor he that bindeth sheaves his bosom. Neither do they who go by say, The blessing of the Lord be upon you: we bless you in the name of the Lord." None that sees them at their work shall bless them, but the wrath of God shall be upon them; the mowers, nor shearers, shall get no good of them, but wrath and calamity shall seize upon them.

There is another thing in this style. He calls them Jacob, and Jacob is the Lord's covenanted people. And so it is as meikle[1] as if He had said, "Fear not, despised and weak people, and yet the Lord's covenanted ones." There is not a cross, misery, or affliction that comes upon the people of God but it is the Lord's, and is sib[2] to Him, for the first word is as meikle[1] as they were despised and silly[3]—a worm; but the next word, "Jacob," is a word of honour. We have to learn here that the very misery of the Kirk of God it is glorious, the very crosses of the Kirk have another sort of lustre nor[4] all the glory that is in the world; for thir[5] two words are as meikle[1] as if it had been said, "Base bodies, and yet highly honoured of God, the refuse of the world, and yet for all that those whom the Lord has taen[6] by the hand to be His people, and He has taken upon Him to be their God." There are three blessed things that befall the children of God in all their crosses that the world has not in its troubles and crosses.

First. There is a moderation while they are under them. We may see the proof of this in this text.

[1] Much. [2] Related. [3] Weak.
[4] Than. [5] These.   [6] Taken.

"*Worm Jacob*" He calls them, and yet He says to them, "I will make thee a new sharp threshing instrument having teeth, to thresh the mountains and to beat the hills to caff."¹ The Kirk under affliction dreeing,² and yet they live, hungered and yet well fed, persecuted but not forsaken. The enemies are doing what they can to put us in the grave; and yet even then, when we are in the grave, we shall live. No; there is such a moderation of the troubles of the Kirk of God and of His children that there is not one ounce of sorrow or trouble that comes upon them but it is all weighed in heaven before it come upon you, and thou shalt get no more of it nor³ the Lord pleases. The Lord will have you to drink no more of that cup nor³ thy stomach will bear. He will not have you to drink till thy heart stand. Such a sweet attemperation have the children of God in all their troubles. This meikle⁴ baseness shall come upon them, and no more; and it shall be mixed with honour.

Another thing that is in the afflictions of the children of God, even a trim⁵ lustre upon them. "Worm Jacob," and despised of the world, yet thee whom I have chosen from among all the people in the world to be Mine. O! there is such a trim⁵ lustre on all the crosses of the children of God, that whatever befall them it is well watered over with the love and favour of God, Rev. xiv. 13: "Blessed are the dead that die in the Lord, for they rest from their labours and their works follow them." What is sourer and more fearful-like than death, and yet death being in the Lord it is sweet, and well watered to the children of God, for then they rest

¹ Chaff.   ² Enduring.   ³ Than.   ⁴ Much.   ⁵ Fine.

from their labours, and Job (chap. v. 17) says: "Blessed is the man whom Thou correctest." Of itself correction is sour, and yet coming from the Lord, and being watered with His love, it is sweet, and so sweet, that it is a thing wherein blessedness stands (Acts v. 41). The apostles when they were scourged before the council for preaching the gospel, it is said of them, "They went out rejoicing that they were counted worthy to suffer for the name of Jesus." There are two trim coverings there put upon their sufferings. First, the Lord's blessed estimation of them. He "counted them worthy." Second, they themselves rejoicing "that they were counted worthy to suffer for the name of Jesus." Well is it that we get a blae hide [1] and bloody shoulders for preaching our Lord's gospel. There is glory in such baseness as that is. Our shame it is a glorious shame. Our hunger is His fulness. With it our Christ is a refreshing Christ. Our death it is a life unto us.

Third. "*Worm* Jacob." This is as meikle [2] as the Lord He esteemed Himself sib [3] to their crosses. There is no cross or misery that befalls the Kirk of God or any of His children, but it is sib [3] to God. There is an excellent word which is spoken by the apostle (Col. i. 24), "I fill up that which is behind of the afflictions of Christ in my flesh;" and (Heb. xi. 26) speaking of Moses, he says of him: "He esteemed the reproach of Christ greater riches than the treasures of Egypt." The sufferings of the Kirk and the children of God, they are Christ's sufferings. Thy wae [4] heart, thy losses, thy sufferings,

---

[1] Livid, discoloured skin.   [2] Much.
[3] Related to or connected with.   [4] Sorrowful.

they are Christ's. The world's afflictions, they are bastard afflictions, they belong not to Christ. There are enew[1] under crosses that Christ has nothing ado. Well's them who are under crosses, and Christ says to them, "Half mine." And you should learn to make use of this and see when you are under crosses how sib[2] they are to Christ. Is it your grief and your sorrow for fear that the Lord's cause and His people in the camp be not well? That is a sorrow that is sib[2] to Christ, and He will comfort those who are under sorrow that way. But if your grief and your sorrow be that ye will be poorer nor[3] ye were before, because there is something sought of you to the cause of God that ye will be in greater danger nor ye were before by entering in a covenant with God ye will get none of Christ's comfort then for your cross and trouble: He has nothing ado with it. Well's them who know their crosses are not their own, but they are Christ's crosses, and then their crosses are well winded[4] up in a web of His love, for then it shall neither hurt you nor kill you, but thou shalt bear it patiently and handsomely. That is a happy affliction that is Christ's affliction, and He has waled[5] it to thee.

"Fear not, worm Jacob, and ye men of Israel," and to speak the word with a warrant, he adds to it: "*I will help thee, saith the Lord, and thy Redeemer, the Holy One of Israel.*" What ground of comfort were this if it were said by one that could not help?—but the Lord says it.

There are three sorts that take upon them to comfort under trouble.

First. There are some who can do more, but only

---

[1] Enough. [2] Related. [3] Than. [4] Wound. [5] Chosen.

speak a good word to them. And that is but a cold comfort, to speak a word, and no more, to a troubled conscience.

Second. There are some who take upon them to comfort under trouble, and they can do something; but it is but man's help when all is done, and we are forbidden to trust in any help of man—Psa. cxlvi. 3: "Put not your trust in princes, nor in the son of man in whom there is no help."

There is a third, again, that helps in trouble, who only should take upon Him to help, for He can infallibly help in trouble. But He is a king of His word. He helps indeed where He promises. When God says "Fear not," albeit thou wert compassed about with enemies on all sides, and there were as many devils round about you as there are piles of grass upon the earth, or as there have fallen of drops of rain since the world began, thou needst not to fear; thou may go through the sea then, and the sea shall not drown you, the fire shall not burn you; thou may'st dance on the grave, for the grave shall not rot you. And so this is a well-fard[1] word: "I will keep thee, saith the Lord, and thy Redeemer, the Holy One of Israel." What if Jeremiah or Isaiah had said this to them! No, certainly that had not been enough, but the Lord says it, and that maun[2] stand sure. Then hang by this word, and this word is putten[3] to to tell us that a trembling and doubting soul in trouble, it can get no fastening word, but only that which the Lord speaks. Albeit an angel or a king should say, "Fear not," or twenty or thirty thousand

---

[1] Well-favoured.   [2] Must.   [3] Added or set down.

armed men should say it, it is nothing; and God grant that we trust not more in men nor[1] we do in the Lord at this time. But if the Lord say to a soul in trouble, "Fear not," we may trust in that word. A doubting soul it gets no sure word to fasten on until it get God's word to uphold it. Bind a ship to a rash[2] bush to hold her by! That is but a slim anchor; it cannot hold her when she begins to be moved. Even so to bid a distressed soul believe in the Kirk, or in the Pope's word, or lippen[3] in a Service-book,[4] it is worth nothing to it, especially to a soul under perplexity and trouble, when many enemies are besetting it. And, you know, a *worm* is a beast that has as many enemies as any beast has, for when it is creeping on the ground it has as many enemies as there are feet going upon the ground ready to tramp upon it, and to put out the guts[5] of it. So is the Kirk and the children of God, environed with enemies on all hands. But there is a binding[6] word here for "worm Jacob:" "*I will help thee, saith the Lord,*" and so they may ride it out against all storms and temptations that can overtake them. You may know how many doubtings are ready to overtake the children of God, especially if there be armies about them, and if the power of those who are against us be great, as, if there be kings upon their side. But even when it is so, the Lord's "*Fear not*" is a powerful word to them who can grip to the

---

[1] Than.   [2] Rush.   [3] Trust to.
[4] The Service-book was a transcript of the English Liturgy, but with some alterations bringing it into nearer conformity with the Romish Breviary. It was accompanied by a book of canons in which the Presbyterian polity was set aside. Both the Service-book and the canons were introduced by royal prerogative. The Church or the nation was not consulted in the matter.   [5] Bowels.   [6] Supporting.

promises of God, who can say in faith, "If I die God's promise shall die with me, for I shall hold by it." When God, who is a king of His word, says, "Fear not," what need you to care for hundreds, or thousands, or fear them when they are about you? The Third Psalm says, "I will not be afraid for ten thousands of the people that have beset themselves against me round about." That is a stout soul, and he is the best sojour¹ and the stoutest that draws a sword that lippens² more to the promise of God nor³ to all other outward helps in the world beside.

Again, some may object and say, "I know that there is enough every way in God, but what is that to me, when I am so unworthy? What the better can I be of His promises, I am so sinful and unworthy?" *Answer*: Whom to is His promises made if not to you? If Christ be thy Redeemer, and thou be in covenant with Him, then all His promises, they are made to thee whoever thou be, though never so unworthy in thy own eyes. But that is our great neck-break⁴ in the point of believing, and in the point of faith, that because we may justly find fault with ourselves, therefore we are ready also to find fault with God and with Christ. O, say we, "There is meikle⁵ guiltiness in me, and so I cannot believe your word of promise that I have anything to do with it." That is as meikle⁵ as to say, that because thou art ill, therefore Christ is ill also. A doubting soul is ready to find many faults with God and with Christ. Thou wilt say He is long in coming, and complains that He lets them not soon enough into Him. The truth is,

¹ Soldier.   ² Trusts.   ³ Than.   ⁴ Ruin.   ⁵ Much.

because thy eye is ill therefore thou believest His to be ill also. It were good for us in looking to the promises of God, to look out of ourselves and to look to them in Christ only; for if ye look for any cause or ground of believing in yourselves, or in the creature, ye shall never believe. That is the surest way of believing to say, "Thou, thyself, art toom,[1] but Christ is full. I am a lost soul, but He seeks that which is lost, and He is found of them who seek Him not." When once we come to this, and rest upon the Lord this way, then we take a right grip of the promises. Now for all that we have heard of, or seen, to be against us, and for as weak as we are, yet we may bless God for what is done in this land: four and twenty or thirty thousand men going into a neighbour kingdom. But they may raise five score thousands to come against them: yet if we could grip to this word of promise, "Fear not, worm Jacob, and men of Israel, I will help thee, saith the Lord, and thy Redeemer, the Holy One of Israel;" and if they resolve (if they be put to it) to fight because they believe; and if we who stay at home can be instant in praying to God for them, that the Lord would make many to favour them and make the hearts of their enemies to faint, what would not our Lord do for them who believe in Him?

The style[2] that God gets here. It is a new style, for God has two sorts of styles in His word. There is Jehovah and God; and the Lord, He would hold these styles albeit the world had not been or any created thing. But if there had not been a world, and lost sinners, and a Kirk, He had not been a Creator, nor a

---

[1] Empty.   [2] Title.

Redeemer, nor a Husband to His Kirk. And so the Lord He has these styles of Creator, Redeemer, the Lord of the whole earth, the Husband of His Kirk, the Holy One of Israel, from us, and our house. And we may say two things of these styles that the Lord has from us. *First:* That they are very humble styles, and very comfortable to us; for by that we may see, that He has married with us, and with our house, because He has taen [1] styles from us: from His lost people He takes the style of a Redeemer; from the covenant that He has made with His people He takes the name of the Holy One of Israel; from marrying with His people He takes the name of Husband. This is even like unto a house that is like to go out of the name for want of male heirs, and there comes in one and marries the heritage of the house, and takes styles from the house, and calls himself after the name of it and so keeps it in the name. *Second:* We may say again that the Lord He has no toom [2] empty styles. Many in the world indeed they have toom [2] names and toom [2] styles. The Lord has made many kings, and many of them fill not the chair of a king; albeit they be princes, yet they have not the minds of princes. And magistrates in the Psalm (Psa. lxxxii. 6) they are called "gods;" and yet they will die the next day, and so they fill not the chair of a god, for God cannot die. And many that are called friends, yet they fill not the rowme [3] of a friend; for either they will change their mind, or they will die the next day, and

---

[1] Taken.
[2] Unsubstantial, shadowy. Toom, as distinguished from empty, is something that has been vacated; emptied out. An empty barrel may never have been full, but a toom barrel has.   [3] Place.

then their friendship is gone. But for the Lord our God He has no toom[1] names at all; Isa. xliii. 3: "*I am the Lord thy God, the Holy One of Israel, thy Saviour;*" and Mal. iii. 6, He says, "I am the Lord that changeth not." This should teach us to put our trust and confidence in this Lord who thus takes styles to Himself from us, and to trust more in Him nor[2] in all the men in the world who are not able to fill their seat—to trust in Generals and Commanders, and such others as these who are not able to fill their seat. No, it is better to trust in the Lord who never yet tint[3] a field and who takes no toom[1] styles to Himself. Whatever God is *called* in His word that He *is* indeed. It is a damnable[4] doctrine that the Arminians teach to say that Christ is a King, and yet it may be that He have no subjects; for they make His kingly office only to stand in this, that He has right to be a King, albeit all His subjects they should be apostates. And they say He is a Husband because He has right to marry a spouse, albeit she will not marry Him. O, but that be a most damnable[4] doctrine to say, that Christ is a King and yet it may be that He have no subjects! That He shall be a Lord and not have a willing people! He taketh no toom[1] names to Himself. Whatever name the Lord takes unto Himself is salvation. The name of the Lord is a strong tower; the righteous run into it and are saved. Is that the letters of the name Jehovah that is a strong tower? No; it is the Lord Himself. The righteous trust in the name of the Lord, and to trust in the name of the Lord is to trust in Himself. So that if we can learn to acknow-

---

[1] Unsubstantial, empty. [2] Than. [3] Lost. [4] Condemnable, odious.

ledge the Lord in His styles, and in His lordship and dominion, and put Him in His chair of state, then no doubt but He will be all unto us that He is called, He will be a friend to you who want thy friend, a father to the fatherless, a king to those who trust in Him, and want no earthly king, or has a king who does not his duty to them. He will be a husband when the husband of those who trust in Him dies, or have a husband who does not his duty to them. He fulfils all the wants that those can have who trust in Him.

"*Behold, I will make thee a new sharp threshing instrument having teeth: thou shalt thresh the mountains, and beat them small, and shalt make the hills as caff.*[1] *Thou shalt fan them, and the wind shall carry them away.*" Lest the Kirk should take ill with this style, "*Worm Jacob*" and "Men of Israel," as base styles—as base styles they ofttimes cast our hearts down—the Lord says to them: "Giving, but not granting, that it be so, yet I will help you, saith the Lord, thy Redeemer, the Holy One of Israel." And the help it is set down in the 15th verse, "I will make thee a new sharp threshing instrument having teeth." There is a doubt met with here in this 15th verse. They might have said, "Why have not we just cause to fear, we being but a worm and *few men* (as the word in the first language reads); and so why have we not cause to fear?" The Lord says to them, "Ye have no cause to fear for all that;" and I shall meet with that objection as there is no ground of doubting in a weak believer, but the Lord He has a wedge to meet it with to ding[2] it out again: "I will make you a new

---

[1] Chaff. [2] Drive by force.

sharp threshing instrument having teeth." How meets this with their objection? Very well; for first they are called a worm, and now they are called a new sharp threshing instrument having teeth. A base and a despised Kirk, and base and lightly esteemed in the eyes of the world; and yet for all that a flail to beat the mountains of the earth to nothing, and to beat them so small that they shall be blown away, so that they are not able to bide [1] their straikes.[2] Then ye see the Kirk, it is a small party in the eyes of the world, and despised of them; and yet for all that the hardest party that ever the powers of the world yoked [3] with. Rise up against the Kirk of Christ who will, they shall find that they never yoked [3] with the like of them. Let kings and antichrist, the Pope and his power, and prelates and Papists, rise up against the Kirk of Christ, they shall find that they had never such a tough party as the Kirk is, for the Lord He has ways anew [4] to make His people strong, that they may prevail.

How is it that they become a new sharp threshing instrument having teeth? The Lord makes them so, and were it not so that they are something of the Lord's making they were nothing indeed. But fra [5] they are something of the Lord's making they are strong enough against all opposers; an' [6] the kirk were slain He can win a battle with them; and [6] they were dry bones He can put sinews and flesh and skin upon them and put life in them to make them prevail; and [7] ye were a worm, ye shall be a new

---

[1] Endure.   [2] Blows.   [3] Engaged.   [4] Enough.
[5] From the time.   [6] "And," if.   [7] If.

sharp threshing instrument having teeth, to beat the mountains of the world and make them small, and to make the hills as chaff. Then the strength of the Kirk it is from God's making of them strong. We are daft [1] that looks to our own strength, and to the number of our men. God grant that our eyes be not fixed upon men for our security! And, indeed, I fear that more nor [2] anything that our eyes be fixed upon men over meikle.[3] Let us look to the Lord's making of us strong. And, indeed, we look all wrong if we look not to our Lord's strength and to anything else. This says that we look all wrong when we look to anything that is in ourselves, and look not only to that which is in Christ. Alas! says some one, "I am a great unbeliever, and will Christ lay His fair face to my black cheeks? Will He kiss me who has so foul a mouth? No." And [4] God make you something, then ye shall be something indeed. It is not our wit or strength or worthiness that will do our turn. It is our Lord and His strength who must do it. Paul he is nothing in himself and in his own account, and yet through Christ that strengthens him he is able to do all things (Philip. iv. 13). And, Heb. xi. 34, it is said, of weak He makes strong—"they waxed valiant in fight, turned to flight the armies of the enemies," through His strength; Rev. i. 6: "The Lord makes us to be kings and priests unto Himself;" and Rom. viii. 37, who are made "more than conquerors through Him that loveth us."

How will the Lord do this to His weak Kirk, to worm Jacob, and to the few men of Israel? There are four

[1] Crazed.   [2] Than.   [3] Much.   [4] If.

ways how the Lord does this. The *first* way is this. Sometimes the Lord He gives unto them worldly strength to overcome their enemies outwardly; as sometimes the Lord He will make some few thousands to rise against many thousands and to put them to flight. The Lord will make good that word which is spoken, Numb. xxiv. 5, 7, 8 (albeit he was a false prophet who spake it, yet it is the Word of God for all that): "How goodly are thy tents, O Jacob, and thy tabernacles, O Israel! He shall pour out the waters of his buckets, and his seed shall be in many waters, and his king shall be higher than Agag, and his kingdom shall be exalted. God brought him forth out of Egypt; he hath as it were the strength of unicorns: he shall eat up the nations his enemies, he shall break their bones, and pierce them through with arrows." This was spoken of the seed of Jacob when they came out of Egypt, and had not a foot of ground of heritage; nor had they a cothouse[1] above their heads, nor a sheaf of corn growing, to show that our Lord He can give security to those who are mean and weak in the eyes of men, and as it is, Isa. x. 33: "He will lop the boughs with terror; and the high ones in stature shall be hewn down, and the haughty shall be humbled." He can make them to bow down under the prisoner. Ay, albeit we of this nation were blocked up by sea and land, yet they wanting the Lord's strength and we having it, they shall fall under us.

A *second* reason of this is, Because they who come against Zion, whoever they be, they have seen their fairest day. Fra[2] once they come against Zion they

---

[1] Cottage or outhouse.   [2] From the first moment.

have never a day to do well again. You know what end Babylon made fra[1] once they carried away the Lord's people to captivity, and Babylon is called the Lord's hammer for beating the earth; and yet fra[1] once they carried away the people of God, their well[2] days are done. And Jeremiah he brings in all the nations about against Babylon; fra[1] once they come against God's people, and His land. And among many other plagues pronounced against them, Jeremiah he pronounces this, li. 26: "And they shall not take of thee a stone for a corner, nor a stone for foundations; but thou shalt be desolate for ever, saith the Lord." Fra[1] once Pharaoh came against Israel and against Moses, there came one plague after another upon him till at last he was made meat for the fishes, and the wrath of God lighted upon him and upon his princes and his people. The Kirk of God is a mite, but crack that mite who will they will break their chaft-teeth[3] upon it, that they shall never eat well again. Be an enemy who will to this covenant that God has made with this land and they with Him (and[4] it were but to be an heart enemy to it), it is a hundred to one if ever they have a day to do well. Can the husband endure that any should come against his married wife to wrong her? No; we believe certainly that the Lord He will take vengeance upon the enemies of our Covenant in Scotland, and of this cause that we are now called to go unto the fields for.

The *third* way, How the Kirk is victorious over her enemies is because her head, Christ, has strength enough for Him and her both. You know what is said of Christ,

[1] From the time. [2] Good. [3] Jaw-teeth. [4] If.

Psa. ii. 9: The Lord has put a rod of iron in His hand to dash all His enemies in pieces therewith as a potter's vessel. All that rise against the Lord and against His Kirk they shall be broken in pieces. In Isa. xlix. 25, there is a terrible word spoken there to the enemies of God's people: "I will contend with them that contend with thee, and I will save thy children; and I will feed them that oppress thee with their own flesh; and they shall be drunken with their own blood, as with sweet wine: and all flesh shall know that I the Lord am thy Saviour and thy Redeemer, the Mighty One of Jacob." So this is all done through Christ's strength. For as He is Mediator there is a promise made unto Him (Psa. cx. 5) that whoever they be who are His enemies they shall never thrive nor do well; and fra[1] the Lord has given Him all power in heaven and earth He may take order with all His enemies, for He may head[2] and hang within His own bounds. He shall fill the pits with the dead bodies of His enemies; and in the pursuing of His enemies He shall be so hot, and in such a haste, that he shall not go into the tavern to take a drink of wine there and to take good cheer, but He shall drink of the water out of the brook until the time that He has brought utter judgment and desolation upon His enemies.

Fourth. The Kirk of Christ it maun[3] be a sharp threshing instrument because of this gospel, for the ill and sorrowful days of the enemies of the Kirk they are contained in this gospel and in this Covenant that Scotland has sworn with God. And whoever they be who will not obey this gospel there is vengeance prepared for

---

[1] Since.   [2] Behead.   [3] Must.

them; to let all the world see this, that it is better to make any party in the world your enemy nor [1] to make Christ and His Kirk your enemy, and to comfort those who are upon our Lord's side of it. Let the world say the contrary, whoever they be who are upon our Lord's side of it when He triumphs, they shall also triumph. And is it not enough that we get a part of our Lord's triumphant victory, and that He will rain vengeance upon His enemies and ours? And it is a part of the Kirk's joy that there is a day coming when no devil in hell, nor no Pope, nor no prelate, nor any whoever they be, who have given wicked counsel against His people, if they have not repented unto Him thereof He shall tread them all under His feet, and He shall say to them, "Bring hither those My enemies who would not that I should reign over them: bind them hand and foot and cast them in utter darkness." That is a sore sentence, and yet our Lord has left it in His Testament to His enemies, and to the enemies of Zion. And they shall have a share of Christ's joy who love His cause and covenant, and rejoice when Zion rejoiceth, and sorrow when it is in distress. Look, what is your greatest fear and sorrow?—that which wakens you first in the morning and is last in your thought at night? If it be concerning the estate of the Lord's Kirk and Zion there cannot be a more blessed mark of a child of God than to be rightly mindful of Zion's case; Psa. cxxxvii. 5, the penman of that Psalm says there: "If I forget thee, O Jerusalem, then let my right hand forget her cunning." If thy joy or thy sorrow be according as the Kirk of Christ is joyful

[1] Than.

or sorrowful, thou shalt then get a share of her victory thou shalt help to divide the spoil with her. When Christ has overcome all His enemies, Rome, and Spain, and Pope, and prelates, and thou shalt sit down beside Christ all sweating, then He shall take the napkin of His consolations to dry thee withal. And He shall then lay thee into His heart and bosom, and shall say: "Come sing a song of victory with Me! All ye who were partners of My woe, come now and take a share of My joy. Come and sit down in a cushion beside Me, and rejoice in Me and in My salvation." Now, to this Lord who has purchased this unto us, and fights for the keeping of it, to His Father and our Father and to the Holy Spirit be all praise, dominion, and glory for ever.—Amen.

Fear not, thou worm Jacob.

No. II.

"*Fear not, thou worm Jacob, and ye men of Israel; I will help thee, saith the Lord, and thy Redeemer, the Holy One of Israel. Behold, I will make thee a new sharp threshing instrument having teeth: thou shalt thresh the mountains, and beat them small, and shalt make the hills as chaff. Thou shalt fan them, and the wind shall carry them away, and the whirlwind shall scatter them: and thou shalt rejoice in the Lord, and shalt glory in the Holy One of Israel.*"—ISAIAH xli. 14-16.[1]

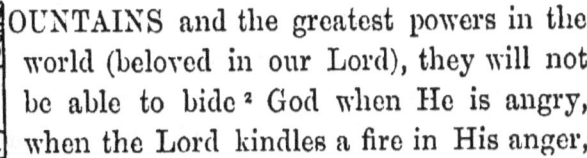OUNTAINS and the greatest powers in the world (beloved in our Lord), they will not be able to bide[2] God when He is angry, when the Lord kindles a fire in His anger, as it is spoken by Himself, Deut. xxxii. 22, He burns up the foundations of the mountains, the mountains they become valleys before the Lord when He is angry; the sea it becomes as dry land. Then all the powers in the world, how great soever they be, they maun[3] bow to Him. Who was there ever that drew a sword against Him and prospered? Who was there that ever exalted himself against Him, and was not laid

---

[1] In MS., "On the Sabbath afternoon," *i.e.*, evidently of the same day, August 22, 1640.   [2] Endure.   [3] Must.

low in the dust? We have here as weak a party mentioned as you could speak of: "*Worm Jacob.*" And here, on the other hand, there is as strong a party as any can be—*the mountains of the world;* and yet, for [1] as strong as they are, and for [1] as weak as the Kirk is, here they are brought to confusion before the Kirk of God. And *the Lord* He does this; for it is borrowed strength from God that does the Kirk's turn, and no strength of her own. "Behold, *I* will make you a new sharp threshing instrument having teeth; and thou shalt thresh the mountains and beat the hills as caff." [2] And who shall get the Psalm and song of victory for doing this? "*Thou* shalt rejoice in the Lord and glory in the Holy One of Israel." It is not thy own arm, and thy own strength, and the multitude of thy own men whom thou shalt thank for this; but thou shalt thank the Lord for it, and rejoice and glory in Him.

Will there be any poor and needy ones within the Kirk at this time? Let it be so, yet, "when the poor and needy seek water, and there is none, and their tongue faileth for thirst, I the Lord will hear them, I the God of Israel will help them. I shall make fountains and rivers for them in the wilderness," when they are thirsty. And they shall want nothing that may do them good.

Is this like the Lord's Kirk and the estate thereof to be in such a case as is here spoken of, who are cumbered this day with the Papists about the falling away of the true Kirk, and what are the marks whereby to discern the true Kirk from the false Kirk? They put this in a question. If Christ shall have

---

[1] Notwithstanding they be so. [2] Chaff.

a true Kirk to the end of the world? And that is but a foolish question for any to propose, "If Christ shall have a Kirk?" for the Kirk of Christ shall never fall away totally, for albeit there be few of the Kirk, and they be silly like[1] to look unto, yet they shall never fail. Many shall be hungry before they die for hunger, for Christ has His Kirk written upon His loof,[2] and upon the palms of His hands. And let hell and devils and all contrary powers rise against them to destroy them; yet they are builded upon the rock, and who can put them off that rock? Well's[3] them who take part with them who are upon Christ's side of it, for all the mountains in the world shall not be able to overcome them and to bear them down.

A second question that may be proposed is this: looks this like the meek saints of God to thresh the mountains and ding[4] the hills to caff,[5] and to winnow them? Are Christ and His Kirk fighting folks. Where fra[6] comes this that Christ, He will make His Kirk a new sharp threshing instrument against their enemies to beat them all to dust? Indeed, the cause of this is not in Christ nor in His Kirk, for they love peace best of anything else. Christ says, "I came to make peace in the world and not for war." And how comes it, then, that Christ and His Kirk, they have aye[7] commonly the fighters' part of it; and His Kirk maun[8] be made a flail to thresh the world, and a wind to winnow them away as caff?[5] Christ and His Kirk, they would live in peace, but the wicked in the world would not let them live in

---

[1] Feeble.   [2] Palm of His hand.   [3] It is good for.
[4] Drive down, break down.   [5] Chaff.   [6] Whence from.
[7] Always.   Must.

peace and ease, since that day that war was pronounced in Paradise between the seed of the woman and the seed of the serpent; they have never been at peace yet to this day. Neither will they ever be at peace so long as the world lasts. The Kirk of Christ maun [1] still be pursued till they be up in heaven with their Father and Lord; except the devil be dead, and so his instruments cease. Christ maun [1] evermore fight so long as He is here and has a Kirk. The mountains and powers of the world they dow [2] not endure Christ. Is this for any wrong that Christ does to them that they dow [2] not endure Him? What is the controversy that is this day between Christ's Kirk and the powers of the world? Nothing else is the controversy but because He is seeking His own from the powers of the world, because we are seeking to have the gospel established, and to have it established in purity and with peace. We are seeking no more, and that makes the pley,[3] and this pley [3] it will last as long as the world stands, and as long as Christ has any followers to follow Him. It is a pley [3] that has evermore been, and a pley [3] that will evermore be; so that it is no new thing to see Christ in the camp. Christ is as oft to be found in the camp as He is to be found in His royal palace. And who are these who are against Christ? The mountains and the great powers in the world. Those have evermore been cold friends to Christ and of His Kirk, and yet for all that they are left by the Lord in this world to be tutors and defenders of Christ, and of His Kirk, for they ought to be mountains to hold the stormy winds off the kirk, that they do her

[1] Must.   [2] Can.   [3] Action at law.

no harm, and to keep the rains of afflictions off her, and, Isa. xlix. 23, it is said, kings they should be nursing fathers, and queens they ought to be nursing mothers to the Kirk of Christ; and yet, albeit they should be so for the most part, they dow[1] not endure Christ. When Herod hears that Christ is born, he says, "He is come to take my kingdom from me, and therefore I will have Him slain now when He is young, that so I may keep my kingdom." Fool! Christ came not to take crowns off the heads of kings in the world. No; by the contrary, there are no such friends for kings, and none so meikle[2] for keeping their crowns upon their heads as Christ is; for, Prov. viii. 16, the wisdom of God even Christ says: "By Me kings reign and princes decree justice." If kings would become Christ's tenants, they might be more blessed under Him than under any other master.

Who are these who are called mountains? Even the great powers of the world who rise against Christ and against His Kirk. And the mountains and these great ones who rise against Christ's Kirk, they agree very well in thir[3] particulars.

First. You know there is no difference between the mountains and the rest of the earth. There are valleys, but only that they are some higher than the rest of the earth is, and by that means the sun when it rises, it shines upon them first, and it shines last upon them at night. Even so the great powers of the world they are flesh and blood as other men are, only they have a glance of glory beyond others when they come into the world, and it may be when they go out of it again; as one when

[1] Can. [2] Much. [3] These.

he is born he may be born a king, and he gets a glance of glory then and another glance of glory at his burial—that is all the difference. They are called gods indeed, but they are only clay gods, for they maun[1] die as well as others. Death and judgment miskens[2] them. No; but it searches upon them as well as it does upon the poorest in the world.

Second. Another difference between the mountains and the valleys is: their uses to come spates[3] of rain off the mountains to the valleys, that do the valleys meikle[4] harm. Even so there has come meikle[4] harm to the Kirk of Christ from the mountains of the world since the beginning: There is a destroying mountain spoken of, Jer. li. 25; the Lord says He will stretch out His hand upon it, and will roll it down from the rocks, and make it a burnt mountain.

Third. Mountains, they are impediments to a servant when they are going a hasty errand of their masters, being in their way. Even so the mountains of the world, they are ofttimes a stone in Christ's gate,[5] when He has ought ado, and yet (Isa. xl. 4) it is said every mountain shall be made low which stands in Christ's gate,[5] when He has ought ado. When will these mountains go out of Christ's gate?[5] As soon as He begins to reprove them, Zech. iv. 7: "Who art thou, O mountain? before Zerubbabel thou shalt become a plain." When Christ is angry at them He can shool[6] the mountains into the sea. What have these mountains for them to boast themselves against Christ our

---

[1] Must.   [2] Make no account of them, overlook them.   [3] Great falls of rain.   [4] Much.   [5] Way.   [6] Shovel, remove.

Lord and against His Kirk, for those of them who are torn away out of the gate,[1] even kings themselves, they are now lying in as little bounds as the poorest bodies that lived with them, and yet those who are behind they will boast also. But the Lord He takes some of them away that all the mountains of the world may know against whom they come, when they come against Christ and against His Kirk, He will make them low valleys.

Here is a lesson to Scotland and a lesson to us this day. Our dear Lord has been letting us see that the mountains in the world they are not able to bide[2] Christ when He is angry. Poor Scotland! that is the outcast of all the nations of the world, the Lord has done this for it when the mountains of the world could not abide it. And there were fourteen great mountains[3] in this land, and there were enew[4] who builded their nests under these mountains, doctors and deans and archdeans, and all these who looked to be prelates; but the Lord He has casten down all these mountains and all the nests also that were bigged[5] under these mountains. And we trust that we may say of them that that shall be upon them which David says of the mountains of Gilboa, "Let never rain nor dew fall upon them, nor any grass grow upon them." So we trust in God shall it be with them. They shall never rise that rain may fall upon them or that anything may grow upon them. The Lord will make them as it is spoken of the Mount of Olives (Zech. xiv. 4), to cleave in the midst toward the East

---

[1] Way.   [2] To endure.
[3] The fourteen bishops deposed "after the serious discussing of the severa processes on many sessions" in the Assembly of Glasgow, Sess. 20, December 13, 1638.   [4] Enough.   [5] Built.

and toward the West, and they who bigged [1] their nests under them shall flee to the valleys for safety. The Lord will make these mountains to cleave in the midst who rise up against Him and against His Kirk. Alas! they have ever far the worst part of it who come against the Lord and His covenanted people; but happy are they who are upon the Lord's side of it, for they shall prevail.

What sort of instrument makes the Lord His Kirk to be? "A new sharp threshing instrument having teeth." Is not [this] against the meekness of the Kirk? for if any want teeth, should not the Kirk and children of God want teeth, for who was more toothless-like nor [2] our Lord Jesus was? When they were putting Him away out of the world, were scourging Him, mocking Him, and doing all the ill that they could to Him, He says, "Father, forgive them: they know not what they do;" "Lord, lay not this sin to their charge." Should the Kirk of Christ then have teeth, seeing Christ Himself had none? Yes; the Lord's Word tells us of three teeth that the Kirk has, and come into their chafts [3] who will, the Lord has given them teeth to bite them so that they shall never do well again (Psa. lviii. 9-11).

The tooth of revenge is given unto them. "The righteous shall rejoice, when he seeth the vengeance; he shall wash his feet in the blood of the wicked." Why, but we may be glad if so be that we insult not over men's persons, but only for their wicked courses, to see our righteous Lord kything [4] Himself to be righteous in revenging Himself upon His and our wicked enemies; and if we sacrifice not the praise of the doing thereof to our

[1] Built.   [2] Than.   [3] Jaws.   [4] Showing, manifesting.

own net, we may justly say, "Blessed be God for it," when we see Rome and Spain and Antichrist, and the mountains of the world that are against Christ and His Kirk and people, fall to the ground.

Second. There is a tooth of justice also which is given unto the Kirk of God. What sort of a direction is that which is given to Saul against Amalek? (1 Sam. xv. 3) —to slay Amalek and all that was within his land, both men and women, infant and suckling, ox and sheep, camel and ass, and to spare none. There is a sword sometimes put in the Kirk's hand to destroy her enemies, and this proves our Lord Jesus to be a victorious Lord over His enemies. These are not the special weapons of our Lord's warfare, for they are not carnal but spiritual for dinging down[1] of strongholds, even prayer, fasting, &c. And (Psa. cxxxvii. 9) there is a direction given there to take Babylon's young ones off their knees and to dash their heads against the stones, and they are pronounced to be blessed who do so.

Third. There is a tooth of the power of the Mediator Christ put into the Kirk's head. Christ and His people are brought in, coming so sonsy-like,[2] Isa. lxiii. 1, and all His garments dyed with blood: "Who is this that cometh from Edom, with dyed garments from Bozrah? This that is glorious in apparel, travelling in the greatness of His strength? I, says the Lord, that speaks righteousness, mighty to save." The Lord and His Kirk have a tooth to eat up all the mountains that come against them, prophesied by that false prophet Balaam, whether he would or not—Num. xxiv. 8: "He shall eat up the

---

[1] Casting down.   [2] Thriving, prosperous-like.

nations His enemies, and shall break their bones, and pierce them through with His arrows." Who will, who will no,[1] the Lord will have the Kirk to have teeth to bite her enemies, so that the enemies they shall stoop and fall under the sword of the Lord and of His Kirk. And the Lord is likely to make it to be so at this time. Who knows but this great work which is begun in Scotland now when it is going into England, and it has tane[2] some footing there, but the Lord He will make it to go over sea ? Who knows but the Lord will make Scotland, who is a worm indeed in comparison of other nations, to be a sharp threshing instrument, to thresh the mountains and to beat the hills to pieces? Who knows but He will make them a sharp threshing instrument to beat Rome and the Pope and Antichrist to pieces, and make all her merchants to cry, "Babylon, Babylon, that great city, is fallen"? O! for to see that great stumbling-block that stands into the way of Christian religion tane[2] out of the way, and then to see the people of the Jews brought in again to Christ, their old Husband, and married upon Him, and the fulness of the Gentiles! O! to see our Redeemer Christ have one fair day of it in the world; to see Jew and Gentile married on Christ, and to see His dominions going from the East to the West and from sea to sea, and to see the whole earth in one sheepfold, obeying the voice of one Shepherd! That is the blessedest day that ever we saw if it were come, and we should pray to the Lord to hasten it that so that may be fulfilled which the Lord promises.

[1] Not.   [2] Taken.

"Thou shalt fan them, and the wind shall carry them away, and the whirlwind shall scatter them;" the enemies they shall be as chaff before the wind. That is a mark of the false Kirk that when Christ and His Kirk rise against them they have no more standing, but they are blown away. Cast the wicked in a furnace of affliction and trial, they will not win out of it again. But cast the godly in a furnace when ye will, they will win out of it unburnt. Cast dross in a hot fire, it will never be seen again. But cast pure gold in a fire, it will come out as good as it was put in. Cast the wicked under the stroke of an angry God, they dow[1] not bide Him, but they are consumed, Isa. l. 9: "They shall wax old as a garment; the moth shall eat them up;" Isa. li. 8: "The moth shall eat them like a garment, and the worm shall eat them like wool." When God is angry at a wicked man, and He begins to strike him, there is no more strength in him to stand against Him than in an old moth-eaten clout that falls out all in holes when any hand touches it; the hearts of the enemies of God's people fail them like water when the Lord grows angry at them. That is a nation that is void of grace that are not able to stand before the Lord when He begins to blow at them. That great and strong city of Jericho, the people heard but news of the great and valiant acts that Joshua and the people of God had done, and incontinent[2] there remained no more spirit in them. There is news of death and of the wrath of God told unto that wicked man Nabal, and incontinent[2] he tynes[3] all his courage. Wherefra[4] is it that all this comes? Will

---

[1] Cannot endure Him.   [2] Forthwith.   [3] Loses.   [4] Wherefrom.

temporal afflictions take away faith, or will it deprive a man of the common gifts of God—as of reason, of sense, of joy? No. No more will any outward trouble take away faith, or take any of these common gifts of God where they are, nor[1] a fire will burn the devil, and that is impossible. But whenever God sets Himself against wicked men, there is another thing backing crosses and troubles nor[1] we see, even the wrath of an angry God backing the judgment, whether it be sword, or famine, or death; and that is the thing that blows away their faith and all their natural parts, and makes them to tyne[2] their strength and courage. Who is the man that will be able to bide a battle, and to stand out when the ill day comes? Only the man who is in Christ and has true faith. Hell shall not fear[3] such a man, nor anything he can be threatened with. Once get saving grace and be in Christ, then thou may be sure thou shalt not be caff[4] before the wind in the day of God's anger. I know if the Lord would kythe[5] in His might and in His power against the strongest in the world, He would make their blaw[6] to fall. But the Lord never tries the strength of His omnipotence upon His own Kirk. But there is vengeance poured out upon His enemies, and upon the enemies of His Kirk, that which the Lord says to Eli by the mouth of Samuel, "When I begin to punish I will make a full end." That is true concerning the wicked. But, by the contrary, the Kirk of God and His children, notwithstanding of all the enemies that be against them, be they never so strong or never so many,

---

[1] Than. [2] Lose. [3] Shall not put such a man in fear.
[4] Chaff. [5] Appear. [6] Ostentation.

they shall be made as caff[1] before the whirlwind. But for the children of God, who are His own Kirk, He says of them (Isa. xliii. 2), "When thou passest through the waters I will be with thee, and through the rivers they shall not overflow thee: when thou walkest through the fire, thou shalt not be burned; neither shall the flame kindle upon thee." And these are the two most merciless enemies that can be—fire and water; and yet He will preserve His own from both. But here is a terrible destruction threatened to come upon wicked men. Have they no more courage nor caff[2] before the wind when God is angry with them? No; no more. There is a terrible destruction told to come upon the wicked—Job xviii. 6: "The light shall be dark in his tabernacle, and his candle shall be put out with him." Woe to that man whose candle God puts out! "The steps of his strength shall be straitened, and his own counsel shall cast him down. For he is cast into a net by his own feet, and he walketh upon a snare. The girn[3] shall take him by the heels," &c. It is cursed ground that he gangs[4] upon. What more terrible thing can be spoken of the wicked man nor[5] is spoken of here? Look again, Job xx. 6: "Though his excellency mount up to the heavens, and his head reach unto the clouds; yet he shall perish for ever like his own dung: they which have seen him shall say, Where is he? He shall fly away as a dream, and shall not be found: yea, he shall be chased away as a vision of the night. The eye which saw him shall see him no more; neither shall his place any more behold him. His children shall seek to please the poor, and his

---

[1] Chaff. [2] Than chaff. [3] Gin. [4] Goes. [5] Than.

hands shall restore their goods," &c. He shall be like a ghost in the night that folks think they see, and, incontinent[1] it passeth out of their sight. They are like a dream that a man cares not for. The Lord shall pull the wicked man out of his sheets, and He shall make him to perish as his own dung from the earth. He shall not swallow down the riches that he gets, or if he swallow them down, they shall be like gravel between his teeth. And (Job xxi. 17–19) among all other judgments prepared for the wicked, the wrath of God is prepared for his children and posterity. The fools of the world, they will not take a lesson of this, for as meikle[2] as God has spoken against them and against their seed. Woe would the hearts of wicked men be, I am sure, if they kent[3] this! I am sure a wicked man would never laugh if he kent[3] this. The fear of hell is a very rare thing. There are few who think upon that what the mystery of hell is. Would ye think upon thir[4] two, ye would think it a very ill thing to go on with the wicked. 1. To think that there is an eternity, and an eternity of wrath, abiding them. 2. To think upon the anger of God, and that it is an anger which will never be quenched. What a terrible oath is that which the Lord swears (Amos viii. 7) against them who sell the poor for a pair of shoes; who wished the Sabbath to be gone that they may sell the refuse of the wheat; who would have the ephah small and the shekel great. By God Himself, "I shall never forget their ill-doing as long as I am God." Woe's ye that have such an oath sworn against you for thy wickedness. Remember what a terrible word is spoken against the house of Eli—

[1] Forthwith.   [2] Much.   [3] Knew.   [4] These.

1 Sam. iii. 14: "I have sworn unto Eli's house, that the iniquity of the house of Eli shall never be put away by sacrifice nor burnt-offering for ever." And there is no greater oath the Lord can swear by nor [1] by Himself, as the apostle says. That is a sore word that there are some whose sins the Lord God has them written with the point of a diamond that they shall never be forgotten. That is a fearful imprecation that is put up against Babylon (Isa. xiii.–xiv.), and against Saul and those who were the enemies of David and of the Kirk at that time (Psa. cix.). Woe unto the wicked, and to them who have tane [2] up a banner against God! Meikle [3] misery and woe abide them. Pre-suppose that a man had a sea of poison to drink, and aye [4] as he drank it filled again, it would be thought a very hard matter. And that sea of wrath that the Lord is brewing for His enemies they shall drink thereof and be mad, and shall fall and never rise again; and yet they fear it not, albeit that be the lot there is appointed for them.

Now whom shall the Kirk thank for all this? "And thou shalt rejoice in the Lord and glory in the Holy One of Israel." God will not have the glory of the victory to go by Himself, and we have more reason to fear this nor [1] any other thing. And God grant that Scotland put not her trust in so many thousands of men and so many gallant spirits. Lord, save us from the sin of idolatry in taking away the thing from God which is His own due. There is an excellent word spoken in Psa. cxv.—when the Kirk had gotten many victories at that time they say, "Not unto us, not unto us, O Lord, but to Thy name be

[1] Than.   [2] Taken.   [3] Much.   [4] Always.

the praise." Not unto Scotland be the praise of victory, albeit we had thousand thousands of men moe nor [1] we have, but unto the name of the Lord be the glory of all. Lord, save us in anyways from meddling with the Lord's glory. It becomes us rather to humble ourselves in the presence of God, and to acknowledge Him in what He is doing. Now the praise of all our works, both in us and for us, be ascribed to Christ's Father and our Father, and to His Son Christ Jesus, and the Holy Spirit for ever and ever.—Amen.

[1] More than.

A Charge to the Lord's Prophet.

"*Set the trumpet to thy mouth. He shall come as an eagle against the house of the Lord, because they have transgressed My covenant, and trespassed against My law. Israel shall cry unto Me, My God, we know Thee. Israel hath cast off the thing that is good: the enemy shall pursue him.*"—HOSEA viii. 1-3.[1]

HE Lord's prophet, beloved in the Lord, he had to do with very rough and hard timber at this time; he had to do with a stiff-necked people. And not only had the prophet of God to do with the ten tribes to prophesy to them; but sometimes also he prophesies against the Kirk and the kingdom of Judah. The most part of this chapter it is prophesied against the kingdom of Israel, the ten tribes, and the last verse thereof it is prophesied against Judah. And because the Lord's prophet he had to do with such a stiff-necked and rebellious people, therefore he uses more threatenings nor[2] he does promises; and he has more threatenings nor[2] any of the rest of the prophets has. For this prophet lived in a time when the people where he lived had no sense, nor know-

---

[1] In MS., "Preached on the Sabbath befornoon," the Sabbath after the fast, August 22, 1640.   [2] Than.

ledge of God. And the kings and princes of these lands, they had set their heads and their shoulders together for bearing down the true worship of God. And, ye know, an ill and a great knot of timber it requires a hard wedge to make it to rive.[1] Even so because they had all revolted from God, and had taken them to a false worship, he maun[2] speak to them as one who kent[3] very well what was in their hearts; and therefore, for the most part, he speaks to them of the wrath and anger of God. And in this chapter, the prophet, inspired by the Spirit of God, he begins with a charge and a proclamation: "Set the trumpet to thy mouth. He shall come as an eagle against the house of the Lord." That is, declare unto them that there is war coming against them from the Lord. And then he gives a reason for it why he makes this proclamation. Some expone this to be king of Assyria, Salmanasar, that was come to against this people, "who should come as an eagle against the house of the Lord;" and some expone it otherways. But this is sure that this was some swift judgment that was to come against them. Some of them thought this judgment is long a coming; but when it comes, it comes with eagle's wings. It is a better judgment, if any judgment can be better nor[4] another, that comes upon feet nor[4] that which comes upon horseback. Against whom shall this judgment come? Not against the wicked folks in the world, but against the house of the Lord, against His own sworn and covenanted people, His main quarrel and controversy that He has is against them. What ailes the Lord to come against His own house?

[1] Split up.   [2] Must.   [3] Knew.   [4] Than.

He maun¹ be very angry when He does so. A father that comes against his own child to strike him if he be wise, he must have a just cause for it and be very angry at him. And the prophet says that the Lord He has just cause to do this. In the first verse He gives one reason of it: "Because they have transgressed My covenant, and trespassed against My law." That is a warrantable judgment that comes for such a cause. When there is sin against God's law and transgressing of His covenant among a people He has just cause to punish them.

What, will Israel make no apology for themselves when the wrath of God comes thus upon them? Yet, says the prophet, they will have their own excuses at that time. "Israel shall cry unto Me, My God, we know Thee." That is the first skonce² that ever the pursued people of God gets to hide themselves under, and a hypocritical people when they are plagued make this objection against the Lord first. Will the Lord, say they, send a destroying enemy against us fra³ Thou art our God and Thou art in covenant with us, and so why should we be put to the worse? Why should Assyria come as an eagle against us, seeing we say, "We know Thee," and we profess Thee to be our God? In the third verse that objection is answered, as there is nothing that a plastered hypocrite can say to God as an excuse of his ill but the Lord has an answer to it. "Israel hath cast off the thing that is good: the enemy shall pursue him." It is not said that they have forsaken

---

¹ Must. ² A shed under which stones are hewed, defence, protection. ³ Since.

good, but they have forsaken the thing that is good. They have forsaken the Lord and tane [1] them to Balaam ; they have forsaken the fountain of living waters, and digged to themselves broken cisterns that can hold no water. And therefore judgment shall come upon them ; the enemy shall pursue them.

Now for the first part that there is a charge given to the Lord's prophet, " Set the trumpet to thy mouth." What is the duty of those who are the Lord's ministers when wrath is coming upon a people ? They maun [2] either tell them of it, or their blood shall be upon the pastor's head. Isa. lviii. 1 : " Cry aloud and spare not, lift up thy voice like a trumpet, and show My people their transgressions, and the house of Jacob their sins." All ministers and prophets of God who would be free of the blood of lost souls are bound and obleist [3] before God to tell them freely of their sins. The Lord says to the prophet (Ezek. ii.), " Tell them from Me what it is that they have deserved." Then all ministers they are heralds sent out in God's name to denounce woe against all God's foes, and to speak peace unto God's friends, and they are messengers sent out from the Lord to tell what is the will of God to His people, to declare whether He be at peace, or if He be at war with a nation.

The *use* of this is, any prophet or minister that changes God's message by the way, and tells it not as God bids him tell it, he is not a faithful messenger, nor a right blower of the Lord's trumpet. He cries not the alarm at the command of the general, as he should that

[1] Taken.   [2] Must.   [3] Obliged.

cries not unto the righteous, "Mercy, mercy unto you for all thy doubting and fainting; salvation to you for all the contrary thoughts thou hast, for there is blood enough in Christ's wounds to cleanse and to save you." And that tells not to the wicked man, "Laugh and rejoice as thou wilt, the anger of God is biding[1] you, albeit thou seest it not." That is a false minister that changes God's wine, and puts in his own water instead of it, that changes God's copy in any point and fills it up with his own devices, that has not his warrant to show you for what he does. As he is a false messenger that will not show his message to you when he summons you. It is a token he is not right. Even so, all these who cannot let you see the copy of God's Word for anything they speak to you, it is a token that they are bastard trumpeters, and are not sent of God to speak to His people. Such ministers run and God sends them not; they speak the lies of their own head without the warrant of God's Word; and whenever there is a service pressed upon the kirk that is not warranted out of the Word of God, that contains such things therein as bowing before altars and sets apart days of man's devising for worshipping of saints, that is a false copy of God's will, and whoever follows it they speak and God sends them not.

Wherefore is a trumpet mentioned here? Because a trumpet is a shrill instrument of war, and a trumpet it is ordinarily blown to waken all and to stir them up who are not thinking of war, nor has any mind of it. So this is as meikle[2] as if it were said, "Set thy trumpet

[1] Awaiting.   [2] Much.

thy mouth; let them hear on the deaf side of their head." The thing that we are to learn here is that a sleeping world and a sleeping Kirk they maun [1] have a trumpet blown to waken them, for they will not be wakened with rounding [2] into their ear to tell them that God is angry at them. But we maun [1] blow a trumpet, and tell you of the wrath of God and of His anger against you. And there are four reasons wherefore we maun [1] blow with a trumpet to waken secure sinners.

First. Because they dawt [3] their own conscience that it may not accuse them for that which their mind lets them see to be wrong. Even as a father does to a dawted [3] bairn lets him not wit [4] by correcting him when he does wrong. Even like unto that spoken by the prophet (Isa. xxx. 10) they "say to the seers, See not; prophesy not," so that sinners have need to be shouted unto as with a trumpet that they may be wakened. Woe's them that can never be wakened with nothing till hell waken them, and if anything in the world be our wreck that same is it, even a spiritual security and sleeping in sin.

A second reason wherefore there maun [1] be blowing with a trumpet to waken sinners is because there is meikle [5] din, and that hinders hearing when God speaks unto us. Gain is crying so loud in some men's ears, and court, and the honour and pleasing of kings, and ease, &c. These things, and the like, cry so loud in the ear of the natural man that all that God's ministers and His prophets can cry unto him of the Lord's righteousness, of His justice, of His truth, they will not hear, neither can they hear. They who know what a disease in the

---

[1] Must. [2] Whispering. [3] Caress, fondle. [4] Know. [5] Much.

ears means say this of it, that when there is a wound within, it makes a crackling there, and it hinders hearing of any sound without; and that is it which makes deafness. Even so, when the day of the Lord's anger and wrath, of His taking vengeance on transgressors is spoken of to some, there is something within that cries louder to them, that makes them not to hear the other, and therefore the Lord He bids sound a trumpet unto such.

A third reason wherefore the Lord bids sound a trumpet is, it is an ordinary thing for the devil to hold men off their compts[1] till they be over the score, to keep them from seeing them till they can do no better, until they come to that that he makes them to think that they are over[2] long a counting with God. Woe's them that let their compts[1] run long, or without taking order with them, for it is a very dangerous thing. Our Lord, again, will have His messengers to set a trumpet to their mouth to tell His people what sin is, for nature will never tell a man what sin is. There are two sorts of convictions for sin that the Lord's Word tells us of. First: There is a natural conviction, and that never lets a man see what sin is. The natural man he is only a patient in that conviction; he never comes to be an agent. The conscience of the natural man may convict him of sin, but for his will and his affections they are mere patients, and join not at all in the work. They know that there is death and hell. But they would have death and hell to bide[3] away from them, and this is the cause of that which is spoken, Isa. xxvi. 11: "Lord, when Thy hand

[1] Accounts. [2] Too. [3] Stay.

is lifted up, they will not see;" Amos vi. 3: "They put the ill day far from them," and fra[1] they think the ill day to be far fra[1] them, and fra[1] they see not the hand of God lifted up, albeit all the world should cry to them, they will not hear nor make them to know what they are doing. Second: The Word of God tells us of a spiritual conviction where God is an agent, and man himself He convicts also—1 Cor. xi. 31: "If we would judge ourselves, we should not be judged of the Lord;" Mic. vii. 9: "I will bear the indignation of the Lord, because I have sinned against Him." There is an evident mark of one who hears the voice of God convicting of sin when they come to that.

A fourth reason wherefore a trumpet maun[2] be blown is because to believe news of the wrath of God and of the Lamb is a supernatural thing, and so the spirit of nature will never make a man to believe them. Nature will never tell a man the thousandth part of the ill and sinfulness of sin, and therefore the Lord maun[2] cry it into the soul as with a trumpet.

Use. Well's that soul whom the Lord works upon in time, and He makes to hear Him when He cries. Well were Scotland if they wakened in time out of their security! I durst say, if Scotland were wakened in the name of that Lord, who sent me here to speak to you, that mercy should be the end of all thir[3] tumults and troubles that have been among us. There is nothing that hitherto has been the wreck of Scotland but only security, and that the sinners of Scotland have never been wakened. There be two things that serve for

[1] From the time.   [2] Must.   [3] These.

wakening sinners out of their security, and we have both these to waken us.

First: The sins of the land wherein we live call upon us to be humbled. And[1] there were no more but the drunkenness, the atheism, the hypocrisy, the ignorance of God, the sins of the families of the land in not setting up the worship of God, we have just cause to be humbled for these and for the like.

Another thing which calls for humiliation is when judgment is already begun, and that is among us. And God knows if it be not time for us now to take our pleasure and ease, and to lay down our heads upon a cod[2] of the devil's stopping[3] when the Lord's ark is in the fields, and when the Lord's people of this land are entering into a strange land; and God knows who are their friends or who are their foes into it; and yet we trust that God will make the people of that land to be for their good, and will cause them sell them meat and drink, and what they stand in need of, and that He who has said, "Touch not mine anointed, and do my prophets no harm," will do for them, albeit they should not show themselves friends to them. But when the Lord's glory is in such hazard, woe to them who are not praying to God for preserving, and for them who are in hazard for it, and are not humbled now for them, for they shall get none of our Lord's comforts in that day when He shall laugh and rejoice, and shall be set up high above all His enemies. They will not do something now when our Lord maun[4] either die, or die when we are like to be an undone people, if He die not for us. Woe to them! but

[1] If. [2] Pillow. [3] Stuffing. [4] Must.

we trust that our Lord's salvation is not far off, but He will help us in time for His covenant's sake, seeing we are a people that are in covenant with Him; albeit the people of this land were all devils and remediless sinners. He will help us now, and take another time for punishing any wrongs of that kind.

There is a reason given for this in the next place why the Lord's prophet should set the trumpet to his mouth: "He shall come as an eagle against the house of the Lord." What king this was that at this time was threatened to come against thir[1] people is differed upon by some of the interpreters. That it was Salmanasar, as some say, it is not likely, and yet it is sure that Assyria was to come against thir[1] people, and to overcome them, and he was to come against them in a fierce and terrible manner, but we leave that. There are two sorts of judgments that come against the Kirk of God. There are some judgments that come upon four feet to them, that come, as it were, upon eagle's wings. And some judgments that come at leisure again, such as the wrath of God that came upon the old world. It was an hundred and twenty years coming upon them or it lighted, and yet for all that it came [at] last. Let the wicked in the world say as they will, yet the wrath of the Lord is long in coming, yet He is aye[2] coming, and His judgment and wrath against the wicked sleep not. Isa. xxx. 18: "The Lord waits that He may be gracious, therefore will He be exalted, that He may have mercy upon you, for the Lord is a God of judgment." The judgments of God sometimes they go at leisure, but they

---

[1] This.   [2] Always.

will come. 2 Pet. iii. 4, there is a reason asked for this, wherefore the Lord's judgments that He has threatened are so longsome in coming? And it is answered, "The Lord delays it, not willing that any should perish, but that all should come to repentance. But the day of the Lord will come as a thief in the night." This is referred to the words that are spoken before; He is long-suffering to us-ward, not willing that any should perish. So that the enemies of the grace of God they can get no ground for their false doctrine.

But the Lord has other judgments that come not slowly but swiftly, and upon four feet as it were. And the Lord's Word, it uses three comparisons to show this swiftness of the Lord's judgments. This text that we have read says that they come with eagle's wings, and this is the king of all flying fowls, and comes with a clap upon the prey thereof. So do the judgments of God upon His enemies sometimes. The second word that is said for that is written, 1 Thess. v. 3, destruction shall come upon the wicked as pains upon a woman in travail. So is it with those who are wicked men. When they think least of destruction to come upon them, and when are preaching peace to themselves, and are bigging[1] their castles upon high that they think no evil shall come near them, then the wrath and anger of God it breaks out upon them and destroys them. The third comparison for showing the swiftness of the coming of the judgment of the wicked, it is in the Prov. i. 27, it is said thereof that their destruction cometh as a whirlwind, and ye know a whirlwind is a thing that comes

[1] Building.

very suddenly. For presently before it there is a calm, and incontinent[1] after the calm there comes a blast of a whirlwind that blows away all light things where it comes. Even so does the wrath of God when it comes upon the wicked. They see nothing but a calm before, and then after their greatest calm incontinently[1] the whirlwind of the wrath of God comes, and blows them away root and branches.

Let our *use* of this be to learn to make use of the time which God gives unto us, for if the Lord's wrath come after such a manner upon His enemies, it is best for all to be looking their counts[2] in time. Well's them that has all their counts[2] laid and fitted[3] before the Lord come upon them to call them to account. He is a blessed soul who can learn wisdom from the foolishness of the five sleeping virgins, and so escapes the wrath of God that comes upon the wicked in the world. O, but that be a sorrowful saying which that man in the gospel says, " Soul, take thy rest, for thou hast enough laid up for many years. Fool!"—is that well said?—"this night thy soul shall be taken from thee, and then whose shall all these things be?" The very time when he is proclaiming peace and ease to himself, aye, when thou art proclaiming rest every way to thyself, it may be that even then the Lord shall send a messenger to take thy soul from you as was done to Him. And what will all thy full barns and thy renewed confidence in the world that thou lippened[4] so meikle[5] unto, do to you then? Well's them who are prepared again the Lord come to

[1] Immediately.   [2] Accounts.   [3] Examined.
[4] Trusted.   [5] Much.

call upon them. They fear not His call when it comes. What if the Lord shall be pleased to send a trial upon this land, and upon us of this congregation who think they shall be most able to stand out against any trial? None shall be able to stand out against the trial as these who can say in effect that there is no new event come upon them but that which formerly they looked might be, and were preparing themselves for the same; who can say there they resolved to be content, and they are content to quit husband, wife, children, life, lands, and rents, and all for their Lord and for His cause? And so let every one take pains to read over the count of their old sins—the night-drinker for his drunkenness, the blasphemer of God's name for his blasphemy, and such as were anyways art and part bringing in a new worship in the Kirk of God in this land, who consented unto the five articles of Perth, &c.,[1] and be humbled before God for them. If ye would have a lap of Christ's garment to cover you in the ill-day, if ye would be safe when the Lord comes against the sinners of Zion as an eagle, count for your old sins and be humbled for them and ye shall be safe.

Another thing that we have to mark in this comparison is, What is it that leads the eagle to come against the prey? Nothing else but the smell of the prey.

[1] In 1618, an Assembly at Perth formed of members chosen according to directions from court, passed the Five Articles, viz., kneeling at the sacrament of the supper, private administration of baptism, private communicating, observance of holidays, and confirmation. These articles were afterwards, amidst much opposition, ratified by the Parliament held at Edinburgh, August 4, 1621. They were enforced with rigour. Ministers were threatened with deposition if they would not submit to them. See Row's "History of the Kirk of Scotland," p. 318, &c.

What was it, think ye, that led Assyria to come against the people of God when they came? Was it the glory of God? No; it was nothing else but the love of the world and the things thereof, without any respect to God's glory. Our Saviour Christ says, Matt. xxiv. 28: "Where the carcases are, thither will the eagles resort." Wherever there is a breakfast for the eagles, they will be there. Even so, wherever the enemies of the Kirk of God may get their vantage against the same, they will be there. It is a plain instinct of nature that leads the eagles to the prey, and hunger is enough to them to make them seek where the prey is. And the thing that leads the enemies of the Kirk of God to come against the Kirk is nothing else but the malice they have against the Kirk and the love of blood. They have such a greedy desire after it. And the Lord's Spirit tells of Nebuchadnezzar that was drunk with the blood of His people, and that he coveted after the same. We may thank the Lord for this that we know what it is that leads on the enemies of the Kirk to come against His Kirk, that it is not the Lord nor His glory. Is the end that they have before them, think ye, the Lord or His glory? No, no! say what they will. They will say the Divine Servicebook which our enemies stand for this day, as one of them imprudently has said of it, that it is a Divine book, and that there is more sound divinity therein nor[1] in all the extemporal prayers of all the ministers, both in our neighbour land and in this land also. But let them say what they will, it is nothing but themselves and the filling of their fat bellies and the pleasures of the world

[1] Than.

which they have been and are still seeking. It is a foolish thing for the enemies of the grace of God to say that man's free will it is a thing indifferent to choose or to refuse anything as it pleases, whether it be good or ill. Is the eagle's hunger a thing indifferent for the eagle to seek to have it stayed or not? No; it is natural for it to seek to have it stayed by the prey. They say there be three things that show this that the will of man is a thing indifferent. First, they say there is in man a thing which they call indifference to do good or to do ill at his pleasure. Second, they say that there is a conscience within those who are enemies to God as well as these have a conscience who are in favour with Him; but that conscience will not keep them in if so be they want grace. Third, they say they have the awe of the Lord in His Word to keep them from sin, and that will be a restraint to them. But there are other three which we may set against these, which are also in every man by nature, that sets them a work to do as ill from their conception. First, there is the habit of natural corruption, that leads them to commit sin; for natural corruption, as they say, is not like a pirate, that comes out of the harbour, and it is a thing indifferent for it to go east or to go west, and so they go where they think they may best find their prey. Nay, natural corruption is not a thing indifferent, but it leads every man captive to the law of sin. Second, there is in every man the habit of acquired corruption, beside the natural corruption which is in all by nature. He has more sin added to that sin wherein he was born, and that leads him on to commit sin. Third, is an individual induration that is come upon wicked men, whereby God has tied them in His righteous judgment to sin and given them over to their own wicked heart, that whether they will or not by reason of that individual induration that is come upon them they maun[1] sin. Well's them that has their will guided by the grace of God, and not by another thing. See what it is that makes ye to stand for the cause of God, whether it be because there are thousands and multitudes upon Christ's side of it, and it would be hard with thee if thou dost otherways? That is a wrong motive, and it will not miss to fail thee if there come any trial. But that is a gracious freewill that resolves to stand in defence of the cause of God, and to stand by the same albeit there were no more upon Christ's side of it, that albeit all others should turn their backs upon Him, yet they will stand with Christ where He is.

What is the quarrel that this eagle has against the house of the Lord, and against His covenanted people, for it would be thought, Who should be free of straik[2] if so be that the Lord's people be not free of it? No; by the contrar,[3] you know it is said, "Judgment must begin at the house of God;" and, Ezek. ix. 1, where those six men are sent out with slaughter weapons in their hands to slay all in the city save only those that were marked by the man with pennar[4] inkhorn, even Christ, they are commanded to begin at the Lord's sanctuary. Whenever wrath is a dealing,[5] professors that have gone on in a wrong course they shall be sure to get the first dint[6] of it. And so think not with your-

---

[1] Must.   [2] Stroke.   [3] On the contrary.
[4] Pen-case.   [5] Being distributed.   [6] Opportunity.

selves that a profession will save you when the ill days [come]. Now there be three ills in a bare profession that will rather hasten wrath upon men nor[1] keep it off.

First. Where there is a profession of religion there is more light, nor[1] where there is not a profession; at least, there should be more light, and that makes the wrath to come sooner, and to light fiercer and hotter upon those who have it, nor[1] upon those who have no profession at all. The more profession and the greater light thou hast, if so be that thou go against the same, thou shalt get the more straikes,[2] and the greater wrath shall light upon you. Of all the enemies [he] that is an house enemy, ye know he is the worst enemy. A minister that goes with a gown upon him, and bears a Bible about with him, if so be that he be false, he is the worst enemy that the Kirk of Christ has. You know who it was that sold Christ our Lord. Even Judas who was one of His disciples, and when he was betraying Him he seemed to be very kind to Him, for even then he would kiss Him, and our Lord says to him, "Friend, betrayest thou the Son of man with a kiss?" and it is very ordinary to be so. The worst enemies that the Kirk of Christ has in our neighbour kingdom are those that are called the heads of the Kirk, and the reverend fathers in God, Canterbury,[3] and those of that kind. Those are the greatest enemies that Christ and our Father and His have, and it is they who betray Him and His cause.

Another ill that comes of a profession is; ye know the

[1] Than. [2] Strokes.
[3] Laud was Archbishop of Canterbury from 1633 to 1641.

Spirit of God in His word uses to reckon from a profession; Amos iii. 2: "You only have I known of all the families in the earth: therefore will I punish you for all your iniquities;" "I made you My chosen people beyond all others, and therefore I will not let you gang[1] unpunished." The Lord cannot endure a people who have a profession of religion to sin against Him as others do. A lord or a laird dow[2] not endure a thrisle[3] to be in his garden, but gars[4] pluck it up by the roots, and cast it over the dike. He cares not to let many thrisles stand in the mountain, but for a thrisle[3] in his garden he dow[2] not endure that. Those who give out themselves to be the Lord's beloved people, and yet are barren of any good fruits, and[5] there be a sore judgment in the world it shall light upon such.

A third ill that comes of a profession is; we trow[6] that a profession makes black sins to become white sins. No; it is not so. David's adultery is adultery as well as the adultery of the greatest reprobate that is; albeit his adultery be tane[7] away, and theirs is to be kept to the fore[8] against them, yet in themselves they are one. The enemies of the grace of God they put a calumny upon us in this, when they say that we say, "God hates not the sin of the elect." No; we say, and affirm it, that the Lord He hates their sin; but withal, He hates not their persons but loves them, and for temporal judgments, albeit they miss spiritual and eternal judgments, they shall not miss them who are guilty of any sin or goes against the Lord's covenant,

---

[1] Go. [2] Can. [3] Thistle. [4] Causes it to be plucked, &c.
[5] If. [6] Believe. [7] Taken. [8] Still remaining.

or seem to be for it, and are not so in heart. Though they were never so dear to God, even as dear as Coniah, as it is said, Jer. xxii. 24: " As I live, saith the Lord, though Coniah the son of Jehoiakim king of Judah were the signet upon My right hand, yet would I pluck thee hence; and I will give thee into the hand of them that seek thy life," &c. And so of all the sore judgments that come upon any people, it shall come upon them who profess the Lord and religion, and are not an honour to their profession. I am sure this is Scotland's note. Some it may be will be ready to say, " I am sure the Lord will defend me, seeing I am a covenanter, and it is God's covenant." No; but if there be a waled[1] straik[2] for any, if thou be not a heart-covenanter, it shall light upon you. The Lord has a judgment prepared for you, albeit thou shouldst never go unto the fields because thou hast no more but a name and a profession thereof. Woe's them that know no more of religion but only the bare name of it!

The prophet goes on in the next verse to tell what a people the people of Israel were, and what they shall do under their trouble. Israel shall say unto me, " My God, we know Thee;" " Thou art our God, and we know it that Thou art our God." This is an objection to what has been said before; shall Assyria come against the Kirk of God as an eagle? No; it may not be so, for we will tell Him that He is our God, and we are His people, and therefore we will cry unto Him in our distress and trouble. There are three things contained in this prayer. First, that Israel in their distress they will

[1] Chosen.   [2] Stroke.

cry. Second, that in their distress they will cry, "My God." Third, they will cry, "My God, we know Thee."

First: That they will cry to God under their distress and trouble; it teaches us this far that hypocrites when they are under the hand of God they are all very holy folks then. In Judges x. 10, and in divers other parts, it is said of the predecessors of thir[1] same people, in their distress they cried unto the Lord, and acknowledged they had sinned against Him; Jer. ii. 27, in prosperity people turned their back upon God, "and not their face; but in the time of their trouble they will say, Arise, and save us." This is an ordinary way that we use when we can do no better, then we cry unto the Lord for help and deliverance; Psa. lxxviii. 34: "When he slew them, they sought him: and they returned and inquired early after God. And they remembered that God was their Rock, and the Most High God their Redeemer." When the vengeance of God was lying sore and heavy upon them, they cried unto the Lord, "Lord, save us." When anything ailes hypocrites they will cry fast to Christ then. O! but there be many who will be content to winter Christ that cannot be content to summer Him also. When worldly men see the hand of God to be upon them; O! but they will seem to be holy and to be devout then. But whenever the hand of God is tane[2] off them again, incontinent[3] they return unto their old ways. This should make us to examine bed holiness, and holiness that comes by reason of crosses very well. For there are many that in their sickness,

[1] This.   [2] Taken.   [3] Immediately.

and when they are under the hand of God any way, they will cry fast for the minister then, and seem to be sorry for their former ill-spent time, and will promise very fair if God will spare them then they shall be better servants to Him in all time coming; and yet when time is granted to them they will return after that to be as ill every way as ever they were before. There are three things that we would [1] try of our holiness in such a case. First: We would [1] try whether it be our own holiness and ease, or if it be God Himself that makes us to cry to Him, and to humble ourselves. Well's that soul that humbles itself under the mighty hand of God, and is brought home to himself by its troubles. Second: In trouble compare thir [2] two together, whether you think it better to be guilty, or if ye think it best to be miserable; if you had rather choose misery before you choose guiltiness; and if ye be more for sin committed than ye are for the misery that come upon you because of sin. There are three things that we look not to in our afflictions. First: For the present our punishment or the afflictions of any, they are not grace. Affliction may well restrain the act of pride for the present, but it cannot restrain the habit thereof. As in Ahab and in Cain when punishment was upon them, the act of pride it was restrained indeed, but the habit thereof was not restrained. Second: We would consider that all the crosses in the world they will do no good unto any, if so be they be not blessed unto us by the cross of Christ. No; they will rather make us worse if He bless them not. The Lord He complains of His people, Amos viii., that

[1] Should.   [2] These.

the more He struck and plagued them the more they ran away from Him. Third: We would[1] remember that affliction of itself is not grace at all, albeit it be a means whereby the Lord works grace in the hearts of His own children, and makes them pliable for it. Fire, ye know, changes not the nature of metals, to make one metal of another; it may well make them hot and soft, yet for all that it cannot make iron gold. Even so affliction cannot make the devil's iron to become God's gold; it may well make it some softer. And so we had need to try whether our afflictions they be blessed of God or not; and we had need to try our holiness then. There are many who make a form to pray to God now, who have their son in the camp, or their husband, that, it may be, never made an errand to pray to God before, and yet for all that has a crooked heart within them. It is not an easy thing to come rightly to Christ. It is no marvel, nor[2] the enemies of God's grace say it is an easy thing to come to Christ and to believe, because they know nothing of it; but it is not easier than that which is spoken of, John xii. 32.: "When I am lifted up, I shall draw all men unto Me." It is a pull of God's arm that maun[3] do our turn to draw us to Him, and not all the afflictions and calamities in the world. Oh, that the Lord will be pleased to bless our public trials in this land, and that He would let all see that it is not good bourding[4] with the Lord now at this time, when the Lord is taking away the husband from the wife, the father from the children, the child from the parents, the friend from the friends, the minister from the flock, &c. It is time for us to

[1] Should. [2] Than. [3] Must. [4] Josting, mocking at.

lift up ourselves in prayer to God, now beseeching Him that He would make His hand to work more and more for us. Well is the soul that comes under the hand of God. Hos. v. 15 it is said, "In their affliction they will seek Me early." Well's that soul that seeks home to God by its afflictions. There is a blessed word spoken (Hos. ii. 6), when the Kirk is running away from God and there is a hedge of thorns set in her way that she cannot win away from Him; when she is following her other lovers and cannot overtake them, she says, "I will go and return to my first love, for then it was better with me nor[1] now." Well waured[2] trouble and affliction that come upon any soul when it comes home to the Lord, and all the dross thereof is tane[3] away, and when a people are brought home, as it is spoken (Jer. l. 5) of Israel and Judah. "Come, and let us join ourselves in a perpetual covenant with the Lord, never to be forgotten." That is a blessed trouble for evermore that leads us home nearer to our Lord. Now the Lord Himself, who is able to do this unto us, draw us nearer unto Himself by all the crosses and afflictions that come upon us. And to this Lord who can do this for us, to the Son of God, Christ Jesus, to His Father and our Father, and the Spirit of grace, be everlasting praise and glory.—Amen.

[1] Than.   [2] Expended.   [3] Taken.

The Weeping Mary at the Sepulchre.

" *For as yet they knew not the scripture, that He must rise again from the dead. Then the disciples went away again unto their own home. But Mary stood without at the sepulchre weeping: and as she wept, she stooped down, and looked into the sepulchre, and seeth two angels in white sitting, the one at the head, and the other at the feet, where the body of Jesus had lain. And they say unto her, Woman, why weepest thou? She saith unto them, Because they have taken away my Lord, and I know not where they have laid Him.*"—JOHN xx. 9-13.[1]

N these passages of our Lord's Word, beloved in Him, we have first set down the earthly witnesses that came to the grave to seek our Lord after He was risen from the dead. And they be of two sorts. The first sort of them are public men in a public charge, Peter and John, the Lord's disciples; and how they sought Christ, and what speed they came in seeking Him! The second sort of persons are private persons coming to seek our Lord, Mary Magdalene, out of whom He had before casten seven devils. And good reason that such think meikle[2] of our Lord, who have gotten renewed souls, or any good

[1] In MS., "Preached upon the Monday after the fast;" that is, evidently the fast August 22, 1640. This sermon is perhaps the best of the series.
[2] Much.

thing from Him. Then we have the fruit that follows the apostles' seeking of our Lord. They go their ways home again and find Him not. Again you have the fruit of this woman's seeking of Him. She will not give over her seeking Him, albeit she cannot find Him at the first. Indeed it is a blessed thing for a poor soul to wait on still at Christ's door till they get Him, albeit they should die there, waiting for Him. And in her waiting for Him, first of all she meets with the angels. And after she was comforted of them, telling her that He was risen from the dead, and was rebuked of them for her weeping and seeking Him there, she leaves them and goes on to seek Him. And she meets with Christ Himself, and speaks to Him, but she miskens[1] Him as many times the children of God are speaking to Him, and He is speaking to them again, and yet they misken[1] Him. She supposes Him to be the gardener, and speers[2] if he had carried Him away, and where he had laid Him that she might know where He was. And then our Lord discovers Himself unto her by a short preaching that He made as our Lord. He is evermore kent[3] by His word, and when she hears Him speak she turns herself to Him, and she being willing to embrace Him she is forbidden to do it at that time. He would not have her to think so meikle[4] of her bodily presence at that time, because there is a better presence coming when He is ascended to His Father. Only she is commanded to tell the Lord's disciples of that which she had seen, and so she is made the first preacher of Christ's rising from the dead.

[1] Mistakes Him for another. [2] Asks. [3] Known. [4] Much.

First: We observe one thing in the general, that concerns the estate of our Kirk at this time. Herod and Pilate, and Jew and Gentile, they have all joined themselves together at this time to do the worst they can to Christ our Lord, and yet, when they have done all that they can, they cannot mend themselves. For now they had buried Him to hold Him down, and yet for all that that mends them not. The worst that the enemies of the Kirk can do to the Kirk is to put her to death, and yet when they think they have gotten that done, it will not do their turn when all is done. For wherever our Lord's bride be, albeit she were even in the grave, she maun[1] rise again, and in a triumph over her enemies. Let our Lord and His Kirk be where they will, He and His Kirk and cause, albeit they were dead, they maun[1] live the third day again, as Christ Himself did, according to that triumphant and glorious word which He spake (Rev. i. 17, 18): "Fear not; I am the first and the last: I am He that liveth, and was dead; and, behold, I am alive for evermore." When John had seen His glory, and fell down dead because he was afraid thereof, He says that to him. There is news to comfort the Kirk of God, and to comfort all those who doubt whether our Lord will tyne[2] the battle that He has against His enemies or not. No; He will make good that word that He speaks there of Himself: "I was dead, but I am alive; and, behold, I am alive for evermore." Fra[3] a dead man cannot do the turn, He will let it be seen that a living man can do it. We need not to doubt of it, but the enemies of Christ they thought that they were quit of

[1] Must.   [2] Lose.   [3] Since.

Him now, that He would cumber them no more; but it is not so for all that yet, for He shall live when all is done, for all the ill they have done to Him. And within these few years our adversaries, they thought with themselves that long or now they should have been quit of our cumber, and that this gospel should [have] been clean borne down long or now. But with their leave Christ is letting us see this day that He will not have it to be so, that He will have that gospel which they thought to bear down so far, to come to some perfection again. So is the Kirk brought in, speaking in Hosea's prophecy (vi. 2): "After two days thou wilt revive us again, and the third day we shall live." This gospel it maun¹ live, whoever they be who are against it, for the bearing down thereof, and the end of it maun¹ be glory to Christ, and so those who are upon His side of it. Now, to say nothing of the race that Peter and John had in going to Christ's grave, it is said the other disciple he outran Peter, and came first to the sepulchre. John is he who is called the other disciple, and he outran Peter. As it is among the children of God, all of them have not a like speed. Some of them get a sight of Christ before others ever get a sight of Him. Christ has some into His Kirk that are old and experienced with His ways, and so they run fast in the same; and He has others also, who are His children and belong to Him, who are young ones, and cannot run so fast. But whoever they be who have the life of God in them, and so are walking on towards Him, they shall, either first or last, meet with Him without doubt.

¹ Must.

He which came first went into the sepulchre and saw, and he believed. He might [have] believed that Christ was risen by that which he had heard, but he believed not till he saw. Many a time had the Lord said to them that the Son of Man must be delivered into the hands of sinners, and must suffer many things of them; that He must die and be buried, but the third day He shall rise again; but notwithstanding of all that He had said, John believed not till he had seen tokens that He had risen from the dead. However it be, yet this is sure, that it is good for every one to use the means that God has appointed for attaining to the knowledge of any thing. For John gat this meikle good by using the means at this time and coming to the grave—that he was assured that Christ was risen. Who was there ever that made a race for Christ but gat some good by their seeking after Him? Seek ye and ye shall find, knock and it shall be opened unto you. Zacchæus, he had a longing desire to see Christ, and because he was low of stature, and the throng was great, he ran before the multitude, and clamb up upon a tree to see Him; and ye have heard what good come of that, as there comes aye[1] good of seeking Christ rightly: He says, "Come down, Zacchæus, this day is salvation come to thy house." He will not fail, but He will make that word good which He has spoken Himself, "Ask and ye shall receive, seek and ye shall find, knock and it shall be opened unto you." Could we be earnest in seeking our Lord—and I am sure ye know that this is a seeking time now, and never was there more need to be seeking

[1] Always.

at the hands of God—as the Lord lives, I durst promise it in His name, if we would seek Him we should see the salvation of the Lord. And so, albeit ill news should come unto us, let us not be discouraged for the same. But let us rest upon this, and put our confidence in the same, that our Lord is to be found of them who seek Him; and He has given signs thereof already unto us, and will do so hitherto if we will seek unto Him.

For as yet they knew not the Scripture that He must rise again from the dead. The rest of the disciples, they believed not these Scriptures that foretold of Christ's resurrection from the dead. Can it be possible that there can be a scholar in Christ's school that has not learned his lesson that Christ taught him? Can it be that any who has heard Christ Himself make so many preachings of His resurrection, that they believe not for all that? Aye, ye may see the proof of it here. The doctrine that arises from this it is clear, that it is not the means, nor hearing Christ as a man preach out of His own mouth, that will do the turn to bring us in to God, and to make us understand things spiritual. Preaching, indeed, is God's mean that He has appointed for that end, and the way that He ordains for bringing in souls to Him. But when all is done, it is not the only mean of bringing us to Him. The special thing is that which is spoken by our Saviour Himself (John iii. 8), that wind that bloweth where it listeth, and no man knoweth whence it cometh or whither it goeth. We may preach unto you until our head rive[1]

---
[1] Be rent.

and our breasts burst; aye, we may preach unto you until doom's day, and yet that will not do the turn unless the inward calling of the Spirit be joined therewith. For an outward sound to the ear is one thing, and Christ's loosing all knots and removing all impediments another thing. Christ says Himself while He was in the flesh (John vi. 44), "No man can come unto Me unless the Father draw him." Christ is speaking in that place to them who had the outward means, and yet He says, it is no strange thing that they come not unto Him, albeit they have the means, because they want the Father's draught to draw them to Him. The scribes they heard Christ ofttime preach, and yet for all that they consented to the slaying of the Lord of glory (1 Cor. ii. 8). Christ is preached there both to the Jew and to the Gentile, and yet for all that to the Jew He is a stumbling-block, and to the Grecian the preaching of Christ is foolishness. We have meikle for us when the Lord's word is preached to pray to Him that He would join His Spirit and His wind with His word. Ay, all means that can be used by ourselves or by others are nothing without that be joined. It is in vain for us to rise early and to lie down late, and to eat the bread of sorrow all the day, if the Lord give not the assistance of His Spirit to the means that we use.

And again, we may learn from this that arms of men are not the thing that will save us, if so be that the Lord Himself watch not over the camp. God keeps evermore the issue and the event of all things into His own hand. And this serves to teach us not to trust in means of any sort whether it be inward or outward matters, we should not lippen¹ in man, nor in weapons, nor any second causes whatsoever, but only in the Lord Himself, that is the only strength of His people. And so learn to overlook second causes when you look that way, and look no lower nor² heaven, to Him who sits there and guides and overrules all battles in the world and all things else, and will let it be seen in the end salvation, salvation, even His salvation to all them who trust in Him.

What gars³ that it is not said, "They believed not Christ," but they "believed not the Scriptures" concerning this point? For there is no part of Scripture so clear as the Lord Himself when He is preaching with His own blessed mouth concerning that article of the resurrection from the dead, albeit it is true the five books of Moses and other Scriptures spake also of this article.

The reason of this is to teach us that Christ and the Scriptures they have but one tongue, and they who believe not the Scriptures they believe not Christ. It is not the sound of Christ's trumpet that many who profess to be preachers blow, but a sound from themselves and from men. This tells us what is Scripture and what is.no[t] Scripture. That only is Scripture and no other that agrees with the will of the Son of God, and is according to His will revealed to us in His Word. And again, that is not Scripture, and so not to be believed or practised, which is not according to the Word of God. And so we may see that ceremonies and inventions of men they are but a dumb Bible, and a ground that none should follow for their salvation. If

---

¹ Trust.   ² Than.   ³ Causes.

we have no other ground for our faith but only this, that the Pope, or the Kirk, has said such a thing, or the great learned doctors have said it, and therefore we believe it. As the poor men yonder over in the north,[1] they have been deceived by believing what grave-like men spake to them, and men who gat the name of learning. That is a blind guide to follow, and will lead us in the mire. But these that are indeed the called and the elect of God, they can discover the voice of Christ from the voice of men, and they only will follow Christ's voice, and will follow no other, whatever they be.

Then the disciples went away again unto their own home. They were oversoon tired of seeking, for they might have waited on as well as the poor woman did. But God has our seeking of Christ, and all our supernatural works of that kind, into His own hand. We believe, pray, repent, seek after Christ and His Spirit, praise, hear, read aright, &c., as long as Christ holds us by the hand, but we do it no longer. A stone that is up into the air is out of its own element, and so long as it has an impediment it will stay there. But take away the impediment that holds the stone from the ground, incontinent[2] it falls to it again. Even so is it with us. When we are employed about these spiritual duties we are out of our natural element; and if the Lord take away His hand from the strongest of His children, a woman will go beyond them in doing good duties. Thank God for any good thing that thou hast, and that thou art kept in a good estate. They never kent[3] Christ's help

---

[1] Aberdeenshire was at that time the stronghold of Arminianism and Prelacy. [2] Immediately. [3] Knew.

well who put man in such a tutor's hand as free-will, to be kept by it; who say that Christ has conquershed[1] salvation to all, and when He has conquershed[1] it, He puts it in the hand of free-will to be disposed of as it pleases, to keep or not to keep it. This is to make Christ a fool merchant, and not to take accompt[2] whether it be misspent or not; but Christ is not so. He knows what shall become of all whom He has bought. You know it is evermore the happiness of the weaker to depend upon the stronger. So it is the happiness of the poor soul to depend upon Christ and upon free grace. The happiness of the ship stands in that to have a good pilot; the happiness of the lost weak sheep depends on a good shepherd to seek it in again, and to keep it from the enemies thereof; the happiness of the weak, witless orphans depends in a good, wise tutor. Even so the happiness of lost and tint[3] souls depend on this, to lippen[4] to Christ and His strength for their salvation, and not to such a changing tutor as their free-will is.

But Mary stood without at the sepulchre weeping. Here is a strange thing to think on. The Lord's own disciples they ran away from seeking of Him. One of them that had said, "If all should forsake Thee, yet shall I never forsake Thee;" and yet here is a woman more forward, and more constant in seeking Christ nor[5] he is, for all his fair profession. It is not fair words and a golden profession that will take a soul to heaven, and will make us to seek Christ rightly. We are all meikle oblist[6] to saving grace in our seeking Christ. Here is a woman

---

[1] Acquired.   [2] Account.   [3] Perishing.   [4] Trust.
[5] Than.   [6] Much obliged or indebted.

more forward in seeking Christ nor [1] all His eleven disciples are. Because she gat not her errand that she was seeking, she could not get Christ, and therefore she will not leave, nor give over, but will wait on and seek Him. A soul that is in love with Christ, they never get their errand till they get Christ Himself. Ye that are seeking Christ, never give over seeking till ye meet with Him, for they shall at last meet with Him who lie at His door, seeking, as this woman did, who say, "I shall lie still at Thy door, let me die there if Thou likest, and albeit it should come to that, I shall die, or I go away and meet not with Him." Ye may know the ardent desire of a soul after Christ can be satisfied with nothing but Himself.

We use to say the thing that one longs for is the thing they maun [2] have, and no other thing will satisfy them. A man that is hungry, and longing for meat, he maun [2] have meat, and meat only, or else he is not satisfied, albeit he get some other thing. A man that is in prison and longs to be free, nothing will satisfy him but liberty. Even so it is with this woman at this time; albeit the disciples were with her, yet nothing can comfort her till she get her lovely Lord whom she was seeking. Learn that lesson of spiritual importunity, never to give over seeking of Christ when once ye have begun to it. Blessed are they that ware [3] their time this way, in seeking Christ.

Mary stayed there weeping for want of Him, and yet looking into the grave to see if He were there. That is a good and blessed desire, and sorrow that is backed [4] with doing. That is heaven's sorrow indeed that is backed [4]

[1] Than.   [2] Must.   [3] Spend in this manner.   [4] Seconded.

with doing and using the means. There are two things said of Jacob (Hos. xii. 4), that he wept and wrestled in prayer with God. What is the matter of a dumb sorrow for the want of Christ? But that is a right sorrow for want of Christ that is joined with using the means to get Him. As it is in Solomon's Song iii. 3, the spouse is wanting Christ there; she uses all means to get Him again. She goes to the watchmen, and says to them, "Watchmen, saw ye Him whom my soul loveth?" She goes round about the city, and to the daughters of Jerusalem, and charges them. That proves her sorrow to be a right sorrow for the want of Christ. And ye know what sort of tears the Scripture says Christ had (Heb. v. 7). He shed tears while He was in His flesh, and withal He offered up prayers and strong cries to Him who was able to save Him, and was heard in that He feared. And that is the grief and sorrow that will only hold the feet when men are sorrowful for want of Christ, and withal use the means to get Him; and not only has a raw wish for Christ, and will not want a morning nor a night's sleep to meet with Him. That sorrow that is so is but a vain sorrow, and will do no good. What followed upon this?

She saw two angels in white sitting, the one at the head, the other at the feet, where the body of Jesus had lain. What needs this guard to be here now when the Lord is risen from the dead? They stay here to be witnesses of Christ's resurrection, and to preach the same to this woman and to the disciples. And Matthew, he has a circumstance of this preaching of the angels that John has not. "Why seek ye the living among the dead?"

Why are ye papists, to seek Christ at the holy grave now when He is risen? You may see that the work of man's redemption it is a very glorious and a very honourable work, for the angels in all the parts thereof are appointed to attend Christ and to wait. When He is born they maun [1] speak to Joseph and His mother to flee for His safety, they foretell His birth, when they are to return with Him again they tell them, and when He was in the garden the angels are appointed to wait upon Him, to dight [2] the bloody sweat off His face. And now, when He is in the grave, they are set to be a guard to His blessed and glorious body, and to preach of His resurrection. When He shall come again at the last day to judge the quick and the dead, He shall come with innumerable multitudes of angels—to let us see that the work of our salvation it is a very honourable work; and the angels they wait well upon it, and upon us. Even like a loving brother, who has his brother lying sick: O but he will run many errands for him in the time of his sickness, and will make all the house ado [3] to get him well and at ease. Even so do the angels to us. They run many errands for us, and O but they are glad of our welfare; and (Heb. i. 10) it is said the angels are ministering spirits for the good of the heirs of salvation. Count ye little or meikle [4] of your salvation as ye will, yet it is the angels' great task that they are employed about. They are appointed to wait on Christ, when is about the working thereof, both in His birth, in His agony, in His burial, in His ascending to heaven, and shall attend Him in His coming again to judge the quick

---

[1] Must.   [2] Wipe.   [3] Astir. See "Letters."   [4] Much.

and the dead. The Lord has them sent out to all the airts¹ of the world to bring in His elect ones. Woe to ye who think little of salvation, fra² the Lord employs such honourable messengers about the same. Alas! the work of our salvation is little thought upon by many. Twenty—a hundred thoughts will come in men's heads fra³ morn to night. And scarce have we one thought of this great work at any time. And what think ye shall become of them who are so careless of the work of the salvation of mankind whereof the angels are so careful?

Thir⁴ witnesses, they were clad in white. The angels, they have not our common country clothes, but they are like heaven in their apparel; to teach all those who are looking to be heirs of heaven to be clad like their country. The angels, they are clad with glory and with majesty, and therefore a sight of them will make a sinner to fall to the ground dead. If we think to be heirs of God in Christ, let us not be like the rest of the corrupt world. The apostle, he has a word for this (Rom. xii. 2): "Be not conformed to the world, but be ye transformed in the spirit of your mind." When ye are drunkensome, and swearers, and break the Lord's day, as the rest of the world does, that proves you to be of the world, and not to have your affections up above. If ye would prove yourselves to be heirs of heaven, strive to be like your father, and like your country, and wear the livery of the house which is holiness: "Holiness becomes Thy house, O Lord." Mind the things that are above.

And they say unto her, Woman, why weepest thou? This would seem to be a needless question to propose to her,

---

¹ Quarters, or parts. ² Since. ³ From. ⁴ These.

for she might [have] said, "I have tint¹ my Saviour; who can blame me to weep? who can reprove me for it, seeing I want my Lord? But there is something in this question that is unseen, that is the reason wherefore they ask it, and this is it: " Your salvation is now finished, and the devils are casten out of you, and so what gars² you weep now?" Our Lord would tell us by this, that ofttimes we weep when we have cause to rejoice. She should have said, " This is the day which the Lord hath made, we will be glad and rejoice in it." "This is a day when a decreet³ is passed in heaven in your favours, that the lost seed of Adam is redeemed; and thou also art in the decree of redemption among the rest, therefore thou should not weep." O that we could learn to accommodate our affections, and all that is in us, to God; to weep when He weeps, and to rejoice when He rejoices. And when our Lord is without in the fields, it is not time for us then to laugh, and to rejoice, and to be feasting. It is a time matter for mourning, now when our Lord is out into the fields, and when His armies are out, and are in scarcity. And yet we trust that our Lord is keeping a day for us of this land, wherein we shall say, " This is the day that the Lord has made, let us be glad and rejoice in it."

Whom seekest thou? This question is speered⁴ at her to make her hunger to be the greater, for the greatest hunger that any has for Christ they may, aye,⁵ be more hungry for Him. And so learn to rap⁶ out all your desires and affections for Christ, not only love Him, but

---

¹ Lost. ² Makes, causes. ³ The final sentence of a judge.
⁴ Asked. ⁵ Always. ⁶ Quickly to throw out.

be sick of love for Him. That is more than ordinary love to be like to die for love of Him. And so all your desires and longing for Christ, strive to make them more, ay, till you come to that which the spouse has; "I charge you, O daughters of Jerusalem, if ye find my beloved, tell Him that I am sick of love. I charge you, as ye will answer to God, that ye tell Christ I am sick of love for want of Him," and till ye come to heaven to sing songs of Him eternally.

"*They have tane away my Lord, and I wat not where they have laid Him.*" This is her apology that she uses for justifying of herself in her weeping, "Why may not I weep, who once had Christ, and now I want Him?" That is a sorrow that may be avowed before God and before the world, to be sorrowful for the want of Christ. There are some who are sorrowful, and it is a shame to hear of it, the cause thereof not being good. Sorrow for want of my bairns, for want of my husband; sorrow for the loss of something of the world, or giving out something for Christ, &c.; that is a shameful sorrow that cannot be avowed. But that is an honest sorrow that comes from the want of Christ. Look that ye ware [1] all your affections that way as ye may avow them, and avow the cause of them before God and man. That is a sorrow that may be avowed that a soul has for want of Christ.

What is the matter and cause of her sorrow?

"*They have taken away my Lord, and I wat not where they have laid Him.*" He is out of my sight, and yet He is my Lord for all that; He is dead, and yet He is my

[1] Spend.

Lord; for that she says, "They have taken Him away, and wat[1] not where they have laid Him," is as meikle as if she doubted yet of His resurrection. And a little after she says to Christ Himself, supposing Him to be the gardener, "Sir, if thou hast borne Him away, tell me where thou hast laid Him, and I will take Him away." "I will think Him a sweet burden to come upon my back for all the pounds weight of spices that are about Him."

The doctrine is clear. To the children of God, *lost* Christ is *their* Christ when all is done. In Cant. v. the Lord's party, the Kirk of Christ, is there sleeping in her bed, and Christ, her husband, standing at the outside of the door knocking, and she says, "I slept, but my heart waked; it is the voice of my beloved." Thy beloved, and, yet for all that, He is out of thy sight. Let the believer's Christ be where He will, yet He is theirs. If they were in hell and He up in heaven, the believer will say, "He is my Christ, albeit Christ should cast me off, and not count me to be His, yet He is mine." So does David's word as the type, and Christ's word as the antitype, testify, "My God, My God, why hast Thou forsaken Me?" He is a forsaking Lord, and yet He is their Lord when all is done. Ay, the believer will say, "He is my Lord, albeit He forsake me, and I will come to Him." Then true faith when it has the back at the wall will claim to Christ, and count Him to belong to them. And that is a very good mark of faith, that when one is setting Christ a speering[2] on all airts,[3] and cannot get Him for no seeking,[4] yet to count Him to be their

---

[1] Know. [2] Asking. [3] Quarters. [4] Notwithstanding seeking.

Christ. This is the thing that the devil would fain be in hands with, to make you to doubt that He is your Christ or your Lord. This was the temptation wherewith he assaulted Christ our Lord. "If Thou be the Son of God, cast Thyself down from the pinnacle of the temple," &c. All that the devil would be at in his temptations is to make us doubt that Christ is ours. But never give it over when all is done, but evermore take Christ for thine.

And, oh, that this land would believe this now, that He is our God, and the God of this land. Then suppose that our armies were put to the worst that are now out into the fields—as we trust in God it shall not be—but albeit it should be so, I say, yet seeing He is Scotland's Lord, if so be that we will wait upon Him, and trust in Him and in His salvation, it shall be found that it is not a vain thing to do so, but that He shall grant us His salvation who trust in Him. And to this Lord, &c.

The Spouse's Longing for Christ.

"I have put off my coat; how shall I put it on? I have washed my feet; how shall I defile them? My beloved put in his hand by the hole of the door, and my bowels were moved for him. I rose up to open to my beloved; and my hands dropped with myrrh, and my fingers with sweet smelling myrrh, upon the handles of the lock. I opened to my beloved; but my beloved had withdrawn himself, and was gone: my soul failed when he spake; I sought him, but I could not find him; I called him, but he gave me no answer."—SONG OF SOLOMON v. 3-6.[1]

"*HAVE put off my coat.*" This is the spouse's answer full of Christ. Like one gone to bed, and having washen his feet, as the custom was in these hot countries, because of sweat after travel. As the friend answereth (Luke xi. 7), "Trouble me not; the door is now shut, and my children are with me in bed." This shows while we are asleep, and bedded with our sweet pleasures, Christ's sweet words, "My sister, my love, my dove," His holy and dear head, frozen with cold, cannot move her to open and let Him in. While the temptation is up

[1] Preached at the communion at Anwoth, April 5, 1647. The *first part*, viz., v. 1 and 2, has been published in the "Communion Sermons."

and upon horseback, and takes us on the right nick,[1] and finds us on a ground of sinning with hot blood, we can hardly stand on our feet and resist, or hold out. The prophets rose early in the morning, and sat late up, and spake to Israel to return from their ill ways; yet Israel hearkened not (Jer. xxvi. 5), for idolatry had taken them on the right nick,[1] and jumped with [2] their ease (ver. 18). David was not himself in commanding to number the people, for Joab, otherwise a bad man, had better light nor[3] David, a man after God's own heart, for he was against the numbering of the people. But the devil stood up, and took David at the right side, when his pride was swollen over the banks (1 Chron. xxi. 1). Job's friends, finding him in a fit of distemper, sometimes through vehemency of his pain, caused him to sclent[4] a little off the line. The devil, winnowing Peter, came upon his right side to put him upon the denying of his Lord when he was upon a cold blood in the fear of his life.

There be four reasons of this:

The first is common—a withdrawing of God's working grace; for, if the dam grow dry or ebb, the mill stands. Psa. xxx. 7: "Thou didst hide thy face"—now the horse is saddled—"and I was troubled." So, then, unbelief makes a road.[5] When free-will holds the bridle, up goes the rider's heels, and he feels his own weight; and so it cannot but be, for obedience is not a web of our making.

2. The temptation in this case is many stone weight, heavier than our shoulders dow[6] bear. Pride, lust, lazi-

---

[1] Point or mark of time. [2] Fell in with. [3] Than.
[4] Slant. [5] A raid or invasion. [6] Can.

ness, and security are the meikle water, the saints are the short-legged horse, and down they go. God gives the devil liberty to break many a weak back. Be humble and fear. He knew us full well when He bade us pray, "Lord, lead us not into temptation."

3. There be two herbs that grow quickly in our souls in summer weather—security and pride. Humility is a strange flower; it grows best in winter weather, and under storms of affliction. When security and pride and other neighbour-like weeds are rank and up, the temptation has us in the nick.[1] Then if ye would be kept from the temptation's black hour, swell not in pride, turn not lazy in the use of good means. If you do, look for a temptation, as God's lance to make a hole and let out the wind.

4. Light is turned blunt and wants an edge, and then the temptation of a hot bed will prevail to hold Christ at the wrong side of the door. For here I provoke[2] to your experience to discern two nicks[3] you will be on. In the one, the temptation goes home without its errand; in the other, ye are taken, at a preaching, communion, a renewed glance of the face of Christ, at the death of a friend, or under a sharp rod. At such a time the temptation comes, and your light is like a new sharp knife. There is much steel into it, and the light shall cut the temptation in the weft at the first wipe. Let that light be a quarter of a year beside you, and it turns rusty and blunt, and loses the edge; and then let the devil come, my friend, say you, and I will foot his boul.[4] The temptation comes on; and by and by without a host[5] it is

[1] Right point of time.   [2] Appeal.   [3] Turning-points.
[4] Drive back his ball.   [5] Without a cough, *i.e.*, without any hesitation.

made welcome and the light stands by looking on like a dead witness, and says nothing.

It were a good *use* of this doctrine to observe the right stots[1] of your soul, to sharp blunted light, to beware of pride and security, and eye well often the case of your heart. Learn to know the gate[2] to the bottom of it. Plumb often,[3] and see how many fathom deep it is. When the heart is up on the devil's nick,[4] now, now take yourselves quickly, guide well, wale[5] your steps, fear and quake, cry to your rock, put your blunt light to the grinding-stone again.

"*How shall I put it on?*" This she says, as thinking it impossible and unreasonable, as Joseph said to his mistress (Gen. xxxix. 9), "How can I do this." There is a dispute here with chiding. "Is not this," would she say, "an unreasonable suit of my well-beloved to bid me fyle[6] my feet, lose my sweet pleasures, go naked in the winter night? Is He not a cumbersome Christ, are not His commandments untimeous, might He not have knocked ere the sun went down, ere I went to bed? It is strange this Christ of mine must have service betwixt midnight and cockcrow, when all other folks are at rest."

We see there be some dainty white and thin-skinned temptations, yea, holy-like, reason-like, and velvet sins, so well favoured to us that they seem to prove Christ to be an unnatural, savage, cumbersome guest, as wild as Turk or Jew. Such reasons will say: "I dow[7] not hold up Christ's cumbersome yeas and nays. He will flay the

[1] Motions.   [2] Way.   [3] Cast the lead.   [4] Point or mark of time.
[5] Choose.   [6] Soil.   [7] Can.

skin off poor nature." For some temptations are of base metal, made of clay, yea they are wholly gross and round spun and ill-litted [1] (Ezek. xiii. 10). The prophets slew souls that should have lived, for handfuls of barley and pieces of bread. But ordinarily Satan has strong and well-spun reasons on his side; and the chief one that makes great din is the world for the world's pleasure, profit, a hot soft bed, well perfumed, daintily made. The devil has drawn the curtains, ushed [2] the house, and kept the chamber quiet that ye may take your headful of sleep; and all these are set against Christ, to hold Him out. No marvel then the hot bed prevails with the spouse. For a mess of pottage prevailed with Esau as a good one. "What? I am hungry; I may not die; you will tell me of the dignity of my birthright, a type of heaven. But answer me this question, Let the birthright go play itself while hungry and famishing Esau breakfasts." This is strong with the whore against God and the seventh commandment. Prov. vii. 17, 18: "The bed is trim and decked; we will get our fill of love; the good man is from home." The robber has his logic on his finger ends. It is not to seek against God and the eighth commandment. Prov. i. 13: "We shall find all precious substance; we shall fill ourselves with spoil." You know that it is a notable token of sanctified light when men are deaf at all reasons that are against Christ and His word. The flesh cries out, "What fyle [3] my feet, lose my place, leave my hot bed for I wot not what?" If the Lord's spirit is in you, answer, "What, fyle [3] my conscience? Better boolie [4] in my

[1] Badly dyed.   [2] Cleared.   [3] Soil, defile.   [4] Weep in a childish manner.

bed, quit my true peace, and lose my Christ." A reason from gold would not be a golden one to Paul; seeing for Christ, all were loss and dirt and dung to Him. The disciples' nets and their lines and their fish-hooks were not worth a straw when Christ said, " Follow Me." Thou who art teddered to thy delights, when Christ comes by and cries, " Follow Me," if then thou canst break thy tether like a rotten straw rope, and gallop after Him, thou hast clear eyes and seest well.

But here is a question that were worthy the loosing,[1] What makes this so hard to us, to go but the breadth of the house barefooted to let in Christ? Certainly the reasons are these.

1. Our light is corrupt and looks awry, and with a gleed[2] eye upon Christ, and it looks with many eyes to the world. Hence when Christ knocketh it says, first, He cannot come here. Second: I doubt if it be Christ that knocketh, because I wish it were not He. Third: I must live. Fourth: I dow[3] not suffer. Fifth: This and this will befal me if I do it. Sixth: If I would let Him in, then my lusts would get no quarters with Him. My will, my affections, and He would never give one jot. They would flee upon each other. Nay, men's lusts are up where eyes should be, and their eyes down at their feet.

2. This is like the first. The devil has litted[4] the world and the pleasures of it. Thirty pieces cast a scad[5] of golden glance upon Judas. His light said, " Sorrow, make care, howbeit the Pharisees had my hungry Master, so be it I had a purse for my part of Him." Colours, and

[1] Solving. [2] Squinted. [3] Can. [4] Dyed. [5] Gleam.

the purple skin of things, and not the things themselves, cross our eye.

3. Our heart and our affections hold us still in our hot sheets, that we dow [1] not rise to let Christ in. Yea, hardness of heart, the worst believer, and the toughest disputer in the world, carveth all, and when we come to choose what to do, then we speer [2] counsel. Again, what sayest thou, lust? what is your will and vote? honour, ease, &c.?—tell me. Shall I let him in? and then we hear not the other side till amen. O but beloved, there is a thing they call "Try all things," and look again and fear always, so needful here that they would pull the covering off all things, and let you see all things, whose skin is black, and whose is white.

"How can I? how can I, spouse?" thou askest, "how can I arise? how can I put on my coat?" I will tell thee how thou canst. Stir thy legs and arms, raise thy frozen fingers. It is strange to make a question how a whole strong man not bound can rise out of his bed! Stir ye, and cast the covering and bed-clothes off, and come to the floor. If men would suffer their light to play fair play, and think judiciously and spiritually on the world, and the delights of it, which is their soft bed, they might open to Christ. Men are but sleeping on a bed of ice. It will melt with the heat of God's anger, and they, and their night sheets, and the bed will swim, nay, men have reason to tire of this bed, both short and narrow. Luke xii. 20: "Thou fool, this night thy soul shall be taken from you;" 1 Cor. vii. 31: "The fashion of this world passeth away." Is not this a short bed? Fools cannot get down their feet.

[1] Can.   [2] Ask.

2. Is it not often hard, and so hard that Ahitophel, a king's counsellor, who could not but have a well-made bed, could not sleep a wink in it? he leaped over the bedstock,[1] and hanged himself, and slipped down to hell.

3. Yea, cold, cold lie they, the clothes fall all over the bedstock,[1] when (Jer. xiv.) nobles cannot get a drink of water. Nebuchadnezzar, with many kingdoms, is driven from them all, and from among men, to eat grass with the oxen (Dan. iv. 33). Here narrow sheets and a cold bed.

4. These who have been snoring and sleeping here are pulled out of their sheets by the Lord, and they leave foul sheets behind them. Job xx. 6: Though the hypocrite's "excellency mounteth to heaven"—a fair and well-made bed—"yet he shall perish for ever, as his own dung" (ver. 7). Are not these foul foldings? "The memory of the wicked shall rot" (Prov. x. 7). When he is gone his name shall stink. It were good then that all who sleep in this bed would waken and rise, and seek rest to their souls, else God shall send three sharp toothed hands—the devil, death, and judgment—to pull them over the bedstock.[1] And when (2 Pet. iii.) the earth and works therein shall be burned with fire, these who lie hottest, and softest, and sleep sound, shall, even they, their bedclothes, and bed straw, shall all be set on fire, and the bed will be burnt to ashes.

"*My beloved put in his hand.*" That is, with the outward ministry of the word. He put in His hand—it is His Spirit (Acts xi. 21; Ezek. iii. 13; Luke xi. 20)—in the hole of my heart, to make a wider hole. I confess this

[1] The fore part of the bed.

putting of Christ's hand in the key-hole of the heart is better felt nor [1] told. But it is this: when Christ sent His voice and tongue through the door, it did not [do] the turn, and therefore He caused His hand to follow His tongue. He gave with the hand of His Spirit such a dunt,[2] until bed, and house, and all did shake, and the door fell on the floor. Who knows not this who knows Christ's working—that when Christ speaks, His Spirit will make in the heart a stirring and such a glowing, that they will find His soft hand rubbing their cold heart? And when a key and lock are rusted, we rub oil upon the rusty part. When Christ cometh, He finds the wards, sprents[3] go in and out at will, and He takes will and heart and affections in His hand, and scours them with His file. Phil. iii. 12: "I am apprehended of Christ Jesus;" Luke xxiv. 32: "Did not our hearts burn, burn within us, while He spoke;" Cant. ii. 4: "He brought me to His banqueting-house." This was a pull of Christ, taking her by the shoulders, and bringing her into the king's pantry. Hence here be two actions.

One of the word, painting out with alluring and soul delighting words, Christ's fair white and ruddy face; this is a moral yoke.

And withal there is a real action of the hand of the Spirit in all His ten fingers working upon the lock, and setting, engraving, and stamping Christ in deep letters upon the soul. As when a fish is taken there are two actions, the bait alluring and beguiling the fish with hope of meat. This is like the working of the word which is Christ's bait; but when He wins us to dry land,

[1] Than.   [2] Blow.   [3] The work of the lock.

then, when the fish is hooked, there is a real action of the fisher, drawing and hauling the fish to land; it leaping and flightering[1] and wrestling while it bleeds with the hook. And this answereth to the Holy Spirit's powerful hauling and drawing of the soul in all the affections, that the soul feeleth joy, comfort, delight, desire, longing, believing, nibbling, and biting Christ's bait.

The *use* is; Because there are odd times, we should take Christ at the right stot.[2] When His hand is thrusting itself down upon our heart you should thrust your hand on above it, and thrust His stamp and His burning iron even down to the bone, that there may be great letters left behind, and all your life after you may bear Christ's marks. Till such a time, you shall never get such fair quarters or such odd conditions of Christ. Therefore make a double knot, neglect not to work with Christ, and set out all the sails of your soul, and write up the time, and this shall help your doubtings afterwards, and shall be a fair seal of your election. It must be a great guiltiness to smore[3] Christ's fire, and cast water on it, by other bye-thoughts, refusing to take Christ's ball at the stot,[4] and strike the iron while it is hot, in the means of praying, reading, conferring, and telling to the daughters of Jerusalem your love-sickness for Christ. But we silly,[5] narrow, and ebb-hearted creatures have not a hand to receive Christ's sweetmeats. We are like the bairn when his father gives him a hearty handful of sweetmeats, his little hand and short fingers let the half of them slip

---

[1] Fluttering.   [2] At the right moment in His movements.
[3] Smother.   [4] Right moment.   [5] Foolish, weak.

from him and skail[1] upon the ground. Our little fingers skail[1] the comforts of Christ, and we lose (1) comfort, (2) confirmation of our charters, and (3) we lose the increase of faith.

"*My bowels were moved for him.*" This is the moving and rumbling of a sorrowful and broken heart and true repentance, that Christ stood while His head took cold, as Isa. xvi. 11: "My bowels shall sound like a harp for Moab;" Jer. iv. 19: "My bowels, my bowels! I am pained at the very heart; my heart maketh a rumbling sound." She would say, "My heart and bowels within me are turned upside down." My soul said, "Woe is me, that my beloved Christ stood the cold winter night at the doors of my heart with His wet head and His frozen hair. O lazy wretch that I am, who could not arise and let Him in." We see in true repentance there is meikle[2] sorrow: (Luke vii.) one woman furnished as many tears as washed Christ's feet. No scant of sorrow there. Ezek. vii. 16: "But they that escape of them shall escape, and they shall be on the mountains like doves in the valley, all of them mourning, every one for their iniquity." Hos. xi. 11: "They shall tremble as a bird out of Egypt, and as a bird out of the land of Assyria," while they, repenting, follow after the Lord. Zech. xii. 10: "They shall mourn for him as one mourneth for his only begotten son, and they shall be in bitterness for him as one that is in bitterness for his firstborn." Jer. xxxi. 19: "After that I was instructed I smote upon my thigh." Ephraim bemoaning himself, did this as one very sorry for offending the Lord.

---

[1] Scatter.   [2] Much.

This reproveth those who know as much of what turned bowels for the loss of Christ means as they know a great burgh town up beyond the moon. They had never wet cheeks nor a woe heart for Christ. They say it not in words, but they think it in heart: "If Christ go by me, and be lordly, I will live without Him. If the gospel leave us, we will get the old law again, and the good old sonsie[1] world." To their comfort, then, be it said, who have a woe heart for Christ's wet and frozen head, and would put in His frozen hair in their bosom, and thaw His head, they have an undoubted mark of Christ's love, and sister and undefiled one.

But what is the measure of sorrow required in those who have turned bowels for holding out of Christ? I answer, this is indeed a needful question, because many deceive themselves here, and many have sorrow who cannot climb so high as to turned bowels for holding out of Christ, and for neglecting of Christ's call. Hence—

1. Beware your sorrow be not too little, or ill-bottomed for fear of strokes, not for love toward Him whom you have offended. The devil can come upon an Ahab with a crack of sorrow like the shot of a child's paper gun, yet it was not humbling sorrow. True sorrow so humbleth a man as—

(1) He dare not play the wanton, and ride the carrie,[2] in sinning as before, as Ahab did.

(2) True sorrow that humbles, sets the party in a purpose to creep into Christ, howbeit He should ding out his harns,[3] as the woman with the bloody issue feared[4] and trembling came to Christ.

[1] Well-conditioned.
[2] A two-wheeled barrow.
[3] Knock out his brains.
[4] Frightened.

(3) The hole made in the heart is only for sin, and this breeds a loathing of ourselves (Ezek. xx. 43): "And there shall ye remember your ways, and all your doings, wherein ye have been defiled; and ye shall loath yourselves in your own sight for all your evils that ye have committed."

(4) True sorrow seeks after the Lord, as here the Church rises and cries after her well-beloved; and these whom Peter converted (Acts ii. 37) were pricked in their hearts, and were at "Men and brethren, what shall we do to be saved?"

2. Some think they do right if they sorrow out of measure for sin, and take their pennyworth of themselves. But God seeks no more of you but as much as to toom [1] your souls of pride, that Christ may come in with His full vessel to fill it. Do not think to buy God's kindness with tears, as if sorrow were a fat feast to God; for some here go so far on as they will overscore and give God a lucky [2] measure, and an inch to the ell, one to the hundred, as the hearty merchant who delighteth to be called "a good fellow." Nay—

(1) Look when you come near to the edge of the brae to a gaping hell. Hold your hand—it is now time to rainzie about [3] your heart.

(2) When you find any smell of the Lord's blood and merits, it is time to look up and smile for joy.

(3) When the desire and hunger for Christ are nipping [4] and sad, speer [5] about for a Saviour. The evil of much mourning is that, first, it is rank papistry. God thinks not a penance of your tears good cheer. You

[1] Empty. [2] Overflowing. [3] Bridle in, control. [4] Giving pain. [5] Ask.

see not that you give suck now to merits. Second: it will make way now to pride. When the water goes out of the bag, wind comes in. When many tears go out, a windy conceit comes in: "I am sure God cannot but be pleased now. He is in my debt now."

So in seeking cooling humility, Satan slips in their neive[1] a hot coal of pride. Men see not that God will hold back an ounce or two of sorrow that you may sorrow because you have not sorrowed enough. If wind came in, it would breed a new boil. Third: it is Satan's gate[2] to despair, and he leads us on in Christ's way to his own lodging, for he himself is a despairing and trembling devil.

But a doubt here seemeth to stand in our way. Sorrow for Christ ariseth from our love to Christ; and as much as we love Him, as much should we sorrow for the losing of Him. We owe Him love with all the heart and in the highest degree, and therefore we owe Him sorrow of that same mould.

Answer. The argument would conclude strongly if Christ were altogether lost to the saints; but the saints have always a hank in their own hands. Second: howbeit sorrow for Christ's absence spring from a love of Him, yet it follows not that love and sorrow should be in alike length and breadth. Joy and love in extremity are commanded because there is no danger in overjoying. Neither is there danger that love for length and breadth rax[3] itself out of joint, and strain a sinew. But there is danger in over-sorrowing, because despair dwells upon the march[4] with sorrow; and so a friend and a foe are neighbours in town-row[5] together.

[1] Hand. [2] Way. [3] Stretch. [4] Separating wall. [5] Side by side.

3. I will conclude with this needful watchword, that we take heed to our high-tuned affections. They are often ravelled[1] through other. When we sorrow extremely for Christ's wet head, it is much[2] if faith fall not a sound,[3] and if joy grow not lean and withered, because sorrow is fat and rank. Again, when the promise comes in and shoulders out mourning, and a blink of His new revealed face, then I will readily borrow a dispensation and sorrow no more, and there, I am fanked[4] and ravelled, ere I be aware, upon security. It is here as when a bairn's little hand holds two meikle[5] apples—as the one comes in his loof,[6] the other drops down upon the ground.

"*I rose up to open to my beloved.*" Inward grief brings out the spouse's seeking of Christ. Why rose she not to open while He spake, and knocked sweetly, and cried, "Open, my sister, my love, my dove?" Here are words to have moved a heart of stone, and no question they moved her with sense in the meantime; but faith was weak. Hence when Christ was away from the door, and she deserted, she makes her to obedience, for obedience is quicker and more powerful under faith, and hunger, and absence, than under feeling and presence. Feeling, or motions at the word heard, will make us soft, foggie[7] and lazy; sweir[8] faith makes us sharp, laborious, and puts us to a doing. In faith, in a manner, we feed Christ. In feeling and presence we feed ourselves. In feeling we take in; in faith we give out; and sense ofttimes makes us idle. While the bairn eateth an apple the book is laid by. But whether the spouse had feeling while

---

[1] Twisted confusedly together. [2] It is a great matter.
[3] *I.e.*, into a swoon. [4] Entangled. [5] Great.
[6] Palm of the hand. [7] Dull. [8] *I.e.*, faith in the midst of opposition.

Christ spake and knocked or not, yet the doctrine holdeth when Christ leaveth off to speak in His word, and when to our feeling He is absent, we are often very humble in doing and seeking Him. When Christ is either not answering or giving rough answers, the woman of Canaan is then busiest, crying and again crying to Christ, following on, worshipping on her knees, disputing the matter hotly with Christ by force of reason to carry away her desires. So His Kirk (Cant. iii.), having lost Him, rises, seeks, and, better seeks in the streets, in the open gates, and, about the walls: "Watchman, good watchman, saw ye him whom my soul loveth?" And so was Mary Magdalene when her Lord was lost. What a din she made with watery eyes. She saith, "Angels, saw ye Him?" "Gardener, sir, have ye carried Him away?" "Grave, hast thou Him?" We, like fools, can complain, "He is away." Fye! "Now all is gone." Fye! Now say ye, "He is away. What will I do?" and ye cry black hunger. But if ye be carefully seeking Him, you are fatter now nor [1] when ye were doated and feasted with His presence.

"*I rose up to open.*" After a refusal of Christ the conscience of the child of God begins to overcast. She had given a short and a dry answer. Now she is woe [2] at the answer she gave Him, and her hot bed cannot keep her. After the saints and Christ are aside, and have broken a straw, I defy you to bide [3] ten days from Him. After you have given Christ a rough and cankered refusal, there is a knot in the conscience that you dow [4] not bide all this time under a refusal of Christ. The conscience has

---

[1] Than. [2] Sorrowful. [3] Stay. [4] Can.

been saying, "Fye upon you, where is love now, where pity, when Christ standeth cold and frozen at the door, and thou wilt not let Him in?" Thus all the time while He knocked was a long thorn or great pricking stob[1] sticking in her conscience. There will, I grant, sometimes be much deadness in the saints after sin, and a purpose to take the play a day or two longer. But ordinarily after sin there is a pulled ear, and God's Spirit crying, "Wrong; come home again." In wicked men after sin there is no scant of false peace, and their heart says heartily, "So be it," and "amen" to all that they have done. After Jezebel had killed innocent Naboth, she said to her husband (1 Kings xxi. 15): "Arise, go take possession of the vineyard which Naboth the Jezreelite refused to give thee for money." This she spoke with an edge, and took a hearty mouthful of it. She would say, "I have taught Naboth good manners, what it is to be a good neighbour to his prince, and to buy and sell with his king. He would not give his vineyard for money, now take it for nothing." Here is Jezebel's "*so be it*," and her seal, "*well done*," put to the murder. When the rulers have crucified Christ, and a stone is above Him in the grave, they say to Pilate, "Sir, we remember this deceiver said while He was alive He would rise again the third day;" calling the slain Man when He is lying under a cold stone "a deceiver." They say they rue[2] not a hair all that is done. I deny not, but sometimes wicked men after sin will halt and clinch[3] like a crazy, tired horse after a long journey. Their conscience, as it were, bearing up a leg, not daring

[1] Small splinter of wood.   [2] Repent   [3] Limp.

to set down both its feet heartily to the ground. But this is not from an ilka[1] day's disposition, but from some holiday notion and a sudden awakening. But a Cain will go asleep again, and leave God and his sick conscience both behind him, and go and build a city. Then try how your conscience dow[2] bear with an outcast with Christ. If you be halting home over to Christ, and looking a greedy and hungry-like look again; if there be a gnawing in the conscience to look home again, because in Satan's bounds, you are out of your own element, you take not with the country nor with the air, home you must be, it is a good token. It is not to be worse thought of that the lazy flesh will say, "Rise not yet to open to Christ. It is too early. It is long to-day. (2) It is a cold night. (3) It is an unreasonable suit. (4) It is an untimeous and hard charge. (5) Give Him not a naysay, but put off awhile, you have no scant of days before you." Howbeit the flesh has all these, yet if ye see through these shifts, and can find nothing but thorns in your way until you return to your first husband again (Hos. ii. 7), you will to the gate again, and Christ and you will, without fail, meet again.

"*My hands dropped with myrrh.*" In the Hebrew, passing myrrh, current myrrh, that is for excellency, passeth well among many merchants.

"*Upon the handles of the lock.*" That is, the Lord left the smell of His words that flowed from His sweet lips (Cant. v. 13). As well smelled as myrrh whereof the holy oil of the sanctuary was made (Exod. xxx. 23). And not only that, but a smell of the effectual working of His

---

[1] Every day.   [2] Can.

grace was left upon the lock of my heart, my will, and consent, which made my hands, that is, my actions, to smell sweetly. We see when Christ is gone Himself He leaves a sweet disposition of obedience behind Him that will do His turn. His grace rubbed and scoured the lock, and made it gleg[1] and easy to open. Christ's fingers wherever they come leave drops of grace behind them. If He go away Himself He leaves a pawn[2] behind Him. Where Christ walketh ye may discern the print of His feet behind Him. After a full sea, and the tide has gone in again, at the utmost point of the coast, the sea has left a white score of foam to tell the sea came to this point, and no further. Luke xxiv. 32, "Did not our hearts burn within us, while He talked with us by the way?" Christ can come by you suddenly in a blast of a whirlwind, in a preaching, and cast in a coal at the window of your soul, and leave it smoking, and slip His way? And He can shoot an arrow of love even to the feathers, and post away Himself, and say, "Pack you out. Here is a bone for you to gnaw on." And with all this He Himself in the joy of His presence is close away only He has left some token, either the gnawing worm of red-wood[3] hunger that is like to eat in at the one side and out at the other, or some work of believing, or of godly sorrow behind Him. Then ye are far in the wrong to Christ who tie Christ and His graces to the running of a sand-glass, and the time of preaching, and eating, and drinking. He can work by His hand when He is absent Himself, and preaching is sowing time, and sowing and harvest, yea, sowing time and growing

---

[1] Easy to work. [2] Pledge. [3] Sharp, furious.

time, are not aye¹ together. Offend not, storm not, because aye when He knocketh He makes not open doors. Thank God for the smell of Christ when ye cannot get Himself. O say ye, "I had rather have Himself nor² the smell of Him." Who can blame you? I know you had rather have twenty thousand crowns of gold as two crowns only. But you get no more for the time. Be thankful and wait on and steward well what you get.

"*I opened to my beloved; but my well beloved had withdrawn himself, and was gone.*" Upon sorrow for not opening follows a further degree of repentance for not opening. But when it is done to her great sorrow He is away, and has withdrawn Himself. This ordinarily follows our refusing to let Christ in that He go His way, and this is sad news. Now take up your hot bed, your lazy sinews, your tender feet, you dought³ not, for cold fyle⁴ your feet, and now you have lost your Lord. See then how far you wrong your Lord under desertions. We can complain and lay all the blame on Him and say, "O unkind Christ." Nay, but lay all the blame on thyself, and say, "Unkind fool that I am, who held Him at the door while His head was wet and frozen." He knocked, and ye would not let Him in. Well warred⁵ you knock and He hold you out.

Use. Then take your pennyworths of Christ while you have Him. We sit⁶ our market, and lose our Lord in the throng, and we cry wrong on Him instead of ourselves. By refusing to let Christ in we incur three great ills.

¹ Always. ² Than. ³ Could. ⁴ Defile.
⁵ Well done. ⁶ Neglect.

1. We are pyned[1] with hungry desires, and we draw at word and sacraments as a hungry bairn sucking dry breasts, and Christ will not let a mouthful of milk down His breasts. This is because we took not our tide of Christ. As Hos. v. 6, " They shall go with their herds to sacrifice, to seek the Lord, and shall not find Him, for they dealt treacherously against the Lord."

2. We lose increase of faith, joy, peace, and much grace, for we do think that Christ knocketh at our door toom[2] handed, and that when He comes in He brings nothing with Him. Nay, this were to judge Christ scarce worthy of His room.[3]

3. We lose in special manner joy and comfort. Sorrow and challenges fill the heart. When the husband is dead and buried let the wife see his coat, it shall cause her heart to bleed afresh for sorrow. The memory of the Lord's crying at the door, " Open to me, my sister, my love, my dove," and your obstinate refusing to let Him in is the coat of absent and buried Christ. The thought of His loving face you once saw, of His sweet tongue you once heard, is the very bleeding of a holed and wounded soul pierced through with sorrow.

" *My soul went out of me* " [Authorized Version, " My soul failed "]. (As Gen. xxxix. 18.) Or, My soul fainted; I fell in a sound[4] because of His speering.[5] But how did she fall in a swoon when He spake? for when He knocked and spake she gave Him a haglie[6] answer, that she would not go the breadth of the house, barefooted, to let Him in. This I take to be the sore and

[1] Pained. [3] Place. [5] Asking.
[2] Empty. [4] A swoon. [6] Rough.

fainting heart she had in hearing Christ's last rap at the door, and His last angry word, like that word of Christ to His sleepy disciples (Matt. xxvi. 45): "Sleep on now, take your rest: sleep your fill, I will go seek My lodging where I best may." And withal remembering His loving words, and remembering her dear Saviour and husband, meaned[1] His dear head in the cold, raw, and stormy air in the night. This brought on a sound,[2] that her soul for sorrow was gone out of her. We see, when the saints remember Christ's sweet promises and fair offers, and, withal, their unbelief and disobedience, it is a sting of conscience and a worm going to the bone, that makes a bleeding heart, and that makes a sound.[2] This, then, is a deep, hot, bleeding wound of conscience, remembering how her Lord spake, and how she refused His offer, for conscience is the two feet of the soul. When the conscience is dashed against a stone and gets a broken leg, the soul halteth, and this is painful and causes a sound.[2] Men know not what danger there is in cutting some master vein that is seated either upon heart or liver, and yet a little chap[3] there may bring on present death. Conscience is the master vein of the soul, and is threaded upon the life of the new birth. Draw blood in this vein by sending Christ away without His errand, and it is a hundred to one that the vein bleed not to death, and the sorrow be excessive even to bring sounding;[4] and in a swooning, man is betwixt life and death. This sickness and swooning are a little matter to beholders. It is easy to stand on the shore

---

[1] Lamented, moaned.   [2] Swoon.   [3] Blow, knock.
[4] Swooning.

and see the swimmer in danger of drowning, wrestling with the floods. But faith has been now at over giving[1] in the Church. Faith and sense are tough in such cases. For the first word of a troubled conscience is, "He is away;" and faith can say, "Liar! he is not away." Sense says, as Psalm lxxvii., "He has forgotten to be merciful;" and faith saith, "Thou liest! this is my infirmity." This should teach us to dote[2] and handle very kindly a tender conscience, and to be loath either to break a wheel of it by some great guiltiness, or to draw blood of it by security, impenitence, neglect of a fair offer. We may soon, with a reckless or sudden chap, call out a lith[3] in the conscience; but none in heaven or earth can stem the blood but Christ Jesus only. If, unseen Christ had not holden up the Kirk's head in her sound,[4] it had been her death.

"*I sought Him, but I found Him not; I called on Him, but He answered me not*" [Authorized Version, "I sought Him, but I could not find Him; I called Him, but He gave me no answer"]. Then under desertion we should seek. Christ is gone His gates[5] now, yet the Kirk lays Him a speering.[6] Peter, after his denial the third day, came to the grave to speer[7] for his Master Christ. The forlorn son, after a long outcast, yet looks home over again, and he thinks him of his father's house. So in Hos. xiv. 2 the fallen Kirk is bidden go home again, and take words with her and say, "Take away all iniquity, and receive us graciously." So also Jer. xxxi. 18, 19. Ephraim, chastised and put out of his father's house, is

---
[1] At the point of giving way. [2] Fondle. [3] Joint. [4] Swoon.
[5] Ways. [6] Sets about asking for Him. [7] Ask.

weeping, and with watery eyes looking home over and crying, "Turn me, and I shall be turned." When the saints are put out of God's house they resolve never to take unto another shift, but lie about God's house, and dree[1] about His door, and greet and weep and howl, at door and window, until God rue[2] upon them and call them in. When wicked men are put from God, they are like the servant put from service that seeks a new master; or like the ship-broken man who, seeing the ship going in pieces and ready to sink, resolves to quit it, and take him to swimming, purposing to make arms and legs serve him for a ship. I love it not when men put from God could resolve to seek about for a new master, and when Christ seems a broken ship they take them to swimming to seek another rock.

But here are two doubts: God will not be mine, how can I be His? *Answer*: Faith will bid you halve the covenant here, and say, "Lord, howbeit Thou wilt not be my Father, yet I will evermore be Thy son;" "howbeit Thou wilt not be my God, yet I will evermore be one of Thy covenanted people." We must learn to hang by little under outcasts. He is a blessed man whom God cannot slay, and a happy man whom his Father dow[3] not forsake. (2) I have sinned. Shall I go home again in my guiltiness? *Answer*: There is but one of two ways. Let me reason with such as saith it is a death for a guilty man to go home to God. Now I will give but not grant you it is death, but it is a greater death to bide[4] away. There are fire and water before you. One of them ye are chased to run to—either to the water or to the fire.

[1] Endure.   [2] Repent.   [3] Can.   [4] Stay.

Of two deaths that you cannot choose but one of them must end you. Take the little death, and pass the meikle[1] death. To bide[2] from God after an outcast, is fire and the great death. Eschew that to creep near Christ's bleeding wounds. Howbeit Christ should slay you to speak to your mind—howbeit it be death, it is but water, not fire; the little death, not the great death.

2. When all is done, it is life, and only life, to go to God after an outcast. Fear not, He will not slay you. Fools! that slandered Christ and called Him a manslayer. The devil lies falsely, for Christ is a sinner saver.

"*I sought Him, but I found Him not.*" A fearful and heavy temptation, as Lam. iii. 8: "When I shout, He shutteth out my prayer." Where His promise now? Prov. viii. 17: "Those that seek Me early shall find Me." Isa. lxv. 24: "And it shall come to pass, before they call I will answer; and while they are yet speaking, I will hear." And now here seeking and not finding, and calling and not answering. We may say here there is meikle betwixt[3] market days. This doctrine is preached daily true[4] to the saints. Let experience be the pulpit. When Christ prayed the same things thrice over (and "O My Father, if it be possible, remove this cup," it was this unco[5] world with Christ), the first two times to His soul's feeling He got but a dumb answer. In this doctrine there is more need to comfort men than to prove it true. The ground would be redd,[6] and all answered that possibly can be said. And—

First: God will tempt His own promise, as we think.

---

[1] Great. [2] Stay away. [3] All are not alike.
[4] Experience preaches the truth of this. [5] Strange. [6] Put in order.

Will not the promise look hungry like then? But there is no hunger at the heart of it. A worm will gnaw and nibble at the root of a plant, and cause it [to] lower to the one side, and droop and change colour; yet it liveth and wants not sap at the root. This same is yet clear, Our Lord will tempt His own word of promise, as we think, and yet the promise bruiks¹ life. "In Isaac shall thy seed be called" (Rom. ix.). A word of promise yet (Gen. xxii. 1, 2): "Abraham," says the Lord, "slay thy son Isaac, whom thou lovest." There is a worm at the root of the promise. The promise lowereth to the one side. This is a sore cross cavil to Abraham's faith. So Luke xxi. 18: "Not a hair of your head shall fall," says our Lord to His disciples. Yet Acts xii. 2: "Herod vexeth the church," and James his hair and head both are stricken off, and fall upon the ground. There was another cross langel² to the apostles' faith. Christ says the gates of hell shall not prevail against His Kirk; yet His Kirk is now as it was long since, and saying (as Jer. viii. 20): "The harvest is past, and the summer is ended, and we are not saved." The Lord stands looking on, and beholds fair play, and we are killed all the day long. Is not here in our seeming a withered and dry promise? What is then to be done here? I answer: Let faith lean not only upon a tottering promise (for if God's promise fall, no great matter, howbeit thy bit bridle faith fall also), but also let thy faith lean upon the very temptation as upon an ordinary and special work of God. When God's honour is impawned in saving His Kirk, He will come

---

¹ Enjoys.
² The rope that fastens the fore and hinder feet of a horse or cow together.

and loose His pawn; and when ye have foughten your fill, and your faith is at the latter swack,[1] He can then come and say, "Poor body! stand thou by, and dry the blood off you, and look on Me, and I will fight My part here." All the several objections are answered.

Objection 1. I am like to let my grips[2] go, and my weakness is giving over.[3]

Answer. Faith is not faith if it yield to carnal fears. Faith should be like the good wrestler who laid on his back yet keeps his grip. Like a man that is drowned with a bush in his hand, if you die here, die with a promise in your fist, and Christ in your arms; and how weak your flesh is, as spiritually wilful should your faith byde[4] by the mark.

Objection 2. Where is Omnipotence so long when I cry with a dry throat and pained breast, and am not heard?

Answer. Omnipotence is in God, and no elsewhere. Be sure not aye[5] at a call to claw your scabbed back. Neither is it Omnipotence's part to flatter you, or, as a pick-thank servant ready waiting on, to say "aye" and "nay" to your "yeas" and "nays." In a word, Omnipotence is at hand to save you when God will, not to humour your impatience as you will. We see not our hasty missing of God's power is not so much faith as the yooking[6] scab of our impatience.

Objection 3. Nay,—but I believe; I am sure I believe, and my very faith is not answered.

Answer. I am far from putting you from assurance of

---

[1] Last drop in the draught.   [2] Hold.   [3] Yielding.   [4] Remain.
[5] Always.   [6] Itching.

faith, and I am sure it is so. But hasted [1] humours and faith riding both in one race, posting together, our dazzled eyes will take the one for the other. He that believes makes no haste. Faith will knock seven times at God's door, and still wait on. You would have at first in your neive [2] what you seek, else you will not play. That faith of yours has soon done with it. A doubt may be made of a hastered [3] faith that it looks like the prophet's cake unturned, and so raw on the one side. Therefore see that it be not a hot, sudden humour; for God has promised to answer your faith, but not your humour; your patient request, but not your hasty command; your submissive desire, but not your wild, fiery passion.

Objection 4. Then you would put me from all assurance that I believe, because I dow [4] not wait?

Answer. Far be it from me; but that faith that ye think faith, in as far as it is so hot-spurred that it will either have a present answer or nothing, it is not faith as ye think. Howbeit it be with faith as smoke is beside fire, but it is not fire. Impatience beside faith is smoke, not fire. Discern, therefore, the one from the other.

Objection 5. My not seeing or feeling God filling my hand, breaks my faith in pieces. Would He let me see He were coming, I would delay.

Answer. Friend, ye may go to your watch, for (Heb. xi. 1) "faith is the substance of things hoped for, and the evidence of things not seen," and faith doth cast an anchor in the night where it sees neither brim nor bottom. Faith is content with a fair unseen God's

---

[1] Early.   [2] Hand, fist.   [3] Hurried.   [4] Can.

venture, and you, a man, may weep and say (Isa. viii. 17): "I will wait upon the Lord that hides His face from the house of Jacob, and I will look for Him."

Objection 6. It is hard to see and believe.

Answer. Then ye say nothing but it is hard to believe, for faith believeth God's bare word with a pair of covered eyes. Secondly, yet ye have the light of the promises, and that is as good as Christ Himself. When it is told a wife, after seven years' absence of her husband, "I saw him: this and this he was doing: he said he would come home by and by to his wife:" this is a next best thing to the poor woman until he come home himself; and believing her husband will not lie, she sets down her stake there in a piece of patience until he come. Hab. ii. 3: "For the vision is for an appointed time, but in the end it shall speak and shall not lie; though it tarry, yet wait for it; because it will surely come, it will not tarry."

Objection 7. It is a wearisome, toilsome, and dreary life that He keeps me in, to hold in His hand and cause me to wait on with little joy, no feeling, and skant[1] and want of old kisses.

Answer. Measure the life by the profitableness of it, and by the sweetness of your submission to God's wise dispensation, and not by your wearying. Little matter ye want sweetness if your faith be on its journey to God. If the traveller be going home, the less matter he be wet to the skin.

Objection 8. I want comfort in calling and getting no answer.

Answer. Faith may be without comfort, and offend ye

[1] Scarcity.

because ye cannot get aye¹ an apple to play the bairn with when ye would. Let it be your comfort that for God's cause, and in a humble submitting of your spirit to an absent Christ, ye can want comfort. He shall get his wombful of comfort that can want comfort, that God may be honoured with his believing and on waiting.

Objection 9. I would believe in the dark, and wink and believe, if I had comfort.

Answer. And little thanks to you to swim when Christ holds up your chin. The greatest praise to your faith, the greatest honour to Christ that can be, is when faith walketh upon fewest legs, neither feeling nor joy, nor comfort, nor experience, nor sight, but only this one: He is faithful who has promised; so said my beloved Christ, and I will believe.

Objection 10. Nay, I see of purpose God holds me off, and shifts me from day to day.

Answer. I grant you, and He well avows that He suspends the subscribing of your bill; for His delay is the seeking of your further kindness, faith, patience, &c. He knows that it is true, " soon had, soon gotten, soon forgotten; " soon heard of Christ, and soon unkind to Christ. A dear² coft³ from Christ is well locked up.

Objection 11. Nay, but His delays are plain judgments, and bode anger.

Answer. Your mind, in my mind, is in a night dream. Expone His delays right, and ye ought to thank God for them. The longer leisure an earthly prince [give] to a poor complaining subject to tell his errand over again and over again, the greater is he obliged to the patience

---
¹ Always. ² That costs much. ³ Purchase.

of the prince. When God is delaying you that ye may pray again, He is like a father saying to his bairn, "Hold up your head, my bairn; speak loud and tell it over again. I heard not what my bairn said." Cant. ii. 14: "My dove that dwelleth in the clefts of the rock, cause me to hear thy voice."

Objection 12. When He delays, I wonder where He is all this time. I fear He come not at all.

Answer. Where He is where He is not, even coming to tryst[1] with your faith's last sob, and purposeth ye shall not die through His lingering. But in waiting till He come, beware ye believe He will never come.

Objection 13. It were great glory to God, and a great confirmation to my faith, that He is a ready help at hand, and heard my prayers at the first call.

Answer. Nay, but His glory is your onwaiting for the trial of your faith and patience and love. When He has gotten this, and is first served, then ye shall be much served in His deliverance of you. But when ye pretend God's glory, and that ye should be served, you are gaping for your own ease, and that ye yourself should be first served in a present deliverance, and no reason but He be first served.

The only principal *use* of all is that we be charitable of our Lord when He answereth not at the first. Love thinks no ill. Far less should it think ill of God. Faith should be long-breathed and not soon tired, and lie believing and praying till the grey hairs. Well betideth all God's on-waiters. They get their errand with meikle joy. The devil takes the word out of Christ's mouth to

[1] Meet.

unbelievers, and saith, "He will not come;" and they take a false answer from Christ. What! shall I wait any longer upon the Lord? And so their faith falls in two in the waft. Wait upon Christ's answer. If it be not an answer of mercy, wait on still, for there is a better one coming from Christ—to Whom, with the Father and Holy Ghost, be glory, praise, and honour, for ever and ever.—Amen.

The Church Seeking her Lord.

" The watchmen that went about the city found me, they smote me, they wounded me ; the keepers of the walls took away my veil from me. I charge you, O daughters of Jerusalem, if ye find my beloved, that ye tell him, that I am sick of love. What is thy beloved more than another beloved, O thou fairest among women? what is thy beloved more than another beloved, that thou dost so charge us? My beloved is white and ruddy, the chiefest among ten thousand."—SONG OF SOLOMON v. 7–10.[1]

N this text we have two things. 1. What befell the Kirk in seeking of her Lord—the watchman gave her straiks.[2] 2. What speeches fell out betwixt her and her fellow friends. And there is a dialogue betwixt them. 1. The Church not finding Christ Himself to her desire, layeth a charge on her companions to take her blessing and her hearty commendations to Him whenever they meet (ver. 7). 2. They upon the occasion of the vehemency of her charge not so spiritually affected as need were, answer, What a walie[3] beloved is this? What din is that ye make to charge us so peremptorily about your Christ? Have you a Christ of your own? Whereof is your Christ made that you charge us this way? And (ver. 9) the Church's stomach arising that

[1] Preached in the afternoon at the communion at Anwoth, April 5, 1647.
[2] Strokes.   [3] Excellent.

THE CHURCH SEEKING HER LORD. 117

her Lord should be despised, falls out in a higher commendation of Him to the end of the chapter in all His proportions.

"*The watchmen that went about the city found me, they smote me*"—with their tongue (Jer. xviii. 18); wounded me, and drew blood of me (Luke xx. 12). No doubt she asked of the watchmen, as chap. iii. 3 : " Saw ye Him whom my soul loveth ? " But they not only refused to tell her, but they wounded her conscience with reproachful words, and persecuted her. We see in the way of seeking lost Christ there are persecutions and troubles. I think Christ is even like dear over-sea wares. Men hazard both life and goods to sea for them, and (Matt. xiii.) He is the pearl that men must buy with the loss of all they have. The woman with the bloody issue gat a thrust in the throng, thrusting in through a multitude to be at Him; and the two blind men crying, for ilk [1] one of them had a pair of blind eyes, gat rebukes of the disciples. We may know, first, we shall never get Satan's goodwill to come to Christ, and therefore he professeth he will wait the gate for us. Second, sufferings and persecutions are in the way to Christ. This is a piece of old rent that lies [2] to Christ's house. He suffered Himself ere He went into glory. Let them put on courage who seek Christ. Let them resolve to take cuffs, blae-straiks,[3] and bloody wounds, in the seeking of Christ and the professing of His name. "If any man will be My disciple, let him take up his cross and follow Me." We will not get this changed. The cross is upon Christ's back. It follows Him and backs Him. Suffer-

[1] Each.   [2] Belongs to.   [3] Strokes.

ings are hard, and we love to lodge in a whole skin, yet we would seek Christ and profess Him, and jouk[1] about to beguile the cross of Christ, and play it a slip; and we think to slip to heaven another way, and therefore men study the art of wiliness now to hide their profession. Nay, that this is not straight dealing and fair play ye must fill the field and throw honestly and fairly, and be marked as one that follows the Lamb wheresoever He goeth.

"*The watchmen.*" Christ's governors are sometimes Christ's persecutors. Scribes and Pharisees and high priests were always against Christ and His disciples. Paul found the rulers of the Jews always against him and the gospel, wherever they had any hand or authority. And Christ told His disciples (Luke xxi. 12), "Ye shall be brought before kings and rulers for My name's sake." The leaders of the people have been their persecutors. Ezekiel xxxiv. 4: "With force and cruelty have ye ruled;" verse 18: "They made the people to eat trodden on grass, and they gave them foul water to drink."

But ye will say: Seeing God has laid a great burden upon rulers, especially upon watchmen, why may not the people lay the same burden on them and commit our souls to them? Nay, but we must know God is Lord of the decree of reprobation, and for His own glorious ends gives some over to corrupt teachers, and yet we sin in selling our conscience to their doctrine. But there is (1) something to be said here for people, (2) something for watchmen.

[1] Bend the head to evade the stroke.

THE CHURCH SEEKING HER LORD. 119

1. Something for people. There be here two extremities. Pride giveth too little, and slavish consciences give too much, to watchmen. Therefore let their feet be pleasant that publish good tidings. Rulers are tutors to Christ's bairns that are minors. Therefore let rulers get all their own, for pride against them stots [1] off them upon God; and when their laws are unjust we owe to them an upholding of the majesty, dignity, credit, and honour which God has given them. Therefore so to disobey unjust laws as that we take at [2] the majesty and face of rulers is unlawful, seeing we are willed to honour the king (1 Pet. ii. 17; Eccles. x. 20). So all comes to this, that troublers of the peace of the kirk or commonwealth condemned (Rom. xii. 18; Heb. xii. 14), and discrediting authority in the very act of refusing obedience to the unjust decrees, is unlawful. Again, the patience of an ass in any man that has a conscience is unlawful. People here stand still without a halter in their head while rulers lay a load of dirt upon them, and their best devotion here resolves in "God forgive our teachers if they lead us wrong, for we know no better." If the watchmen forbid or command, and load your conscience under the pain of straiks,[3] he is but an ill market man who would give much for such people's part of their inheritance. Men forget that we watchmen can put a toom [4] spoon in a bairn's mouth, and cry, "The Church rulers! authority, authority! the law, the law!" as if the Bible were long ago burned. But know ye not that watchmen in Christ's matters can totter; yea, the chair and the pulpit can reel; and therefore if your light be your Scripture, God

[1] Rebounds.   [2] Oppose, or use freedom with.   [3] Strokes.   [4] Empty.

help you. I will not give much for your faith, for our faith often sits door-neighbour with the world, and the world prisoneth light. Go over sea to Rome and learn this. In the doctrine of the law of nature, of the Godhead, of two natures in Christ, for the most part they are sound, for this truth has little trafficking with the world's fatness. But because Purgatory (denied by a famous Papist to have any just claim to truth by any patent in Scripture) doth lie in the world's fat arm, gain, giving milk and suck to it, therefore this chamber in hell is stiffly maintained, because this lie is a ship that bringeth home much gold, and one dying will toom[1] his purse to ease his conscience. Therefore when the command of rulers has ease, honour, the world and the fatness of the earth on the one side, and on the other there is nothing but losses and sufferings, the question speaks clearly the world's side is thief-like and to be suspected. And this is too ordinary in rulers, as also in us all by nature, to seek the truth as the wanton child doth his book, wishing he may not find it, and fearing the finding of his book cost him the loss of his pastime. Would men in the fear of God dig for wisdom as for gold, they would find it. But as if men forsaw the less light the more false peace, they take as much of conscience as makes for them, and no more. And when light of conscience cries on them too fast they wish it wanted the tongue, and in their heart pray a sorrow to the well-shod tongue of an enlightened conscience.

"*The keepers of the wall took away my vail from me.*"

[1] Empty.

Either they took away the scarf that covered her face, or her vail, or kerchief that did cover her head, which was both an ornament (Isa. iii. 23) and a sign of subjection of the wife to her husband (1 Cor. xi. 7); for because (Ezek. xxiii. 25) they took away the vail from lewd women, as a token they were harlots, whereas the vail is a sign of modesty. It is clear the rulers beat the Kirk from obedience to her Lord, and called her a harlot, heretical, and schismatical, and covered her with a vail of traditions. In Solomon's days rulers have been playing and encroaching upon the woman's vail and her subjection to Christ, her husband in hearing, and obeying his voice only; and this is again decorous and modesty to pull the poor woman's vail off her head and send her out barefaced and bareheaded among the enemies to be laughen at and mocked. This has come in rulers and tutors under pretence they owe obedience and subjection to the watchmen. Because watchmen think they get not in commanding too much (whereas Christ allows them in commanding only the chair[1] of sent servants, straitly bound with a written commission from the Lord), therefore they make a hole in the poor woman's vail, or they pull the kerchief off her head, and busk her with a vail of human traditions, a vail of fig-leaves, not a kerchief of Christ's fine linen. This is pride in men of eminent place in the Kirk; and pride is an ill and cumbersome neighbour beside Christ. It is always going over the line, and not content with its own side, and thinking its own bounds strait and narrow. It will be over the march in Christ's hained[2] pasture. It is a curse in the

[1] No other authority than.   [2] Enclosed.

law to remove our neighbour's landmark, and take in a piece of Christ's furrow. Watchmen have power and authority here, and it cannot be denied but they are often like the man who shearing away the hair, that he cuts both quick hide [1] and flesh. Rulers, in cutting off hair and exercising what power Christ has given them, they too oft cut Christ's quick hide and come in upon the flesh with their knife, meddling with the woman's kerchief and vail, which only should be of His busking, for it is His own kingly power to govern His Kirk and to busk her as He pleases. When men take upon them to do it they cut the quick flesh; and therefore our Lord had good cause to say (Psa. ii. 10), "Be wise, be instructed ye judges of the earth; guide well; look to your tackling;" but the mischief is, honour is an apple so sweet that Balaam will stem the spirit of prophesying, howbeit the form should nip in pieces. To come to the purpose, and men's honour and their unbounded appetite to be at the chair of it and to keep it has often made a wide hole in the kirk wall, and such a slap in the Confession of Faith as an idol as great as a kirk has come into Christ's house. Men would fain be at this to clip in length and breadth the woman's vail, to make it as meet for policy as a strait coat for a woman's body until it pain her, and she pains it until the seam skaileth [2] and loupeth out. The woman's vail is most seemly when rulers suffer it to keep the just quantity and length and breadth of the Lord's pattern on the Mount, and it is the wife's part to stick by the vail and put on no other. Better lose her tutors than her husband.

[1] Living skin. [2] Parts and bursts.

"*From me.*" The Church gat this ill turn of the watchmen because she held her Lord at the door. For this cause, because (Lam. i. 8, 10) " Jerusalem had grievously sinned. . . . The adversary hath spread out his hands on all her pleasant things (and so also upon her vail); for she hath seen that the heathen hath entered into her sanctuary, when Thou didst command that they should not enter into Thy congregation." The Kirk of God gets carnal lords to rule over her, and gods of wood and of stone to serve every day and night—Jer. xvi. 13; and verse 11, "Because your fathers have forsaken Me, saith the Lord, and have walked after other gods, and served them and worshipped them." We can complain of our Lord's absence and of His unkindness, and of cruel watchmen, and we are only to be blamed. We made the broust ourselves, and we can lay the blame of spoiled drink upon God. Would we keep good quarters with Christ, we should get pastors according to Christ's own heart. People under blind shepherds should rather then cry out against themselves who are wandering sheep, than against their shepherds who cause them to err. A repenting man is more angry at his own heart that consented to sin than he is at the devil who did tempt him to sin. There is oft too much crying out against rulers who have not always hap to steer the rudder of the ship cannily,[1] and too little godly sorrow for our sins, that procure that " leopards and lions shall watch over our cities" (see Hosea xiii. 7, and Jer. v. 6).

"*I charge you, O daughters of Jerusalem.*" The Church with much ado hath escaped the hands of the watchmen,

[1] Cautiously.

and finding small and very cold comfort from them, and no news about her beloved, turns her to followers and companions, and conferring with them to tell her well-beloved that she is sick of love for Christ.

This teaches what duty the saints owe one to another, to love one another (1 Thess. iv. 9), and to teach one another (Col. iii. 16); "Exhort one another daily" (Heb. iii. 13); "Provoke one another to love and to good works, not forsaking the assembling of yourselves together" (Heb. x. 24, 25); and among themselves to speak that which is good to the use of edifying, that it may minister grace to the hearers (Eph. iv. 29), having speech always with grace seasoned with salt (Col. iv. 6). This God commanded: "Say to your brethren, Ammi; and to your sisters, Ru-hamah. Plead with your mother, plead." This charge is given to every one of the faithful to plead with the apostates of their time. And Mal. iii. 16, "Then they that feared the Lord spake often one to another; and the Lord hearkened, and a book of remembrance was written before Him." Our Lord thinks so meikle of the sweet and comfortable speeches among the faithful ones, that He lays to His ear and hears it, and writes it up in a book; and Zech. viii. 21: "And the inhabitants of one city shall go to another, saying, Let us go speedily to pray before the Lord, and to seek the Lord of hosts; I will go also." This speaketh and crieth aloud against those who confine all exercise of God's worship within the walls of the kirk, making all their worship holiday worship, using godliness for holiday as they do their Sabbath clothes. But Abraham had religion within his house. He taught his children sitting and walking in his house, and in the field, lying down at night, and rising up in the morning; and Philemon had a kirk at his house. Are not ministers Christ's stewards? and who knows not the bairns may possibly not be disposed to eat at the set time of the ordinary meal, and in the public ministry, for the Word's working and Spirit's working are not always confined to the hour of the sand-glass, neither is the Spirit tied to a pulpit, and a gown, and a minister's tongue. Shall we then think Christ's house is so narrowly holden and his pantry so scant that He will not allow a four hours' drink upon His bairns or a piece between meals? Shall not hungry bairns get no more nor public allowances in church assemblies? Nay, our Lord allows His bairns to carry home to their houses grapes and apples off the tree of life, and eat at home. For many coals make a great fire, and private Christians will rub one another's memory and their cold hearts; and often what ministers cannot do in public, God's Spirit with private helps will do it at home. It is seen when a great doctor of physic has given over the man, an old wife has come in after him, and wrought the cure, and made the man sound whole. This doctrine should be right understood, for it warrants not the conventicles and unwarrantable meetings of Separatists and Brownists, who despise public meetings, and make a kirk in private houses of their own. They learn not this from Christ, who honours the Pharisees' preaching sitting in Moses' chair with His own presence, and commanded others so to do; howbeit they had leaven in their doctrine. We will not get a church of clean paper and of new velvet as

Separatists and Anabaptists would have, and it is a fearful sin to make a rent and a hole in Christ's mystical body because there is a spot in it; and this place will not help the conventicles of Separatists, for the Church here has conferred publicly with the watchmen, as chapter iii. 8. She so honoured the public means that she said, "Saw ye Him whom my soul loveth?"[1]

"*Tell Him that I am sick of love.*" This is a broken, fiery, and passionate kind of speech, wherein she lays a charge upon her companions that they would in their prayers to God show Christ her errand, and take her hearty commendations and blessing to Christ because for the present she cannot get Himself. In a desertion anything is good meat to a hungry soul. When the Church had Christ, and was near to Him, there being a thin door only betwixt Him and her, she counted little of Him, and would not fyle[2] her feet to let Him [in]. To a full soul even the honeycomb is loathsome. But now, having lost Christ, with a great desire she is content to get one that will carry her commendations to Him. Hunger for Christ is good cheer, and a good feast. Experience may confirm this doctrine, for sometimes a kiss of Christ's mask when ye cannot get His bare face is a full dinner. When David is at home the worship of God and His tabernacle is not so sweet, when he may have the best rowme[3] in it. But in Psalm lxxxiv. he would be content with all his heart of the swallows' rowme[3] in the bowers of the house, and then a psalm was sweet-

---

[1] See this clause more fully expounded and applied at pp. 307-327 of Rutherford's treatise, "Influences of the Life of Grace."
[2] Soil.   [3] Place.

meat. But when he yoked [1] with Bathsheba both the tabernacle and Psalms dreed [2] of cold, and were laid up to a full sea. Compare here faith and sense together, and you will find sense prouder nor [3] faith. Sense will have nothing except it find an open door to go into God, and faith will be content to busk and to look in through the key-hole to see but the half of Christ's face or one of His ruddy cheeks. The Kirk's sense is at this—Cant. i. 2: "Let Him kiss me with the kisses of His mouth." That is a piece of pride to rest with nothing as content but the Lord's bare face, His breath, and a kiss. But (Luke vii.) a poor woman is content to kiss His feet. "Set Me as a seal upon thy heart," says the Kirk (Cant. viii. 6). Sense there will be in no place except at the board-head, and the first mess and the hand in the plate with Christ. But the woman of Canaan's hungry faith is glad to lie under the table with the dogs, and to eat the crumbs that fall from His table. Thomas his sense has not except he see Christ and put his finger in the print of the nails and his hands in the hole of His side. The silly [4] hungry woman with the bloody issue will be content to touch the hem of His garment. Servants' bread is good cheer to the home-coming forlorn son. It was once another world when bairns' bread was no delicacy to him. This reproves doated lovers, who when they have full wallets and abundance of Christ's love and their armful of Him, misregards Christ, and makes small reckoning to anger Him, and set not by [5] His presence because wealth causes wit to waver. Such spoiled bairns in a wealthy world let wisdom's good

[1] Joined himself to. [2] Suffered, endured. [3] Than. [4] Feeble [5] Value not.

meat spoil and sour. And when that world is away they would be glad of the licking of Christ's trencher. O, but humble hunger will think meikle[1] of half a smile and half a kiss of Christ. And the reasons are these :

1. Desertion and absence of Christ is a great scourge to pride and security. When we have Christ at will and access, presence, sense, and liberty, ere we are aware we turn wanton and secure, and count little of Christ's sweet tongue and His lovely knocks. It is even so here. Beggars dow[2] not bear wealth, Christ's lordly beggars, His full spoiled and doited[3] louns,[4] find the ground of their stomach then. And because you are too full and know not well wherefore the well serveth you till it go dry, it is the wisdom of Christ that ye go over hungry grass, and seek after the half blinks that ye counted little of before, and eat sweetly the last year's leavings, and be glad of Christ's mouldy bread.

2. Humility is never well-fed, and fat till sense grow traiked[5] and lean, and then when sense is traiked[5] and lean, and like to starve in a famine, spiritual humility (to speak so) gets checks, and grows fat, under desertion, while hunger makes a wide mouth: then comes David's "How long, Lord?" (Psa. v.)

"*I am sick of love*"—or, as the Hebrew word beareth, "weak through love." That is, feeling wrath and the curse of the land, and wanting the sense of His pardoning love. I am sick through longing to have reconciliation and forgiveness, as is exponed well in Isa. xxxiii. 24: "The inhabitant shall not say I am sick; the people that dwell therein shall be forgiven their iniquity." So is it

[1] Much.   [2] Can.   [3] Stupid.   [4] Worthless persons.   [5] Weak.

in this song at chap. ii. 5; at Matt. ix. 12: "They that are whole need not the physician, but they that are sick." He means Saviour-sick for the physician Christ; and, Psa. ciii. 2, 3: "Bless the Lord, O my soul, who forgiveth all thine iniquities, and healeth all thy diseases." This is her pained conscience saying: "I am pained, I am in a fever, the health, constitution, and frame of the life of my soul is troubled because I want Jesus." To take the thing up that aileth the Kirk now we must know that it is not the bairn's truant sickness, nor the loun ill that aileth the Kirk, for there is pain and sorrow in this sickness: "My soul panteth after Thee, O God. My soul thirsteth for God, for the living God: when shall I come and appear before God?" (Psa. xlii. 1, 2.) "My soul longeth, yea, even fainteth for the courts of the Lord: my heart and my flesh crieth out for the living God." When the heart panteth and the flesh has a tongue to cry, David was not at himself. It is with the saint's longing for Christ as when a woman's husband has been long over sea; every ship she sees makes her both blith[1] and sad, for hope deferred is a breaking of the bones. The first sight is half joy, but with pain, when all the passengers land and her husband is not there, then her heart breaketh. Every one that knocketh at the door makes her both blith[1] and sad when she sees it is another, she sighs and says: "Alas! it is not my love." In this Saviour-sickness the soul in the word and sacrament waiteth for Christ. When it is not He, oh! then the heart is woe: "I missed Him and I got Him not." Second: As in other sickness

[1] Glad.

so here, meat and drink do the sick man little good, and sleep can he not. The sick man now has no mind of sleep; his absence holds her waking. Word, sacraments, reading, prayer, conferring, have no taste. They feed not. The soul is ill-like and sick, until Christ come Himself, with a drink of cold fountain water of the well that runneth out from the sanctuary from under the throne of God and the Lamb (Rev. xxii.) The poor soul gets never a kindly cool of love fever. Third: In this sickness there is fear of wrath, a fire in the soul, and a sort of unbelief and fear He come not, for hunger is hard of faith. When hunger and faith run together hunger is speediest of foot, and out-runneth faith. Old Jacob hearing this that his son Joseph liveth, he believeth not, for his heart fainted (Gen. xlv. 26). Yet he would fain have had it true, but desire made such a wide mouth and racked itself so far until faith took the cramp. It is as we say, "What good news! Alas! I fear they be not true," and say to a sick soul burnt up with God's wrath, "Be blith,[1] Christ is coming;" he will let out a look with a watery eye, and death, earth hunger. "Alas! I fear it be not He, I would so fain have it Him. I dow[2] not believe it. Fear fills my heart, and that fear is a pain of the fever."

But is it not a dangerous case, may you say, to be thus sick? *Answer:* As Christ said in another sense, so may we here: "This sickness is not unto death, but to the glory of God," for there are speaking and crying tokens of life here. And, first, this sickness has a fair long tail. It is drawing Christ down out of heaven to the broad side of the poor soul that is Christ-

[1] Glad. [2] Can.

sick. Christ comes always to the cooling of the fever. Nay, He is always in the house, howbeit the person in the fever know Him not; He is at the sick man's bedside preparing drugs and washing herbs for him. He is looking on. Her groans and her sighs are of my well-beloved Christ, my dear husband, and His groans and His sighs, howbeit not heard by her, answer hers behind the curtain. Oh! for my dear bride, the Lamb's wife. And—

Second: There is here another good token, a sweet impatience in this love-sickness. Every hour for absent Christ is a day, every day a year. "And oh!" says the soul, "Saw ye Him. . . . Oh! He is long in coming. He goes slowly. Oh! run, well-beloved like a roe, or a young hart upon the mountains."

Third: This one sympton of a Saviour-fever is also that there is a deadly sorrow until He come again. The harp of joy [is] laid by and hanged up until Christ come again and put in tune.

Fourth: All this time there is a fire of love to Christ in the heart, and His absence is like a fan to cause it to burn faster.

Fifth: The special prevalent mark that proveth it will end well is hunger and thirst for Christ, and a rude working hunger, and hunger that has hands and feet, and it is the only choice token of life.

But a question may be asked here in this sickness. That there is here a heart fainting and hunger for Christ, pronounced by Christ to be a mark of those whom God shall fill (Matt. v. 6); yet the hungry soul will not accept of this mark, and because he has the mark of hunger rather reasoneth the contrary, he is none of God's? *Answer:* Because extreme hunger would so fain believe that often out of desire to have it true that Christ cometh, it unbelieveth, as is said before.

Second. Hunger is of kin and blood to want, and is of its own nature a toom,[1] empty thing, and thereupon the man thinketh he wanteth all.

Third. God disposes it to be so because hunger is given to man that he should not rest upon it, but seek meat. But we may learn how to spain[2] our desires, even to send them out in love-sickness for Christ. If the pulses of many souls in our time were graiped,[3] they would be found not sick of love, but sick of lust. Some have, alas! sickness for their neighbour's vineyard, others Haman's sickness after he led Mordecai through the streets, sick of court because his honour got a scad.[4] This age is full of sick men, fevers are rife, every man seeks for this world.

If ye find my beloved what shall ye tell Him [Authorized Version, "If ye find my Beloved that ye tell Him"]. The Church must find Christ ere she can tell Him. It is only a found Christ we must pray to. If we start Him not, and snapper[5] not on Him where He is, we cannot pray to Him. This condemns those who tell Christ's news and they never find Him. They pray and speak to Christ, and they never meet with Him. They must then be dumb prayers; and so they are. When men get not access at all, they but cast away prayers in the air. He that prays in one measure or other, must win in to the King's chamber of presence, and to the feet of King

---

[1] Empty. [2] Wean. [3] Felt. [4] Scald. [5] Stumble.

Jesus' chair of state: "By whom also we have access by faith into this grace, wherein we stand" (Rom. v. 2).

Objection: Oh! I pray often, and I think I have not found Him. Are all these prayers then lost? *Answer:* All find not Christ in a like measure, yet little faith is faith, and every weight of gold is gold, a mool[1] as a mountain of gold. Second: If you have found yourself in prayer, you may soon find Him. If you get but in prayer the sense of a pair of blind eyes, and a dead heart, it is a degree of finding Him. Third: Know there be three degrees of those that find Christ. First: Your Lord gives you sometimes but the beggar's welcome, a closed door, and liberty to set your mouth to the hole of Christ's lock, and cry through that ye find Him, when ye find but the very hole of Christ's lock. Second: Sometimes the half-door is casten up, howbeit your weak arms dow[2] not cast up the door to the wall; and this is more than the first, and here they lie whining and scraping at His doors with some degree of motion and liberty, wrestling with an unbelieving heart. Third: Sometimes you find the whole door casten up, and your bridegroom taking an hearty armful of you, which is possibly a feast by the common.

Any of these are a finding of Him. Only beware of fashionable and dead prayers coming from custom, not from conscience. One of the marks whereof, is that men cast in their bill to Christ, and never ask whether it be heard or not. Then ere ye go away, leave a loud, last knock, and observe what God sayeth, and always so pray as that you instantly urge the answer of your bill.

[1] A crumb or particle. [2] Can.

Objection: Then when I cannot find Christ, shall I not bide [1] aback, and pray none till I find Him?

Answer: This is a deep one of Satan, that some men will not come to Christ until they be so busked that there is not a wrong pin upon them. Nay, it is best to go to Christ with ragged and rent clothes. Necessity cannot blush. Young children rive [2] two or three books ere they learn one. Better spill [3] a prayer or two and fumble at it, as be deluded of Satan to wait until your heart be on a good blood. Nay, a cold man must walk and stir himself until he be hot. Prayer is like God's file to stir a rusty heart; blowing helpeth a cold fire, and by moving, working, and stirring upon the new birth, the heart will grow warm. To stay from praying until the heart say, "Now, God, now I am prepared," is the way to lose what ye have, but not to find more. Be doing though weakly. If there be something of yours and something of Christ's, He will accept of His own, and pardon yours freely and fully.

"*If ye find my beloved.*" Then Christ is a seeking, and [is] lost in the Kirk's feeling, yet notwithstanding is her well-beloved, as ver. 1. Christ standeth without at the wrong side of the door, yet is her well-beloved. Nay, the covenant standeth if ye were in hell and He in heaven at the right hand of the Father, yet He is my Lord and my God. We see want of present possession of Christ depriveth not the saints' right and just claims to Him. A man year and day our king's rebel loses his life-rent of present possession, yet the heritage is his and his heirs. He loses the use, but not the right. A

[1] Remain.   [2] Tear up.   [3] Mar, destroy.

nobleman having three houses to dwell in, the king for his fault confines him for all his life within one of them. His confinement forfaults the use of the other two, but his right remaineth. So right doth it fare with the saints; they, being Christ's outlaws for some offence, do often lose a very life-rent of spiritual joy and comforts, and so are Christ's confined rebels, and they lose joy, comfort, and present access, liberty, feelings, love blenks;[1] Christ in His felt presence being under a wadset[2] to them; yet faith all this time will not deny They will say, "My Lord, my Saviour, my well-beloved;" Isa. xlix. 14: "Zion said, My God hath forsaken me." Well, Zion, think on of that! "Thy God," and yet He has forsaken you that is thy God and not thy God. Your tongue makes you a liar. But here under the forefaultery[3] the claim standeth still. Jonah ii. 4: "Then I said, I am cast out of thy sight." I said, whilk[4] I? "Even I roving, dreaming, Jonah said." God said it not, for Jonah's claim, right, and title to God stood still. They are fools, then, who hang up all the rights of their salvation upon a felt presence; a loose, rotten pin. Money lent out upon bank is a man's proper goods, howbeit not in his coffer. Christ to the saints is sometimes lent-out money, yet is He yours. You see the furnace making for you, and finding Christ behind the wall you learn to *swim*, howbeit a wombful of feeling be not at hand to hold up your head. Daunted[5] bairns, you must learn to go your alone, howbeit your mild

---

[1] Gleams, glimpses.
[2] A legal deed by which the debtor hands over his heritable property to his creditor that the creditor may draw the rents in payment of the debt.
[3] Forfeiture.   [4] Which.   [5] Caressed, fondled.

nurse Jesus be not at the bairn's back to hold you by the two shoulders. If you can do this and keep your assurance, howbeit hell and wrath were in the shell of your heart yet Christ and heaven are in the yolk of it.

"*What is thy beloved more than another beloved?*" The companions of the kirk being somewhat carnal and not well acquainted with love-sickness as the Church is, giveth her a sore check, for the Kirk spake with feeling, and took an hearty mouthful of it in charging of her well-beloved. And therefore the companions of the Church double[1] the question, and they say, "Have you any beloved of the new cut. Whereof is your Christ made more than other Christs? There is fell[2] great din of your beloved. What needs all this? You are fell[2] hot in the chase that you come on with adjurations and charges. I would not have you overfine. Be like neighbour and other. Neighbour-like in holiness is very good." We see in as far as we are carnal we dow[3] not bide heat and forwardness in religion. We love still a moderation in God's matters. We need not think but the old world thought Noah too holy and too just. He will make a great vessel on dry land far from the sea, and he will have all the world but seven moe[4] and himself drowned for sin. Noah in all the world, and none like him; he is the only man. You know Jeroboam in bringing in the golden calf in 2 Kings xii. 28: "It is too much for you to go up to Jerusalem to worship. Behold thy gods, O Israel! which brought you up out of the land of Egypt." He would say: "It cannot be denied but it is God's law to

[1] Repeat. [2] Strange, unusual. [3] Cannot abide. [4] More.

go up to Jerusalem to worshipping, but, saving his own wisdom, it is a strait one, it is too much and more nor[1] necessity. If God be worshipped I doubt not but the place where is indifferent. Therefore it is not good to be fiery and lay too sore a burden upon the people, to pain ourselves to take the young ones, the male children, thrice a year up to Jerusalem." Therefore Jeroboam with a piece of desertion would slack the girth. There is a thing now in religion that they call discretion and a wise moderation. This is the only safeway. Let cold, politic, canny[2] men go before you, and follow them and dance ye as they pipe, and that is now sure work. "He is old enough, ask himself," say the parents of the blind man. They thought the rulers burdened their discretion with a tempting question, and therefore they would not take the tale ere it came to them. "I love Christ," says the middoway man or the half-lan[3] man, "but I would not make a blowing horn of my religion. They shall never know upon what side I am. Fye! fye! for wisdom to this age. I hope I am as good a Protestant as any of them. I hope I have a soul to keep, but ill mot[4] I thrive if I endure too great preciseness, and that men should start at a strae[5] and carry so kittle[6] stomachs, and they will not do as neighbours and others do, having forgotten what common people say, 'Too holy was hanged.' I would not have men's consciences too small spun. A conscience of small linen and cambric dow not,[7] for the thread will soon break. It is good to be holy, but not over[8] holy." It

---

[1] Than. [2] Cautious. [3] Or halting; one not fully grown.
[4] May. [5] Straw. [6] Nice, squeamish. [7] Profits not. [8] Too.

can hardly be thought but such men as seek this way, and they live as they speak, believe that God's law is too high a tuned lute, and therefore let moderation slack the string. When David says (Psa. xvi. 4), "The idols' drink offering of blood will I not offer, nor take up their names in my lips;" such men would judge David had precise lips who would not name an idol. This midcourse Christ blamed. People thought they might come to heaven, and there was no necessity to be so holy as Scribes and Pharisees. But Christ said: "Except your righteousness exceed the righteousness of the Scribes and Pharisees ye cannot enter into the kingdom of heaven."

Men are gone so far that atheists have taken this course as to think, not to swear, drink, and not to follow the ordinary chambering and wantonness of the time, is to be precise so as lewdness is no moderation. Nay, I wish men were persuaded in the contrary, and would know that Christ's pass to heaven is either go quickly and with all your speed to heaven, or then miss your lodging at night; take even your choice. The old job-trot,[1] the old mid-course, well-a-ways brother, will not do the turn. Therefore no marvel nor[2] this world think that the saints have another beloved than the rest of the world has. It is known our divines think not in matters [of] faith much of what Papists say; as learned, as holy as you believe other ways, and we hear this daily, "Others have a soul to keep as well as you." What then? Must not every man be his own herd here? Men think with one stroke of the hammer they have felled a man cold dead to the ground. And yet all

---

[1] Jog-trot.   [2] Than.

they have said is no better nor [1] a rotten argument from excellent logic that is not sure in the dry land, and very dangerous in the sea. Let the pilot say to the passengers, " A better seaman nor [1] even I was, or will be, and who loveth life, goods, ship, as well as we do, sailed upon yon rock. Come, I will try my skill to follow him that way." Is not this unhappy sea logic? And conscience in God's matters sailing by another man's compass must then be in danger. It were better ask for truth; then, whither he goeth, truth cannot go in the mire, but men may.

"*More than others.*" That the companions of the Church ask this question, " What the Kirk's beloved is more than others?" shows they were not so well acquainted with Christ, nor with the fits of spiritual ague and fevers for absent Christ. The Lord has bairns in His house, and Christ's bairns must creep ere they gang.[2] All within the Church have not a like experience of Christ. 1 John ii. 13 makes some fathers, some young men, and some little children. There may be two sons of one and the same father, and the one be thirteen years of age, and the other a sucking child that can neither speak, stand, nor walk as yet.

The *use* is, that the aged bear with the infirmities of the younger and weaker, and if a weak one fall and break his leg, the apostle (Gal. vi. 1) will have those that are spiritual to put the broken leg in joint again with the spirit of meekness. Love should bind up softly and tenderly. Spelk [3] the broken bones. Who are in this carriage toward men to keep these rules?

[1] Than. [2] Go. [3] Support by splinters.

First: The wilful and proud Pharisee is not to be borne with in obstinacy. No man owes his tongue to lick his neighbour's running boils.

Second: It is rashness to break up a window in any man's soul, and fly upon his conscience at the first. Let God sit judge there.

Third: In Church controversies, in a great wood of sundry controversies anent matters of faith, we should attentively go by the thorny bushes, and walk so with men who worship one and the same God with us, albeit they err in some things from the truth as we put on a compassionate mind towards them. Know Christ will send no man to hell for errors coyning[1] from mere weakness.

Fourth: We are to look as well to that which men have as to that which they want. We look always to the blind and bloody side of a man, and to men's cloudy part. Men would say, "Turn the leaf and cast up the other page, and look upon the enlightened part of the man and his moon side." We are like the fly that cannot sit down upon the whole skin, but with eyes, smell, and tongue, we fall down upon the sore boil at the first.

Fifth: Let them be wicked men, we are then not only to look what they want, but what possibly the grace of God may give them. Fish playing in the sea to-day, for aught we know, may be ordained for Christ's hook the morn.[2]

Sixth: A common fault in us all that we look to sick men with pity, and not to sinful men with pity. Christ

---

[1] Arising. [2] To-morrow.

wept for Jerusalem, and yet Jerusalem slew Him. Samuel wept for Saul and envies him not, howbeit he had taken his office over his head. Pity in place of grudging, thankfulness for what Christ has given us, a humbling fear for what justice has denied them, would turn our spirits if we considered the matter right.

Seventh: The judge not perversely wicked claimeth the largest share of every subject's love and charity. Thou barkest at him and smitest him with thy tongue, but little knowest thou he sits in the cleaving of a windy mountain. Four temptations from all the four airts[1] come on him every day. Thou art on the shore and he is in the raging sea. And this is one of Solomon's ills, the poor man can lie in his cothouse. Under David and Solomon the music went not unpleasant to all men's ears. Many eyes are on government, and to many it seems to crook and bear a leg; but men are ready to give authority more judgment nor[2] mercy.

Eighth: All men have holes and wants, but here is the matter. Some men have a crooked toe, and yet it is not seen; and some a crooked nose, and that is soon seen; because some carrieth the blot on their face they are soon seen and spitted at. You pity your own crooked toe and offendeth at your brother's crooked nose. You pity yourself, and summon your love home to lick all your own sore. Lend charity and love to others, and send some of it from home to love and pity others, and so much the more because fire will be under much ashes, and if the man be good gold will you cast him off because he wants some grains, or because his King's

---

[1] Quarters. [2] Than.

stamp is clipped in the edge, and it wants half a letter? Christ will pay the skaith,[1] and take him in His own treasure, whom you have casten out of your heart; and beware of that when God is taking in you are casting out. That is to be feared. In a word, where there are weak and strong in a Kirk, every man should have a back and saddle in readiness to bear in love his brother over the water. Our Lord Jesus will not cast away a bruised reed, or deny a poor, weak bairn of his kindred and blood, because he has a little crook or halt. Neither should we cast away any but in love. Wait on, pity, help, and be thankful for what our Lord has given us.

"*That thou so chargest us*" [Authorized Version, "That thou dost so charge us"]. The adjurations of the Kirk sick of love are to naturally disposed daughters of Jerusalem, [as if] uncouth things and miracles. "O what means the woman," say they, "to come on with fiery cannon yell? We have seen many holy folks before, but we saw never the like of her who cometh on with cursing and oaths to bid us speak to Christ for her." We see in as far as we are carnal, we are ignorant of God's true wisdom and God's way of spiritual love and fever in the conscience of His own children. Paul heareth this of Festus, " Too much learning hath made you mad." And so did they to Christ. Others say, " Why hear you Him? He is mad." 1 Cor. i. 25 : " But the foolishness of God is wiser than men." That which men call foolishness and stark daffing[2] in God, is wisdom above all worldly wisdom, and they think God's saints silly gouks,[3] and God's bodies climbing crow-nests, and they wot not what they are

---

[1] Damage.   [2] Folly.   [3] Weak fools.

seeking. "Honest man," say they, "he means well, but he has no wit. There are bees in his head." And in so far as men are natural they can put Christ till an assize, and hold a justice court upon the power of godliness, and give out a doom¹ that holiness is plain fancy. Howbeit nature had now to be God's scholar, yet it will needs put a book in God's hand and be His master, and teach God a lesson. Jehu and his companions call one of God's prophets a mad fellow (2 Kings ix. 11). And what was Jeroboam's natural estimation of obedience to God's law? 1 Kings xii. 26, 27: "And Jeroboam said in his heart, Now shall the kingdom return to the house of David: if this people go up to do sacrifice in the house of the Lord at Jerusalem, then shall the heart of this people turn again unto their lord, even unto Rehoboam king of Judah, and they shall kill me." Does not here [the] head of wit speak a fool's tale? God had said that by obedience to God his throne should be established (1 Kings xi. 38). He says in plain language, "If I be holy I shall never do well. If the people worship God as He has commanded in His word, then farewell good policy. I and my new honours shall shoot short." Any man that has nature in him let him take up his cross and follow Christ, and when it comes to obedience with a hazard or seen danger, his wisdom shall say, "Take heed what you do. Look ere you loup. You resolve well, but you walk upon coals covered with ashes. You spit further nor² you will loup, and these that obey Christ because natural reason leads them, they obey natural wisdom, and not Christ." In God's matters

¹ A judgment.   ² Than.

men had need to take heed to their natural wisdom else it will lead them in the briars. When God calleth you either to do or to suffer, hear no voice but one, even Christ's own word; for our wisdom has a rank smell. Go at leisure, pity yourself, see to your own standing. Christ sayeth (Matt. xi.), "Wisdom is justified of her children." Then God's wisdom is condemned of His own bastards. They can call God's wisdom rash folly. The ill-step bairn will never speak good of its stepmother. Worldly minded men are not wisdom's full gotten bairns, and therefore they speak ill of their mother; but the full gotten and lawful sons of God's wisdom speak good of their mother, and follow her footsteps. It is not good to obey God upon conditions, and the condition comes home to his door. "Carnal wisdom, shall I do it?" This wisdom is the devil's wife, and will lord it out against Christ; but it does always dance as the ill world pipeth, and thinks it folly and ill manners to be out of tune and fall out with the multitude and come to daggers, as Christ did with the Scribes and Pharisees, and court, and time, and the doctrine of the elders. Oh! learn to deny yourselves, and be in tune, and keep measures with Christ Jesus. A good conscience is a good, soft, well-made bed. He is wise enough who is wise to salvation, and has saved his own soul, and shall hear God's "Well done, good servant." What is well done must be wisely done. Goodness cannot be a fool.

"*My beloved is white and ruddy.*" The Kirk with an edge of words takes Christ's part. "My beloved, my beloved," I would you wist what you say when you speak of my beloved. I scorn He be made fellows with any [one, be] he in heaven or earth. One thing is here worthy in the Kirk.

First: That hearing Christ laid in an uneven balance, she starts quickly and takes the temptation presently by the nose, and with a long speech sets Christ even up presently in the skies, and dings[1] speedily, with force of words, her companions out of an opinion that Christ has any mortal match. This is right, not to let the temptation go on. We should not let men away with it when they would put a ruffle upon Christ Jesus. Nay, true grace will borrow strength from a tentation,[2] as Paul, seeing idolatry at Athens, and God put out of His room,[3] he grew hotter nor[4] he was before, like a horse that cannot endure the spur. So when Christ says (John vi.) to His disciples, upon occasion that Capernaum had played turncoat, and left Him, "And will ye also leave Me?" Peter answereth with a piece of stomach: "Leave thee, Lord! To whom shall we go?" Leave you! Whither then? To the devil. The disciples (Acts iv.) were charged to speak no more in the name of Jesus. Peter and John draw out a strong one against that. They will not leave it so, but speer,[5] "Whether it be righteous to obey God or man, judge ye." This speaks right against such as will hear Christ ill-spoken of, and will hang their head and let a reproach, lighting upon Him that died for them, blow over their shoulder, and misken that there is a good friend ill-spoken of. Nay, ye cannot be fiery enough when Christ gets a tout; when the black-mouthed dogs in the world bark agains-

[1] Throws down.   [2] Temptation.   [3] Place.   [4] Than.   [5] Ask.

that well-given stranger Christ, there should be a staff in your mouth. Now the curse of God be on them that love not my well-beloved. You hold with your own; ilk[1] one takes part with his own country. A man will speak for his own father, brother, bairn, wife, or friend he will plead for; but not a word in favour of his own Christ. He will go his own errands and speak his own business to his prince, but not a word for Christ. Christ has tongue enough, let Him speak for Himself. Well, well, nobles of Scotland! I dare not say; so be ye served when your eye-strings break and your life is come to your lip; but God forgive you. And what better are they who will stand at Christ's back and see His head broken in His cause, in His members, in His Church, and not party their well-beloved, and never say it is ill done. True zeal makes a quarrel of a wrong done to Christ, and He gets too many wrongs now; and He is like the man that has many kin and few friends. Many now are with Christ, and few for Christ. He is worn out of friendship in the world.

"White and ruddy" is the best temperature, and strongest and most lively constitution of a man, and seemeth to note his Godhead—white, pure, innocent, holy —as (Dan. vii. 9) He appears in the vision all white as snow and as pure wool; and in His glory His face shineth as the sun, and His raiment white as light (Matt. xvii. 2); in Him dwells the fulness of the Godhead bodily (Col. ii. 9). And read the Hebrew Adam, the last Adam (1 Cor. xv. 45), flesh and blood with us (Heb. ii. 14). This shows that Christ is the beautifullest and fairest among the

[1] Each.

sons of men (Psa. xlv. 2). Fair things delight us much, and perfect white and perfect red make a beautiful person. Beauty be a great conqueror of love, and will take a castle in the heart. We love fair things, as fair sun, fair moon, fair roses, lilies, men, women, &c. But put out all the beauty of the creatures in one; they are all but caff [1] and sand to fair-faced Jesus. I had far rather have one look of fair-faced Jesus as have all the world, and ten worlds, with sevenfold more beauty than they have. See Isa. lxiii. 1: "Who is this that comes from Edom, with dyed garments from Bozrah? this that is glorious in apparel, travelling in the greatness of His strength?" The Kirk, wondering at Christ's beauty to see Him go so manly-like, says, "O, who is yon goes so manly and so sonsy-like?[2] He is a lucky-like[3] person." It would rejoice one's heart to see Him go in the greatness of His strength. Is not yon fair, glorious Jesus, in red scarlet, having all His clothes dyed in blood? And the answer is made, "It is I, even I that speak in righteousness, mighty to save." John i. 14: "He dwelt among us, and we beheld His glory, as the glory of the only-begotten Son"—like the heir of a great king. His beauty is answerable to all that is said here (Col. i. 15-19; Rev. i. 13-16, and x. 1-3, xix. 11-13). If any fair thing allure your heart, and fair, lovely Jesus do it not, ye must be lordly, and ill to please.

You make a good *use* of this doctrine if you take Him with all His forms and fairness as your husband whom you love, as your Master whom you fear and serve, as your King and Lord whom you obey, as your Shepherd

---

[1] Chaff.   [2] Well-conditioned-like.   [3] Altogether prosperous.

and Guide whom you follow. And for[1] all His beauty, He is not proud, nor lordly; He will match with black ones. Surely Christ's beauty helps to marry Him. He is always white, ruddy, and most when He wooeth. I marvel not that He seem black and dun to some men who get a sight of Christ but[2] in Satan's dark glass (for there be two sights and representations of Christ); and in that He is all black, for He comes upon men's wrong side with His beauty.

First: Natural men, without faith, with only natural eyes, see Him, and they see but Mary's son—not Christ white and ruddy; they see not the King in His beauty, nor in His holiday clothes.

Second: Some see Him in His law of commandments, commanding hard things to flesh and blood—to deny themselves, to enter in at the strait gate which leads to life. Men would love Christ's beauty if He only shined with light and love; but His light commandeth, accuseth, summoneth, challenges, condemns, and this makes Christ both gray and black-skinned. Men should love light as well because it commandeth and convinceth as because it shineth as light; and should break the devil's glass, and learn out of love to obey; and then Christ's yoke would be easy, and then you would say, "O, fair Jesus! O lovely, white, and ruddy Jesus!"

Third: Man looketh to His cross; and this is Christ's black skin and His black dool[3] clothes. Isa. lii. 14: "As many were astonished at thee; His visage was so marred more than any man, and His form more than the sons of men." Then to many He cannot be white

---

[1] Notwithstanding.   [2] Only.   [3] Mourning.

and ruddy, if He have under His sufferings a marred and a holed¹ face, blue and black, and all bleared with strokes. These that cannot rejoice in Christ's cross, and think it exceeding joy when they fall in divers temptations, as in their crosses they have communion with Jesus, they see only but Christ's outer half, and start aback at His marred visage; but faith here shall look Christ within; He is well lined within, even under sufferings.

"*The armour-bearer among ten thousands.*" In the Hebrew it is, *Bannerer*² above ten thousand. The banner, or standard, is a war-like thing. He that carries it is the chief of the thousands that follow him. So Judah (Numb. ii. 2, 3) was the tribe that was chief standard-bearer; and out of this tree Christ sprang (Heb. vii. 14), who is the lion of the tribe of Judah (Rev. v. 5). He standeth for an "ensign of the people" (Isa. xi. 10); Him the armies and thousands in heaven follow (Rev. xix. 6, 14); He ruleth over the Gentiles (Rom. xv. 12). Put white and ruddy, which betoken health and strength, with this, that "He is the standard-bearer," then we see that Christ is a strong, active soldier, and the prettiest man of His hands in all the company. Bring ten thousand—that is, many—yea all the armies in heaven and earth together, and Christ is the fairest, prettiest, bravest, and ablest man among them all. One look of Jesus is worth them all. So speak of all Christ's virtues, this is among the first of them, that He is a tried man of war; for who but He fought the Lord's battles, and fought it out with the curse of the law, with sin, with the devil, with death, with hell,

---

¹ Pierced.   ² The Lord of the standard.

and goes with many crowns on His head to conquer. He His alone has laid many a pretty soldier on the broad[1] of his back. But this description bodeth[2] that Christ will have ado[3] with His strength; nay, ay, while there is a devil, ay, until he be bound and cast into the lake of brimstone, and locked up, Christ will have but the fighter's life. Christ and the ten thousand, His brave bairn-tyme[4] at His back—God bless them all—must fight. It would even do a man good, and rejoice his heart to see Jesus fight. It sets Him to fence and wale[5] His sword. But take Christ at His best, He has the soldier's life; therefore, all you that come to take or leave, you must come upon these terms—either to do or to die; either to fight with your standard-bearer, or lie down and be slain. "O," say you, "suffering is a hard life. Will Christ and His Kirk never get rest?" Certainly little until they be at home together. It was never otherways with Christ. He was aye[6] oftener in the camp, watching, than in a soft bed sleeping; and therefore, as you who would follow Him, rise up off the hearthstone and from the fireside, and to the camp with you! Put on your shoes and all your armour — blood, the blood, the cross of Christ, for you to your dying day until you be at home! It is proclaimed at our King's Market-cross, in Jesus' name, red war betwixt you and three—the devil, the world, and sin. But Christ bears the colours; He is well worthy of that place. He ventures foremost with white and red, God and the Kirk's colours and their

[1] Breadth.   [2] Intimates.   [3] Business.
[4] Brood of children.   [5] Choose.   [6] Always.

arms. Silly,[1] tempted, wounded, crossed soldier, look up to the standard-bearer, Ensigner Jesus, in red and white! Take courage and buy a heart from Christ. "O, but," you will say, "Jesus is often in His cause, and members put to the worse, and His colours slapped[2] with cannon bullets." *Answer:* Nay; but God sews the holes in Christ's standard again, and we may certainly say two things of Christ—

First: This text makes Him white and ruddy, and so strong, lively, able. Our Captain is not sickly; He is able of person to fight, to watch, and ward, and not take sickness. Neither cannon bullet, arrow, nor spear will go through His corset of proof. He is God, and not man only; the strength of Israel, and He wearies not.

Second: I dare lay a wager He will win yet; and when it comes to the last onset, He will make bloody brooks; the ark will be sent home again, and glory shall dwell in our land. Christ will mow down His enemies, and loose the belt of the rulers of the earth that are against Him. When Christ puts His finger in the loop, both belt and sword will fall from them; and how will they then fight? In Rev. xvii. 14: "These shall make war with the Lamb, and the Lamb shall overcome them: for He is Lord of lords, and King of kings: and they that are with Him are called chosen and faithful." And in end, when Christ and we shall lay down our swords together in heaven's entry, and put on our crowns of glory and our king's robes, Christ shall be all in all. To whom with the Father and the Holy Spirit be dominion and glory for ever.—Amen.

[1] Feeble. [2] Broken into gaps.

The Deliverance of the Kirk of God.

"*In those days, and in that time, saith the Lord, the children of Israel shall come, they and the children of Judah together, going and weeping: they shall go, and seek the Lord their God. They shall ask the way to Zion with their faces thitherward, saying, Come, and let us join ourselves to the Lord in a perpetual covenant that shall not be forgotten.*"—JEREMIAH l. 4, 5.

N this Scripture, beloved in our Lord, we have a prophecy of the fall of Babylon, the golden city. And in it we have a description of the full and final wrath that shall light upon all the enemies of Sion, and the enemies of all them who have such a bill to give in to the Lord's court as the Kirk has in this chapter. "The violence done to Me and to My flesh be upon the inhabitants of Babylon." There is a violence done to the Kirk of God by Babylon, and their complaint is put in before the Lord; and the complaint is heard by Him, and there is a prophecy given out here before the people of Israel be carried away to their captivity, for this prophecy is given out in the time while they were in the way of carrying away captive. And the Lord here He gives out a prophecy—first, of the ruin of Babylon; and, secondly, He has another prophecy here of the deliverance of

Jerusalem. Now to take the words as they lie in order. (1) The time of the deliverance is set down: "At that time and in these days saith the Lord." (2) We have the parties that are delivered: these of Israel and the ten tribes, and with them the children of Judah. (3) We have the union and sweet fellowship of a divided Kirk and the people of God who before could not join with either: "The children of Israel shall come, they and the children of Judah together." They were separate from others for many years, because the ten tribes they had desertion from the true religion, as that is the thing that makes a separation among people; and, upon the other hand, there is nothing that is such a needle to sew people together as when people join all together in the truth of God—when we have all one Lord, and faith, and baptism, and hope, and inheritance, &c. The (4) particular is, What shall be the thankfulness when they are delivered from their captivity? And this is set down unto us in many particulars. The first is, they shall take a journey from Babylon towards Zion. Second: We have the manner how they go to Zion—they shall go weeping while they are going there. Third: The errand wherefore they shall go to Zion, shall be to seek the Lord their God. Fourth: They shall speer[1] the way to Zion, and while they are speering[2] it, their faces shall be towards the same. And then, lastly, while they are thus going to Zion together, there is a conference between them, and, in their conference, they resolve both of them upon this: "Come, and let us join ourselves in a perpetual covenant to the Lord that shall not be forgotten."

[1] Ask.   [2] Asking.

Now for the first, To wit—*The time when the Lord will deliver His people* from their captivity and bondage. Look unto the time when this prophecy is given out, and that is, They are not well come to Babylon at this time, and yet there is a triumph promised even before they be sent away. And there is in this chapter a prophecy of the destruction of Babylon, and that is for the heartening [1] of the people of God, who were carried thither; and before utter misery and desolation come upon them, there is a prophecy of their delivery and of the destruction of their enemies.

The *first doctrine* arising from this point is, The Kirk of God never sooner enters in any trouble, but they have the Lord's backband [2] given unto them that they shall be brought out of it again; and they have law burrows [3] and caution of the Lord that death, hell, and all sort of trouble shall not do [4] at them to destroy them (Psa. xvi. 10). When our Lord Christ is put to that strait that they get Him put dead into the grave, that any would think He is gone now for evermore, He has it backed with that promise: "Thou wilt not leave my soul in grave, neither wilt thou suffer Thine Holy One to see corruption." Blyth [5] may that subject be to go into prison who beforehand has his king's pardon and assurance that he shall not die into the prison. And the Kirk and children of God, they have this meikle [6] for them when they go under any strait or trouble, or, as it were, to prison, that they shall not die into that prison, but Christ shall bring them safe out of it again. And there

---

[1] Encouragement.   [2] Bond.   [3] Legal security.
[4] Take effect upon them.   [5] Happy.   [6] Much.

are two special reasons wherefore this is that the children of God, albeit they be under trouble, yet they succumb not under the same.

The one is, If there be anything in the world that sees over the water, it is faith, and so it sees over beyond the trouble, and therefore succumbs not under it; as ye see it is said (Mic. vii. 8) : " Rejoice not over me, O mine enemy : when I shall fall, I shall arise ; when I sit in darkness, the Lord shall be a light unto me." There is a stout look of faith looking over to the other side of the trouble, and taking the answer before the answer come, and gathering faith that all shall be well, albeit, for the present, it stand hard with them. The 118th Psalm, it was penned when the servant of God was in very great trouble; and yet in it he promises to himself in the Lord's name : " I shall not die but live, and declare the works of the Lord." There faith on the one side, and yet looking to the other shore and believing life in death. And he believes salvation when all is black about, and that foul winter will turn in a fair, clear summer. He believes, and the Kirk of God in trouble believes, that He that will come, will come, and shall not tarry, believing this, that none shall die in prison who look out at the window of their prison to God. And this, indeed, should hearten[1] us, and make us not to cast down our hearts for any appearance of ill that yet we see, although they were greater than they are. But this I speak only to the children of God, who when they are in trouble, or it is in coming on them, they can send letters to their friends, as faith does, and say, " I shall live, and not die, and declare the works of the Lord."

[1] Encourage.

Another reason of this promise of delivery beforehand is by reason of that fair promise made to the Kirk and people of God, that the waters shall not drown them, the fire shall not burn them, nor the flame kindle upon them—a promise made that even death itself, which has so awesome a grip, and so strait, yet it shall not slay them, as our Saviour says (John xi. 26) : "He that believeth in Me shall never see death." And having such promises as these, it is no wonder that good news He preached to the Kirk beforehand that their King and their Lord lives, and so His salvation is near to them who wait on Him.

Now the *second thing* we observe upon the time, it is said "in these days." What days were these? Days wherein the vengeance of the Lord lights upon Babylon and upon the enemies of the Kirk. Then Israel and Judah shall come back to their own land to seek the Lord and to join in a covenant with Him.

So that the *second doctrine* is this, that the fall of the enemies of the Kirk of God, and the rising of the fallen Kirk, these go together; for the enemies and we laugh not together, and weep not together, but when we weep they laugh, and when we laugh they weep. When the Lord drowns Pharaoh and· his chariots and all his army in the midst of the Red Sea, then Moses and the people of God they are set safe upon the shore to sing of the praises of the Lord. When the land of Canaan spews out the inhabitants thereof, as a foul stomach spews out the meat that is in it that troubles it, then the Lord He plants His people into the land, and as it is in Psalm xlii. 4, the Lord has a safe house to

THE DELIVERANCE OF THE KIRK OF GOD.

keep His children in, while there is a pit digged for the wicked (Psalm xciv. 13). When Haman's cup is full, and he is at the top of the ladder in his court, that he must fall down again, then Mordecai and the people of God they must be delivered. It is even here as it is in war. When a sojour [1] has watched out his glass,[2] and has bidden [3] the night and the cold, when his glass is gone, another is put in his place, and he is sent to his warm bed. Even so is it here. When the people of God get rest, then the enemies of God they fall, and these go aye [4] together, the rest of the people of God, and the trouble of the wicked. And therefore a word of terror to those who are the enemies of the Kirk of God. You, who are enemies to the Kirk of God, laugh as ye will before noon, I will assure you there will be a change afternoon. I would not have your next day in another life, and be in your case afterdays, for all the world. Albeit they have a fair-like blink in the morning, yet it is but beguiling, for they will have a foul afternoon of it. Sorrow and indignation will come upon them. And therefore, I beseech you, eat none of their dainties, nor take no part with them, for the Lord laughs at them, as it is Psa. xxxvii. 13.: He laughs at the wicked, for He sees their end afar off; He knows what will be the end of all their good cheer and all their merry days. And therefore woe is that man who has no more, but only a part of the laughter of the wicked, for that is but like the crackling of thorns under a pot, that is but a blaze and away. This looks very much like us and our time, that wicked men and the enemies of the Lord, they must

[1] Soldier. [2] The sand-glass. [3] Remained over. [4] Always.

come into the rowme¹ of the Kirk of God and His people, who before were in distress and calamity, and yet He will perform that word (Jer. xx. 12, and Isa. x. 12). When the Lord has performed His work in Zion, then He will fall to and punish the stout heart of the king of Babylon. When the Lord has humbled His Kirk, and done His work with His fire there, then the wicked they must fall on it and be consumed thereby, that we may know that it is good for the children of God to wait upon Him. And that is the second part of the *use*, that faith and hope are evermore waiting for good at God's hand and for daylight. We never heard of any who waited upon the Lord, but at last they might say: "This poor man cried unto the Lord, and the Lord heard him, and delivered him out of all his troubles."

Again, thirdly, that the delivery of the Kirk of God is not for the present, but "in those days and at that time." We learn here, that there are none who wait upon God but they must frest² Him, and as men frest² well so God pays well that which is frested.³ It is not salvation in hand, but an onwaiting life that the Kirk of God has while they are here. And this is to meet with a doubt and a knot that thir⁴ people could not loose for the present. They might say, for all that the Lord says of the destruction of Babylon, yet we are there captives, albeit the wrath of God be pronounced against them, yet the sparks thereof have come upon us. And we have sore drink of that cup, and, for the present, we have sad days; for the temple of the Lord is burnt, our princes are hanged, our priests massacred, and we ourselves are carried away

¹ Place.   ² Prove.   ³ Proved.   ⁴ These.

captive from mount Zion. How shall this then be that Babylon shall be destroyed and we restored? The Lord answers this, that the deliverance is coming, but it would not come until that day that He had appointed for it. To teach the Kirk of God to give God that mickle [1]—as alas! He gets over [2] little of that kind of us—that He will do for His own people at length, though not for the present, and to look to that word in Psalm xxv. 22, that the Lord will redeem Israel out of all his troubles, and Psalm lxii. 5: "My soul wait thou only upon the Lord, for my expectation is from Him," even to make God's omnipotence the object of their faith and of their hope, and learn to wait upon God only. "I would do that," says some, "but I have nothing in hand." But we must remember that all their stock is in God's hand who hope rightly in Him; for if they had anything in hand, it were not hope, as it is, Rom. viii. 24: "Hope that is seen is not hope." But the thing which one sees not is properly the thing that he hopes for. And so the less we have in hand we have the greater reason of hope. That no man may be troubled with this, I have nothing for the present; but in such a case learn to believe in God, and then ye have the more. How many rich men are there in the world who have no more but only pieces of paper for all that they have, and yet men will account them rich, albeit there be not two pence in their purse. The hoper and on-waiter upon God is this way rich, yet all his sums are in God's hands, who pays His annuals [3] well, so that His annuals [3] they are better than the world's principal sum.

[1] Much. [2] Too. [3] Quit rent due to a superior.

A third objection: "I have waited long for deliverance but it cometh not." The text answers, "At that time and in these days," to teach us to set no time to the Lord the creator of time, for His time is always best, and as it is Hab. ii. 3, "Albeit it tarry, wait for it; for it will surely come;" and as it is 2 Peter iii. 9, speaking of the Lord's general coming to judgment, "The Lord is not slack concerning His promise, as some men count slackness," &c. The Kirk says that the Lord is long in coming, and slack of His promise; but He says He is no [1] slack as men count slackness, but will come and will show mercy to His people and deliver them. As meikle then as we frest [2] God as meikle faith and hope indeed have we. He that will go to heaven and have nothing at all in hand, his faith and his hope are strongest; he that believes in Him when he sees not, but believes in the mirk,[3] that is likest faith. Let no man then call godliness fancy, or say, "What have the children of God for the present? They have moe [4] weary hearts here nor [5] the kye [6] of Bashan, and moe [4] tears nor they who laugh and rejoice in the world." Let it be so, yet it is an unseen heaven and happiness which the children of God believe. And, indeed, the thing that is seen is not believed. If they saw heaven they could not be said to believe it. As the man that sees Rome, he cannot say that he hears only of it but by report. But believe life, and what is said of it without any more, and that is true faith. To say I believe in God, and I love Him, albeit I never saw Him, as the Apostle Peter

---

[1] Not. [2] Prove. [3] Darkness. [4] More.
[5] Than. [6] Cattle, *i.e.*, strong ones.

speaks, "Whom not having seen, yet ye believe with joy unspeakable and glorious." And ye know the Lord's word He spake to Thomas, "Blessed are they which have not seen, and yet have believed." Blessed are they, blessed are they who believe when they see nothing but contrary appearances; who will die, and yet will hope and wait for the salvation of God, and were at that, as it is in Psalm xxiii. 4: "Albeit I should walk through the valley of the shadow of death, yet will I fear none ill." When a man is under the shadow of a tree he is near it then, so when a man is within the shadow of death, that is, to be near death, it is faith then to believe in God.

Now the second particular in the text is, *the parties that are delivered*, and these are Israel and Judah. Israel that was hardly handled by proud Assyria, that was the rod of the Lord's anger and indignation, as ye may read Isaiah x. 5; and poor Judah that was carried away captive to Chaldæa by that proud tyrant who was the hammer of the devil to beat them. What nation would have said that ever they should be a kingdom?—the one of them being in Assyria, and the other of them in Chaldæa, the temple burnt, their city sacked, the land spoiled, and more, the anger and indignation of God lying upon His people; where we learn this shortly—he is in a weak estate whom the Lord cannot help; he is near death whom He will not quicken. Fatherless! and will not the Lord be a Father to you? Comfortless! and will not the Lord comfort you? Let Israel and Judah be in as hard and miserable a case as they will, the Lord, who is the help of the poor and needy, He will deliver them.

The third particular is *the union that is between Israel and Judah* at this time. And there is a number of marks of this union. First: That they shall come together to Zion. Second: That they shall serve the Lord together. Third: That they shall speer[1] the way to Zion, weeping. Fourth: That their faces shall be thitherwards while they speer the way to Zion. And, lastly, that they shall all of them have this common resolution: Let us be joined in a perpetual covenant with the Lord, never to be forgotten. So then here the Lord giving unto us a proof that when He sews a Kirk together, that not only people of sundry families, but even people of sundry tribes and of sundry kingdoms, their fellowship shall be seen, and especially in this that they shall worship God together. They shall both have their faces one way, and shall ask the way to Zion together, seek the Lord together. And they shall have a common covenant and band with the Lord, never to be forgotten. Now, whether or no was this ever historically true that Israel and Judah took such a journey as this towards Zion after such a manner and for such an end, there is no necessity to stand upon it now, because many of thir[2] prophecies they are accomplished in the Messiah. But there is a ground here to prove the lawfulness of that private service and worship that Israel and Judah performed to the Lord together, albeit they were of sundry kingdoms. And before this they were of contrary worship, for Israel was filled with idolatry, had a calf at Dan, and another at Bethel, and corrupted and changed the whole true worship; yet now they come together and

[1] Ask.   [2] These.

say, "Let us join ourselves in a perpetual covenant with the Lord, never to be forgotten." Now that not only they of sundry towns and of sundry families, but even those of sundry kingdoms, may meet together this way, this text will bear; and that they may worship the Lord privately, it will bear that also; for some to come from one politic kingdom to another, and join together this way, for them to come to Zion, and ilk [1] one of them to speer [2] the way at another, and to make a covenant and to have conference amongst themselves: "Let us be joined in a perpetual covenant with the Lord, never to be forgotten." Now in the public worship of God there is no such speeches among private persons: "Let us be joined in a perpetual covenant with the Lord." Neither, as Calvin says, is there in the public worship by words a public spurring up one of another. So, then, this text it will warrant that which all our interpreters and our divines allow, that those who are of diverse kingdoms and diverse families, when they meet together, they may speak one to another, exhort, comfort, instruct, admonish every one another in the mutual duties of the worship of God, ilk [1] one of them lending their shoulder to another before they come to the part where the public worship of God is.

It may be said that this concerns not us meikle, that the kingdom of Israel and the kingdom they shall worship God together, and shall speak good words one to another, that they shall enter in a covenant together, but what is that to us? We are another kirk than they were. And so it concerns not us. But remember what

[1] Each.   [2] Ask

the apostle says, "What is written is written for our instruction upon whom the ends of the world are fallen." And howbeit this prophecy should never be historically fulfilled in the persons of Israel and Judah, yet it will serve to warrant the children of God on this point, to exhort, instruct, comfort, rebuke, and to speak of those duties that the Lord requires of His children, and of them toward another before they come to the public worship of God. Now for the better understanding of this, the Lord would have private Christians to be considered in a threefold relation. The first is as they are a master of a family. Second, as they are fellow-members of the grace of God. Third, as they are extraordinarily graced [1] of God above others. For the third and last of these, we need not to speak meikle of it; for a private Christian so graced and qualified it has not been found fault with that they write commentaries, and do other things of that kind.

And for the first again, the duty of a private Christian as he is a master of a family, that is also far out of controversy, that a Christian as he is the head of a family, and so has the charge of them who are within the same, ought to discharge himself in this. To say nothing of that place (Deut. vi. 7) which warrants this point, and of the Lord's commendation of Abraham (Gen. xviii. 19): "I know that He will command His children and His household after Him, that they shall keep the way of the Lord," &c., and (Exod. xii. 26) where the master of the family is commanded when the children shall speer [2] at him what the Passover means,

---

[1] Favoured. [2] Ask.

the Lord says, Ye shall tell them it is the sacrifice of the Lord's passover, who passed over the houses of the children of Israel in Egypt, when he smote the Egyptians and delivered our houses. There the master of the family, albeit he be not a minister, nor a public man, has a charge to expone[1] the doctrine of the sacrament of the Passover to his family, Psa. lxxviii. 5: "The Lord established a testimony in Jacob, and appointed a law in Israel, which He commanded our fathers that they should make them known to their children, that the generation to come might know them, even the children which should be born, who should arise and declare them to their children." So that the fathers they are bound to teach the children, and the rest of those who are in the family. Now under the name of a family, ye know we must expone[1] it according to the fourth command, when that is set down that masters of families should be careful to have those within their families keeping the service of God. Ye know there is set down "the manservant," "the maidservant," "the stranger that is within the gates." So when the charge is laid on masters for their families, it is laid on them for all the members of the family, and for all the strangers that are in the same; for while he is there, he is a fellow and joint-member with the rest of the family. Now all the question is about the duty which the Lord requires of private Christians, as they are fellow-members of the same body one with another; as they are hands, feet, eyes, &c., of the blessed body of Christ. What seeks the Word of God in this case? Hear the Word of God. It is clear also

[1] Expound.

—Lev. xix. 17: "Rebuking one another;" Col. iii. 16: "To teach and exhort;" Mal. iii. 16: "To speak often one to another;" Heb. iii. 13: "To exhort one another daily, while it is called to-day." And that is recommended as a special means for preventing hardness of heart; and there are none, I am sure, but they will acknowledge that whatever is recommended as a means to prevent hardness of heart, it is a duty commanded and ordained of God. But so it is that this duty of exhorting one another is recommended as a means for preventing hardness of heart, and therefore it is a duty commanded of God, and so lawful and necessary. And 1 Thess. v. 11: "Comfort yourselves together, and edify one another as ye also do." "Warn them that are unruly, comfort the feebleminded, support the weak."

Now these places they will not only warrant the master of a family to do so, but also all Christians as they have commerce with others, that they join with others in such a manner, and the moe¹ coals be together the hotter will the fire be. And there is another place not far from this—Psa. xxxvii. 30: "The righteous man he speaketh of wisdom and of judgment, and the law of God is in his heart;" and Prov. x. 21: "The lips of the righteous feed many." This is not to be understood of a pastoral feeding, that because one is a righteous man he should go to the pulpit and take the charge of souls upon him; but he feeds many in a private way, and it is a meaning unknown to the text to restrain it that otherways.

Anything that can be said against this is, that it is

¹ More.

very like the public teaching, that if they may exhort, instruct, comfort, rebuke, admonish, &c., one another, what difference is there between this and the public teaching, except only in the place, that the one is done in public and the other is done in a house. For answer: This is not so much against us as it is against the Scriptures of God, and yet the difference is clear; for every Christian is commanded to exhort, instruct, rebuke, comfort, &c., one another; but for the other it is said, none can preach except he be sent. And so the conclusion of this argument it is as much against the Scriptures of God as against these who defend the lawfulness of this ordinance. And this argument will be as much against these who speak one to one, as against him who speaks one to twenty. And, thirdly, there is very great difference between private exhortation and public preaching; even as when a common sojour[1] gives warning to the army that the enemy is coming on them, and he who is appointed watchman, he gives also warning of the same. Now speer[2] the difference between these warnings. It is clear the one has a calling to it, and authority from the general and the army, to give warning. The other, again, is not so bound. But yet, as he is a part of the army, he is obleist[3] to give warning when he sees them in any danger though not in such a public, and failing therein, he does wrong. And as the difference is between a master, who is clad with public authority for teaching of scholars, and one of the condisciples teaches another on that same lesson that he teaches. Now there is none who will say that either the one usurps the watchman's

[1] Soldier.   [2] Ask.   [3] Obliged.

place or the other the master's charge; but the one does what he does by a special designation for that effect, and the other as he is a member of that body. Again, the one has his place by public authority; and there are two wrongs done when he is disobeyed, one against the Lord's calling and authority, and another against his message and that which he bears. But disobedience to the other is not so great. Again, the public watchman he is ordained to use all means ordinary and possible for the good of people; but the other is only to do in an ordinary way. A private Christian he ought to help others in the way to heaven; but he ought not to make that his study—to study divinity for that effect.

Again, another objection is that this is like interpreting of Scripture, and this is a thing that is altogether unlawful for any but for them who are authorized persons. For answer to this: All who know the controversy between us and the Papists, know that Bellarmine[1] he lays this to the charge of the heretics, as he calls us, that they will not have the interpreting of the Scriptures bound to any kind of men as to pastors, but they will have it a thing common to all. And another of no less note than Bellarmine, to wit, Becan,[2] says, while he is reasoning about the Scriptures: "Wherefore would the Lord have the Scriptures to be obscure, but only because He would have the order of pastors and teachers and doctors and people to be kept and observed." And in his 1 tom. quest. 10, he makes that question, "To whom belongs

[1] Robert Bellarmine, a cardinal, a noted defender of the Papacy, died in 1621.
[2] Martin Becan, a Jesuit, died in the year 1624. He has left three volumes of writings.

the interpreting of the Scriptures?" And answers, "Only to the Kirk, that is, only to Kirkmen." But this is our judgment in this point, that the power of interpreting the Scriptures in public is due to the pastor only and to no other; but for the private spirit of interpretation of the Scriptures it is a thing that belongs not only to pastors, but also to all Christians. And this is not a thing that is only my device, but that which our divines do approve; for Junius says,[1] in the third chapter of his book, these: "We will not have interpreting the Scripture bound to particular men, but to be a thing belonging to *omnibus fidelibus* (all the faithful) in a private way and manner." Trelcatius[2] he says also the like, and also Rivetus.[3] And Luther and Calvin agree unto this while they are exponing that place. They say of ministers their public interpretation of the Scriptures is not to say that none has power of interpreting the Scriptures but Kirkmen, but all have power and yet difference—the private interpretation from the public. And all our divines, they acknowledge thus far; and Rivetus, while he is answering that Jesuit, he says: "There is a twofold interpreting of the Scripture. The first is public only belonging to pastors, a second is private belonging to *omnibus fidelibus;* and the professors of Leyden they agree unto this also." And yet this is not to put private persons, whosoever they be, in the

---

[1] Franciscus Junius, or Francois Du Jon, Professor of Theology at Leyden, died of the plague in 1602.

[2] Lucas Trelcatius, Professor of Theology at Leyden, died in 1602. He wrote a synopsis of Theology.

[3] Andre Rivet, Professor of Theology at Leyden, and then at Breda, died in 1651. He was the author of many books.

chair of ministers, but only this—it is impossible for them to believe the Scriptures unless they can apply such Scriptures for rebuking, comforting, instructing, &c., one another, and to reclaim such as are wandering out of the way. Now if this be true, that the word of God thus gives place to exhort one another for comforting one another, rebuking one another, &c., then the meeting of Christians together for that end cannot be unlawful, for there is none who will meet that way but those who are bairns of that same house.

Again, it is objected that this rebuking, comforting, instructing, &c., is but only of one to one, and no further. But if ye will compare this form of speaking with the original, both in Greek and Hebrew language, and ye will find that it comes very far short of their mind who say so. If ye will look for the Greek language (Rom. xiii.), you will find the apostle says there : " Owe nothing to any man but love one to one." Now will any think that the law of God will bind one to love only and no moe[1] ; or rather does it not bind us to love all those who are called our neighbour ? And Gal. v. 13 the apostle says, " Serve one another in love." The meaning of that place is not that only one man should serve another man, but the law of God it binds moe.[1] And sicklike, " Bear ye burdens one of another." Is that only meant of one man ? The Word of God will carry it towards all men in so far as a good conscience will permit; and James v. 16 : " Pray one for another, and confess your faults one to another." The meaning there is for all the members of Christ's body, so that

[1] More.

the Word of God it will not bear us to this, that it is only one to one this duty belongs.

And then, if ye will come to the Old Testament, ye will find the word not so strict. As Gen. xlii. 21: "And they said one to another, We are verily guilty concerning our brother, in that we saw the anguish of his soul," &c. The word is that every one of them spake to his brother. The text there is about Joseph's brethren. When they saw the hand of God upon them they spake thus. Now will any think that this was one to one, or rather not every one of them to another; and 2 Kings vi. we will find the like also. There was a whole army there, and will any man believe that one of them only spake at once, speaking such a word as they do?—there so that this is nothing else but a subterfuge and a way of escaping. And so they will find no face for this, that this duty it should be only of one to one.

A second objection is, that anything that is done in this, it must be done but by way of occasion, for it is not a direct command that we should be about any such thing, and have set time and place for the same, but only as it is occasioned by the way.

Answer. Anything is called occasional that is occasioned by us and by our blindness and ignorance, and this way the preaching of the word is a thing occasional, and a worthy divine, Rollock,[1] he said this, and so in this sense men might carceir [2] public preaching.

[1] Robert Rollock, born 1555, died 1599, a Regent in St. Andrews, the first Principal of the University of Edinburgh, and for a short time before his death one of the ministers of that city. [2] Imprison.

Again, secondly, the meaning is, Ye shall not intend such a thing, but what ye do therein ye shall do it by your intention. And certainly, that cannot be a fair way, as the philosopher could say. They failed in this who said, Men should do anything that is good by their intention. And they who write of moral philosophy, they say thus far, that a good action is the better that it be intended, and where a good action is [not] done by the intention it is so much the worse.

A third objection is that it is not lawful to appoint such a set time, and a set place for such actions. Certainly if it was lawful for Job's friends to meet together to comfort him, then this was not unlawful, neither that they made a meeting to come together for that effect. I believe that that place says that both the time and the place were appointed beforehand; and is the action the worse of it? No, certainly; for if the ordinance of God be lawful, then the fore-setting of time and place for the same cannot make it unlawful, except they will put religious worship to be used in an unlawful time and place. As to preach upon a day of man's invention to make it holy, that must not be. But for the other part, again, the appointing of time and place for a religious action makes it not worse but rather better. And we should beware of that, to distinguish in these things where the law of God distinguishes not. If it be lawful for a man to pray in private, there is none who will say that for him to appoint six hours in the morning, and such a house [to] pray in at that time, makes his prayer unlawful; and sicklike for preaching in the week time, will that make it unlawful to appoint Tuesday and Thursday for preaching?

Another objection is about the number of those who may together discharge this duty. Say they, "If two or three or some moe[1] may meet together for such an exercise, then why may not as well three hundred or a whole congregation meet that way?"

That is an objection soon answered. Solomon he might have houses to dwell in, but he might not exceed in the number of his houses. So Christians, they may thus meet in a private way. But if numbers of them meet together, then it is not a private worship, but a public. A man is bound to give to the poor, but he is not tied to give all that he has to them; that is superfluity and ostentation.

The last objection is: "All that is yet said," say they, "will not authorize a manner of conference that has been used by some, that two or three private Christians should meet together, and that every one of them should pray about." I believe there be none against this. But they say there is no warrant for three or four persons to pray *per vices*[2] at one time. And the argument they use is this: say they, "What ever point of worship wants either promise, practice, or command of God, that is an unlawful point of worship. But so it is, that praying thus *per vices*[2] is a point of worship that wants practice, promise, or precept, and therefore it is unlawful. But I would answer this with retortion to them who object, the same praying privately is not commanded, and is therefore unlawful to pray in private. No man will say that, I believe. And, again, if it be a thing lawful to preach, will that make it unlawful that one preach after another?

[1] More. [2] In turn, one after another.

A third reason is, because all the public actions of the worshippers of God, they are this way ordered by the public worshippers, even so are the private actions of his worship by the private worshippers. If this were retorted to us: "What Scripture have we for that in our public worship, to have first prayer, then singing of Psalms, then prayer, then preaching, then prayer, then singing, &c.," I believe no man would think it needful to give particular Scripture for that, for it belongs to the office-bearers in the house of God to order these things. So if it be lawful for one to pray in private with another, why may not as well one pray after another? And we will find preaching thus allowed (1 Cor. xiv. 31, and Acts xv.). Peter begins, and then Barnabas, and Paul, and then James. So that all this proves clear enough that there is no necessity of objecting against this point of worship, providing that all things be done in the right manner, as the Word of God allows.

Now a word of *the manner of their seeking to Zion.* They go weeping to seek the Lord. They weep because they had angered the Lord, and weep for the desolation of the holy city, and truly a work of reformation it requires weeping. And it should not have so meikle [1] rejoicing and so meikle [1] security joined therewith. And it looks the liker a judgment, that so few are drawn to repentance by this work of reformation, for the former breach of our covenant and our turning away from the Lord. The work of reformation should draw us to this, as the harlot wife who has been put out from her husband for her harlotry, when she is brought home again

[1] Much.

to her provoked husband, and he delivers to her again the keys of the house. If she be honest, it grieves her and makes her heart to melt, that she should have provoked such a loving husband. Even so, when the Lord has dealt so graciously with us after our falling away from Him, should there be so many dry cheeks among us as there are? It is not honest [1] like. But withal—

"*They speered*[2] *the way to Zion.*" All the tears in the world without this, they are but like to Esau's tears, for he resolved in the days of mourning to kill his brother; and like Judas's tears of desperation. But these are better tears that are spoken of Acts xx. 19, when the apostle was there leaving the Ephesians to serve the Lord, with many tears and temptations. It is nothing to weep for sin for a time, but to have their faces towards Zion, and asking the way to it, and to weep, that is more. That is an excellent stance their face has. While they are serving the Lord, and wat [3] not where to find Him, yet they have their faces towards Him. There is nothing more easily describes the seekers of Zion and of the Lord than their right look. They know not the way to Zion, and yet they have their face there away, and so speer [4] the way thereto.

There are three excellent looks spoken of in the Word of God: Psa. lxix. 3: "My eyes fail while I wait for God;" and David's comparison that he uses—"As the eyes of the watchmen wait for the morning, so wait we for Thee, O God." And then to wait upon God in the day of trouble, that is an honest look also, that look spoken of Isa. xvii. 7: "At that day shall a man look to his Maker,

[1] Becoming. [2] Asked. [3] Know. [4] Ask.

and his eyes shall have respect to the Holy One of Israel." What day is that spoken of there? That day when the Lord shall visit Zion, and the Kirk shall be left desolate, and there shall be only as it were gleaning grapes in it; even that which is spoken of, Isa. viii. 17: "I will wait upon the Lord that hideth His face, and I will look for Him."

To look to the Lord when the wind blows motes and sand in your eyes, that is an honest look, and then to look to the kingdom of heaven, and farther nor[1] time into eternity; as it is, Heb. xi. 9, Abraham, content to dwell in tents, and to seek no abiding city here, because he looked for a city which hath foundations, whose builder and maker is God. And to have Moses' look in the twenty-sixth verse of that chapter. He esteemed the reproach of Christ greater riches than the treasures of Egypt, because he had respect to the recompense of reward. Moses looked higher nor[1] all the courtiers in Pharaoh's court did—beyond time to eternity.

And a third good look is to look to slain Christ. When the Lord shall refine the house of David, and pour the spirit of supplications upon them, then they shall mourn when they look upon Him whom they have pierced. This condemns all the thrawn[2] looks that sinners in the world have, whatever they be. There is a look, Prov. xxi. 4, a high look, the Lord cannot endure it. And Prov. xxiii., for the eyes to behold strange women; and Isa. lvi. 2, "They all look to their own way, every one for his gain from his quarter;" and that look, Ezek. xviii. 15, that the house of Israel has its

---

[1] Than. [2] Distorted.

eyes toward the mountains and the hills. They look not to the Lord, but to their own gods. The Lord condemns all those who look not to Himself. And that is sure, every man who in faith looks to God and Christ and heaven, he will follow his look. O! that we had hearts and eyes to seek Him, and to look after Him, and to Him who is able to do this for us, to draw our hearts and eyes towards Himself; to that Lord, only wise, eternal, immortal, invisible, to Christ's Father and our Father, and Himself and the Holy Spirit, be all praise, glory, and honour now and for ever.—Amen.

The Kirk's Holy Resolution.

"*In those days, and in that time, saith the Lord, the children of Israel shall come, they and the children of Judah together, going and weeping: they shall go, and seek the Lord their God. They shall ask the way to Zion with their faces thitherward, saying, Come, and let us join ourselves to the Lord in a perpetual covenant that shall not be forgotten.*"—JEREMIAH l. 4, 5.[1]

E have heard, beloved in our Lord, a holy resolution of two kingdoms, to wit, Israel and Judah, after their deliverance from their captivity, to join themselves together to serve the Lord and His house, where He dwells, to ask the way to Zion with their faces thitherwards, and weeping. And their manner, how they went to seek the Lord—they went weeping. And their weakness when they are in the way—they speer[2] the way because they know it not. And then their encouraging one another into the way; they say, "Come, and let us join ourselves in a perpetual covenant with the Lord, never to be forgotten." Anything of that which was spoken the last day I repeat nothing of it. Only this would[3] be remembered, that the Lord's people

---

[1] No date or place is given to this sermon or the preceding one, but from its contents the two would seem to have been preached at the same time as the sermon on Isa. xli. 14-16. See note p. 1.

[2] Ask.   [3] Should.

of Israel and of Judah, every one of them encourages another to seek the Lord, and they set their shoulders together to help forward His glory, and for their brother's weal, and they come weeping one to another, and they speer[1] the way to Zion with their faces thitherwards.

Whilk[2] teaches a lesson that is most necessary for us, and is most worthy of our observation; and that is, that the Spirit of God allows[3] the communion of saints, and that every man be careful for the soul of his brother, that so we have not Cain's answer to give unto the Lord, "Am I my brother's keeper?" And that according to the calling and station the Lord has put us in, we be careful to exhort, instruct, comfort, and admonish one another, to edify one another in our most holy faith.

Now what I spake concerning this, I speak nothing thereof again. Only a word of that which I spake concerning the mind of our divines disputing against the Papists and Jesuits in that controversy between us and them about the interpreting of the sacred Scriptures, where they avow this to be a point of Popery, that the gift of interpreting the Scriptures should be only bound to the Kirk and to Kirkmen. Now it is not their meaning, neither is it my meaning, in defending this point, that all private Christians they have warrant from the Lord either to expone the Scriptures in public to the people, or yet to expone them after that manner that ordinarily we take for exponing the Scriptures, and that is to expone them as doctors and professors, or yet as pastors, who may expone the same, and are declared

[1] Ask. [2] Which. [3] Commends, approves of.

of God to be such as should understand and expone the Scriptures, and raise doctrines, and apply them to the people's use. Neither is this the mind of our divines, or of any in our Kirk, or of those on whom they lay the blame of Separatists. But the mind of our divines and our mind in this is—

First: That the faith of the people of God, in understanding the Scriptures, should not so depend upon the interpretation of Kirkmen, as that they themselves should be altogether ignorant of the sense thereof, for that were indeed to have a blind and implicit faith, and to believe as the Kirk believes. Again—

Secondly: That it is not against the Word of God, but agreeable thereto, that private Christians in a private way, they may apply the sense of Scripture to themselves and others, and that meaning that the Spirit of God has in such places of Scripture, and that they may confer, exhort, warn, rebuke, &c., one another. And this is not so meikle[1] exponing of Scripture as it is applying thereof rightly. But we are so far from giving anything which is due to the pastors or doctors who are in the house of God, or of any who are called to that holy function, or minds to follow the same, that we say with the apostle, Heb. v., "No man taketh this honour unto him except he be called of God for that effect." He ought not to meddle with what belongs to them.

Now the main thing that Israel and Judah shall do while they are in their journey this way—they shall seek the Lord their God, and shall ask the way to Zion with their faces thitherwards. Now a word of them.

[1] Much.

First: It is said that they shall be a company of seekers of God. That is the main thing that takes up the essence and the name of a believer, and a seeker of God, that he seeks the Lord. Now this seeking the Lord, it pre-suppones losing of Him. And having a reference to this losing of Him, God is sought this way, in four considerations. The

First is when the Lord's face is sought. This is when His favour and loving-kindness are sought, which is better than life. So it is said, Psa. xxiv. 6: "This is the generation of them that seek Him, of them that seek Thy face, O God of Jacob." These are the generation of them that seek the Lord's favour. So also Psa. xxvii. 8: "When thou saidst, Seek ye My face; my heart said, Thy face, Lord, will I seek"—that is the Lord's favour that is there spoken of. Sick-like, Hos. v. 15, "I will go and return to My place, till they acknowledge their offence, and seek My face: in their affliction they will seek Me early." Our natural condition and the state that we are in, that we have lost a sight of God's face and His favour, should put us to this. These who want should seek the Lord and the sense of His love. They who stand in need thereof should seek His face and loving-kindness, and blessed are they who seek this indeed.

A second thing that we are to seek under this, is to seek the image of God which we have lost. To seek wisdom, as it is Prov. ii. 4, 5: "If thou seekest her as silver, and searchest for her as hid treasures; then thou shalt understand the fear of the Lord, and find the knowledge of God;" even to seek that which we lost in Adam at his fall. For as it is, Rom. iii. 23, "All have sinned and come short of the glory of God;" they have missed that glorious image, as it is well exponed, and therefore it would[1] be sought for again. And this is the Lord's complaint, Jer. v. 1, that there is no man that seeketh the Lord; and it is the charge given unto His people, Zeph. ii. 3, "Seek ye the Lord, all ye meek of the earth;" and Isa. i. 17, "Seek judgment." The people, they should be careful of seeking God, and they ought to seek the image of God, which is true sanctification. And this is the main and essential way of seeking God. Again—

Third: We have lost the kingdom of heaven and paradise; and therefore that would[1] be sought. Matt. vi. 33: "Seek first the kingdom of heaven, and the righteousness thereof, and then all other things shall be casten[2] unto you." They who profess to seek, and seek not this, they fail in their seeking, and walk not with them of whom it is said, Rom. ii. 7, "who by well-doing" purchased a good report unto themselves; nor follow the example of Abraham, Heb. xi. 10: "He sought a city which hath a foundation, whose builder and maker is God." And then—

Lastly: To seek the means of salvation; that is, to seek God. Psa. cxix. 45: "I will walk at liberty, for I seek Thy precepts;" that is, "the thing that I make search for is Thy precepts," which is the way to salvation; and ver. 155, "Salvation is far from the wicked, for they seek not Thy statutes." It is a note of them who seek not the way to heaven that they seek not the Lord's statutes.

[1] Should.   [2] Given.

Now the *use* of this is, to condemn a multitude of seekers in the world, who albeit they seek God yet they seek not God nor His face, seek not His image, nor are they about the seeking of heaven, nor seek they after His precepts and the means of salvation. There are a number condemned, Phil. ii. 21 : " All seek their own things, but seek not the things of Christ." How many are there in the world who in their callings seek nothing but to get gold for their god, but cannot say as Christ says, and clears Himself from being guilty of such wickedness : " I serve not Mine own honour, but the honour of Him that sent Me " ? The most part seek their own honour and glory, and seek the world, but they seek not God. They seek corn, wine, and oil, but seek not to have the light of the Lord's countenance lifted upon them. And whoever seeks after these things, they shall not find what they seek, or if they find them they shall lose better. It were better to obey that, Isa. lv. : " Seek ye the Lord while He may be found; call upon Him while He is near," &c. ; and certainly whoever has their task to seek the world and the things thereof, they seek not the Lord nor His face, and image, or heaven, or salvation. Oh! if we knew what we have lost, and that we could leave our care of seeking things in the world, and set to to seek God and His face, His image, and heaven, and the precepts and testimonies of the Lord! And, out of all doubt, that is the best seeking in the world, and there is no man but he is seeking, and every man is seeking some good thing. But O! how many are there who come short of that which they should seek, who are seeking lying vanities, and forsaking their own mercy.

This is the world's conquersh[1] and their search; "Lord, save us from it."

Second: We have set down unto us, what the people shall seek—"They shall seek the Lord their God." The thing that is called seeking the way to Zion, it is exponed to seek the Lord.

And here we have this *doctrine* arising clearly unto us, that in the means of the worship of God, God Himself is to be sought, and not the means themselves. They are now coming from their captivity, and in their coming, they seek not the dry hill of Zion, or the temple, or the external means of God's worship, but they seek the Lord in these; for that is the fairest flower that grows there. The Lord Himself is better than preaching, or sacraments, or prayer, &c., and all the means of His worship; for all of them serve but only for leading to Him. And therefore none should content themselves in the worship of God until they get God Himself. Look unto Psalm xlii. 1, 4, and it will show this. The first verse says, "As the hart panteth after the water-brooks, so my soul panteth after Thee, O God;" and in the fourth verse, "When I remember these things, I pour out my soul in me: for I had gone with the multitude, I went with them to the house of God." At this time David was banished from the means of God's worship, and that is his heart-break, and the only thing that he misses at this time was God Himself, and so he missed the means for God. So, also, Psa. lxxxiv. 2: "My soul longeth, yea, even fainteth, for the courts of the Lord." Now was that no more but to have

[1] Acquisition.

a rowme¹ where the sparrows bigged² their nests, and the swallows kept their young ones? No. He expones it in the other part of the verse: "My soul crieth out for the living God." So also in Psalm lxiii., where David was banished into the wilderness—his heart was seeking the Lord, and so was longing for Him as thirsty land does for a shower, and then adds: "That I may see Thy power and glory so as I have seen Thee in Thy sanctuary."

Use. In all the means of the worship of God, whether ye have the use of them or want the use of them, seek ever God rather nor³ the means, whether it be in preaching, praying, hearing, reading, &c. Strive to be in at God Himself. And this is the difference between an hypocrite and a true seeker of God, for the hypocrite he seeks after the means, and no more. That is enough for him if he hear the word, and get the communion, or if he be a preacher, that he preach the same and no more, that he put his hand to a covenant. That contents these who are not true seekers of God. But the true seeker of God he learns to miss Him in the means of His service, and he thinks he has not things well at that time, when he finds not Himself; and, therefore, let us remember that praying, preaching, praising, reading, hearing, even all the means, they are as chariots and torches to carry us to God. But if so be that the Lord Himself be not sought for in the means, then we speer⁴ not the way to Zion rightly, and there are thousands in the world who mistake this way, for they seek only Zion and the outward means; and thus they miscarry in the worship of God.

¹ Place. ² Built. ³ Than. ⁴ Ask.

"*They shall seek the Lord their God.*" He is their God, and yet for all that they are put to seek Him. If He be their God, how is it that they want Him, or what necessity is there of seeking Him, for they have Him already, if He be theirs? Yes; He may be lost, and yet for all that be their God, because they are not in possession of Him, nor have they the sense of His presence, and that being their God is only by covenant, but He is not presently theirs in possession. Even as a man who has a number of houses, and yet he is so confined to such a house to dwell there all his lifetime for some crime committed by him. All the rest of the houses they are his in heritage. He has only lost the possession of them for a time, but he has right to them. Even so is the Kirk of God here tyning [1] access to God, and losing the comfort and joy of the Holy Ghost by sin; and yet for all that, the charter it stands still unviolated anent the decree of election, albeit for the present they dare not take possession thereof.

And this answers a case wherein many of the weak children of God are oftentimes, that they dare not apply the promise of God to themselves, or say Thomas's word, "My Lord and my God!" and yet for all that, for the world they dare not say the contrary. This is in effect to brangle [2] their own right, for He is the Lord and He is the portion of His children, albeit they dare not say, "The Lord is the portion of my inheritance." He is their rock and their strong tower, albeit they see it not; He is their Lord and their God, albeit they have not still assurance of the same.

[1] Losing.   [2] Shake to pieces.

"*With their faces thitherwards.*" This says that they had a mind to be there. And their asking of the way tells us that they knew not the gate [1] to it.

Here we may learn, that Christian souls and seekers of God, they will have a great desire and a great affection to be at Him, and yet, for all that, be ignorant of the means and of the way how to win to Him. And we may see that a true heart and honest intention in seeking the Lord, and weakness also, both these may stand together, as Nicodemus—he has a good mind to be at Christ, and yet, for all that, he is ignorant of the point of regeneration. And Mary Magdalene, she sought dead Jesus at the grave. That was weakness in her, and shows her affection to Him. But she should have sought living Jesus. And the apostles they dare not leave Jesus when the Capernaites left Him; and Peter says, in the name of the rest, "Whither shall we go if we leave Thee? for Thou hast the words of eternal life." And yet, for all that, they were not well grounded in the art of Christ's suffering and of Christ's resurrection, as we may see John xx.

This tells us that many of the children of God who have their faces towards heaven, they have their own ignorance, and know not where to gang.[2] And this should teach all of us to put a difference between weakness and wickedness. God knows the one by the other well enough. These who have an honest purpose to be at God, and know not the way how to win to Him, He will fley [3] none away from Him for that. But He is angry at wickedness, and dow [4] not abide it. But those

[1] Way. [2] Go. [3] Frighten. [4] Can.

who would fain be home over at the Lord, although they be weak and know not the way well, those who waken with that thought in the morning, and fall asleep with it at night, who mind the honour and glory of God, albeit otherways there be slips and falls in the way, the Lord He will give mercy, providing there be a habitual intention to seek God. Woe is the man that has his back to heaven, and has a habitual intention to seek the world; for his disease is not weakness, but wickedness. When a man's whole practices are how to get the world, if a man only mind this, and have his back upon Zion, God will not lift such a man when he falls. But if a man have his face towards heaven, albeit his legs be so weak that they will not follow him, yet He who leads the blind by a way that they know not, that breaks not the bruised reed, nor quenches the smoking flax, who deserts not any who minds after Him in truth, He will eye such and not let them fall, but when they fall He will raise them again.

Now in their resolution there are two words to be looked to. First, they say "*Come.*" Second, the words of their resolution are set down: "*Let us join ourselves to the Lord in a perpetual covenant, never to be forgotten.*" The first word, "*Come,*" is a word of many men, every one of them encouraging another. "Come, and let us all have one purse," as it is in the Proverbs (i. 11, 14). Ilk[1] one puts at another and strengthens the hands of one another in the work. As we have the word, Isa. ii. 2: "Many people and nations shall say in the last days, Come, and let us go up to the mountain of the Lord, to

---
[1] Each.

the house of the God of Jacob," &c. Such a word as is used Cant. vi. 1: "Whither is thy beloved gone, O thou fairest among women, that we may seek Him with thee?" There ilk¹ one of them says they will help another in seeking Him. And I am sure this is a better fellowship nor² other "Comes" that are set down in the Word of God. "Come ye," say they (Isa. lvi. 12), "I will fetch wine, and we will fill ourselves with strong drink; and to-morrow shall be as this day, and much more abundant." There the drunkard encouraging the drunkard to drunkenness. And (Gen. xxxvii. 19, 20) when Joseph's brethren see him coming, they say, "Behold, this dreamer cometh. Come now therefore, let us slay him, and cast him into some pit." And every one of them gives wicked counsel to another for taking his life. Such a "Come" as that which is Isa. xli. 7: "The carpenter encourageth the goldsmith, and he that smootheth with the hammer him that smote the anvil, and every one of them helps another to set up a golden image, and to fasten it that it should not be moved." There is over meikle of this good fellowship used in the world, and this is a woful and miserable pit to catch many souls in when ilk¹ sinner encourages another in ill. O! if the world would take notice of this, that ilk¹ one of them has their "Come" and their fellowship together this way: the drunkard and the worldling have their come. But "Come, and let us join ourselves in a perpetual covenant with the Lord." There is no blessed Brotherhood and fellowship of this kind. Where is this sort of "Come," where ilk¹ one encourages another to set God upon high?

¹ Each.   ² Than.

Now what is their resolution? They come not home to Zion to take the play, but when they are come home, they do it that they may be "joined in a perpetual covenant with the Lord, never to be forgotten." That is the end of all deliverances the Lord bestows upon us, that we may serve Him and be joined in a covenant with Him. That is a blessed cross that the end of it is to draw us nearer to God. "Before I was afflicted I went astray, but I have learned to keep thy statutes;" and Luke i. 74, 75: "That He would grant us, that we being redeemed from all our enemies might serve Him without fear, in holiness and righteousness all the days of our life." Then the end of deliverance from enemies is that we might serve the Lord in holiness and righteousness all the days of our life. And certainly such a deliverance as this is blessed, and there is no man that is lawfully delivered from a cross but he who does so.

Wherefore are afflictions called visitations. O! but that is a kindly word, and crosses are so when they are blessed of the Lord. They are visitations. And such crosses and visitations leave drinksilver[1] behind them where they come. When the Lord stells[2] a cannon foranent[3] their pride or worldly-mindedness, &c., and then they are amoving and purposing by His grace to set against it. When the Lord does this to make them deny themselves, and become humble in their own eyes, O but that is sweet. There is a word that expresses this well—Ezek. xvi. 63: "That thou mayest be confounded and remember, and never open thy mouth any more because of thy shame, when I am

---

[1] A vale given to servants. [2] Places. [3] Right against.

pacified towards thee." The shame of the cross and the confusion come upon them by their captivity, shall work this in them when they are reconciled to Him. And the like of this word is used Ezek. xx. 42, 43: "And ye shall know that I am the Lord, when I shall bring you into the land of Israel. And there shall ye remember your ways, and all your doings, wherein ye have been defiled. And ye shall loathe yourselves in your own sight for all your evils that ye hath committed." And therefore every man speer[1] at his own soul when he has been under any cross what good he gat of them. God brought you unto poverty, and art thou still as proud as ever thou wast? That is a stinking-tailed cross. Has the Lord delivered you from sickness and the gates of death? And art thou delivered therefra[2] and yet art as worldly-minded and as irreligious as ever thou wast? That is a cursed cross that is sealed with the feid[3] of God. And, by the contrary, a soul that is delivered from any cross, and speaks out of the dust and is humbled thereby, that is a blessed and sanctified cross.

"*And let us join ourselves in a perpetual covenant with the Lord.*"

This tells us that all that are joined in covenant with God He and they are made one. And if ye will look to three things ye will find it to be so.

First: A covenant is a band of friendship, and so they are made one. And certainly that is no small favour that the Potter and the clay should thus enter into covenant; for when the sinner is thus entered in a

---

[1] Ask.   [2] From.   [3] Enmity.

covenant indeed with the Lord, then they get forgiveness of sins, and getting it makes the Lord and them to be of one spirit.

Second: Being in covenant with God, they have one heart, a heart like God. Ezek. xxxvi. 26: "A new heart also will I give unto you, and a new spirit will I put within you; and I will take away the stony heart out of your flesh, and I will give you a heart of flesh." The Lord is there speaking of the promises of the new covenant, and the word that is used Ezek. xi. 19 is not unlike this same: "And I will give them one heart." It is meant that He will give them a single heart. And it may have this meaning also, that they shall have one heart with the Lord. These who speak of the understanding, they say when one understands a thing, the understanding and the object are knit together; even so is it here. The Lord's spirit and the heart meet, and thus they are made one.

Lastly: They are made one with the Lord because the tenor of the covenant it runs so: "I will be your God, and ye shall be My people," and Cant. ii. 16 the spouse says, "My well-beloved is mine, and I am His." There is a mutual claim and a mutual union between two things here; for the one of them is the possession, and the other is the thing possessed even of them both.

Now the *use* of this is: To speak against many covenanters in the land who indeed are anti-covenanters. That soul who is not one with God, and he who makes not God's foes to be his foes, and His friends to be his friends, is not in covenant with Him. He who can hear His name blasphemed, and will not join with them

THE KIRK'S HOLY RESOLUTION.

who serve the Lord, but is against them, that man has not truly subscribed the covenant. He has sworn away ceremonies, but he has not sworn away that ceremony of drinking healths; and those who dare ordinarily take the name of God in their mouth, such are anti-covenanters in God's account, and He will reckon them for His foes. And therefore let every one try who has putten[1] his hand to the paper, and sworn and subscribed, that he shall mend his life among other things, and yet his life is so scandalous that it gives offence to others. Remember that he is a heart opposer of the covenant, and so is an enemy to God.

Now a word of the perpetuity of the covenant: "Let us be joined *in a perpetual covenant with the Lord, never to be forgotten.*" That is, let us be joined in a covenant that cannot be broken. Is there none of this people who are in covenant with God that can sin against the covenant? and is not a sin against the covenant a breach of it? It is one thing to sin against the covenant, and the mercy of a Mediator, and another thing to break the covenant. All the elect and all believers, they sin against the covenant, but the elect and believers break not the covenant. The breach of the covenant is only proper to godless and wicked men, who are within the compass thereof outwardly. But for these who are within the covenant, they break it not. And the reason of this is—

First: Because of the Lord's eternal election of them, and then because of that habitual grace that is in the child of God. Even as every wrong look that the spouse

[1] Put.

gives breaks not the band of marriage that is between the husband and her, and puts her not away from any right to her husband's goods and to be partaker of his honour; even so those who are within the covenant of grace, their slips and their faults break not the covenant with God, because of God's eternal election and because of the habit of grace that is in them, that are the bands of the covenant, and that which makes the believer a formal covenanter. Again—

Secondly: If we will look to both the parts of the covenant, it is eternal; for as God is the one part of the covenant, so God-Man and Man-God is cautioner for the other part thereof. The Mediator Christ being on our side of the covenant, and cautioner for us, it is sure; and there was no doubt of breaking the other side of the covenant. But Christ, He is on both sides of the covenant, for all the promises of the covenant they are made to Christ as He is Mediator. And in Him they are Yea and Amen, and made over to us as it is (2 Cor. i. 20). Now among all the rest of the promises of the covenant this is one, Jer. xxxii. 40: "And I will make an everlasting covenant with them, that I will not turn away from them, to do them good; and I will put My fear in their hearts, that they shall not depart from Me." And our Lord says, "My sheep hear My voice and I know them, and they follow Me; and I give unto them eternal life, and they shall never perish, neither shall any man pluck them out of My hand." Thir[1] promises they are not fastened upon our free-will, for that indeed is a rotten pin, but they are fastened on

[1] These.

Christ Jesus as Mediator of the covenant, and He is also the Principal in the covenant. He is cautioner, undertaking for our part, and it is He who has undertaken: "I will put My fear in their hearts, yet they shall not depart from Me." A

Third reason of the perpetuity of the covenant is because the party in covenant with God is not man and man's free-will, but man graced of God and man standing under the decree of election, and as he is a new creature in Christ and in God. If so be that free-will were our tutor, and we had our heaven in our own keeping, then we would lose all. But because we have Christ for our tutor, and He has our heaven in His hand, therefore the covenant it must be perpetual.

The *use* of this is, to show us the misery of all those who are not within this covenant, for they are in another covenant, even in a covenant which may be broken. Jer. xxxi. 31, 32; there are two covenants mentioned there; the one whereof is broken, that covenant that He made with them when He brought them out of the land of Egypt; and then there is the covenant of grace called the new covenant that cannot be broken. They that are under the first covenant they are worldly men and reprobates, and strangers from God, and what grip has such of heaven, or of salvation, or what assurance of remission of sins? There is no more, but if they can win it[1] have it. But there is no promise made for it, not from the first to the last of the Revelation.

O! but that be a miserable case, He has nothing for salvation but such a word as Israel had, and lost the

---

[1] Succeed in reaching to.

good of it; and Adam also. But O! how fair is the state of the children of God who have such a strong Lord to be our staff, and such a guide to lead us in the way, [and who] have him to be a Lord to work in us to will and to do of His good pleasure. If ye knew what this were, there would be more pains taen[1] to be in covenant this way.

Learn, not only to be under God as Lawgiver and supreme Judge of the world, for so are the devils and reprobates in the world, but learn to be so in covenant with God as that ye may be assured of your election and of true grace wrought in you. That is an anchor that will not break, but will carry you through in all storms, gloom[2] at you who will. Thou wilt be able then to ride out against all their glooming, and in the strength of the Lord thou shalt be a conqueror, and more than a conqueror through Him that has loved you. To this God, Christ's Father, and our Father, to Himself and the Holy Spirit be ascribed all glory, praise, and honour, for ever and ever. So be it.

[1] Taken.   [2] Frown.

The Forlorn Son.

"*And he said, A certain man had two sons: and the younger of them said to his father, Father, give me the portion of goods that falleth to me. And he divided unto them his living.*"—LUKE xv. 11, 12.[1]

N this parable, beloved in our Lord, we have to consider these particulars, the meaning of the parable, and then Christ's scope therein. All parables in the Word of God they are no other but only continued similitudes and metaphors illustrating some spiritual thing. In this parable there is a man and a householder spoken of, a father who has two sort of sons. For the meaning of the text, we have to understand, first, what is meant by a house here; second, [who is the father]; and third, what is meant by the two sons.

[1] In the MS. there is no date given to the following sermons further than "Sermons preached by Mr. Sam. Rutherford;" but one or two phrases in them would seem to fix them to about 1640, when the Scotch army was in England. Rutherford seems to have been fond of courses of sermons on a particular book or chapter of Scripture. The sermons on the Song of Songs, on Zechariah, and Revelation, in Dr. Bonar's edition of Rutherford's "Communion Sermons," are evidently parts of courses that he had delivered on these books. "Forlorn" in the sense Rutherford here uses it occurs in Shakspere, Henry VI. part iii, iii, 3.
Henry.
Is of a king, become a banish'd man,
And forced to live in Scotland a *forlorn.*

Now for the first. Ye know it is ordinary for the Lord in His word to resemble His Kirk or the kingdom of grace to a house or a family; for Christ our Lord He holds a house here wherein all the bairns[1] of the house are free to the table, for there is a difference even here between the bairns of the house, and those who are only servants, and goers and comers as it were.

Then, secondly, what is meant by the father? There is greater difficulty in that to know what is meant thereby, because the Word of God it does ordinarily call the first Person of the Trinity, the Father, distinct from the other two persons. And yet there are three good reasons wherefore this is to be understood of Christ, the second person of the Trinity.

First: If we will look unto the scope and drift of the parable, it will say this much to us, for the text tells us that the Scribes and Pharisees murmured at Him saying, "This man receiveth sinners, and He eateth with them," and so they thought He could not be the Messiah and the Saviour of the world, who used[2] such company that haunted among godless and profane persons. Now to take away this scruple and objection, Christ our Lord uses this parable that now we have read, and so labours to let them see how welcome such are to Him, who have been runaways, who have been lewd and lascivious persons, if so be they will come home, and will indeed acknowledge that they have need of Christ. He will show that He has the mind of a father towards such, and welcomes them home again as kindly as the father does his lost bairn,[3] who has spent all that his father

[1] Children.   [2] Frequented.   [3] Child.

gave him to live upon, and, having spent all, repents of his misspending, and comes home again to his father in a submissive and humble manner. Again—

Secondly, to prove that it is Christ that is here meant is clear by this: This parable in substance is all one with the former two parables in this chapter, concerning the lost and wandered sheep, and the lost piece of silver. If a shepherd be careful, having lost a sheep, to seek it in again to the flock, and will receive it in gladly, meikle[1] more will He, who is the Good Shepherd, have a care of those who are His sheep, to seek those who are lost, and welcome them when they come. In John x. 11 Christ says, "I am the Good Shepherd, the good shepherd giveth his life for his sheep." If, then, this parable be one in substance with the other two parables, and these be spoken of Christ, that it is He who loses the groat, and from whom the sheep wanders, and He seeks them in again, and will not rest till He find them, then it cannot be another father who receives a prodigal waster, runaway child, than Christ. And—

Thirdly, thus to call Christ Father is not against Scripture neither, but is agreeable to divers places therein. And to leave all the rest, and take to this one place it makes it clear Heb. ii. 13; it is said there that Christ has many bairns[2] and sons for glory, and therefore having many bairns He must be a father. That is brought out in the words cited out of Isaiah, "Behold I and the children whom the Lord hath given Me." And this style[3] it is also given unto Christ, Isa. ix. 6: "The Everlasting Father," so that both the scope of the

[1] Much.   [2] Children.   [3] Title.

parable itself and of the parable going before, and other places of Scripture clear unto us, that here, by the father, is meant the Son of God.

Now, the third word is, we are to consider, what is meant by the two sons. The younger son some have taken to be the Kirk of the Gentiles, and the other son to be the Kirk of the Jews. And there is reason for this, because the Kirk of the Jews they had the morning market of Christ, and He made a covenant with them before He made a covenant with us, who are Gentiles. But however it be, the text it will bear further than this. As Christ, He casts none away who come to Him, Jew or Gentile, and repents of their sin's provocations. By the older son we take to be meant all they who live within the visible Kirk, who profess themselves to be Christ's, and yet, in the meantime, they are nothing else but rotten hypocrites. And by the younger son, who craved his portion of goods of his father, and went away having gotten the same and spent it riotously, and then came home and confessed this wandering, is meant any sinner who sees his wanderings and is ladened with sin, and comes to Christ and makes his moan to Him.

The purpose of the Son of God in this parable is to take away that slander laid against Him, that He could not be the Messiah, because none of the honest[1] people, none of the kirkmen and bishops, none of the clergy, haunt His company; but His ordinary company is debauched, wicked men, that such will no[2] keep company with. Publicans and sinners are His ordinary company, and therefore He cannot be the Messiah.

[1] Honourable, creditable. Latin, *honestus*. [2] Not.

Now our Lord takes upon Him to prove that this same proves Him to be the Messiah, because He makes such welcome when they come to Him.

Out of this ye may see, then, what has always been the judgment and opinion of natural men of Christ. Ye may see by this that they have always taken their marks of Christ by the moon. "Scribes and Pharisees follow not this man, and therefore He cannot be the Messiah, seeing they countenance Him not." And this is yet the opinion the world has of Christ and the gospel. The kings of the earth, and the clergymen, and universities, and velvet gowns follow not Christ and this way of the gospel, and therefore it cannot be the right way, for if it were the best way such would follow it and countenance.

But this form of reasoning is against Scripture, for the Scripture says: Not many rich, not many wise, not many [noble], not many learned, but the poor, base, and contemptible things of the world are the followers of Christ. Because there are few scarlet clothes and crowned kings at Christ's back, that proves not that He is not Christ and the Saviour of the world; but because He has publicans and sinners to be His followers, that makes Him to look like the Messiah than otherwise He would, albeit the world think not so. For such a Saviour as Christ should always be beside lost sinners. Such a physician as Christ is should be beside sick and diseased persons. And to let the world see that Christ's kingdom it comes not with observation and outward pomp and glory, therefore He would haunt the company of publicans and sinners. Let none then be scared away from Christ as a lordly Saviour, but come in humility to Him, as the woman who had the bloody issue durst not come to speak to Him or to touch His skin, yet she touches the hem of His garment, and that cures her. Such are nearest Christ who are aye[1] complaining of sin, and think themselves to be furthest from Him; for whole folks need not Christ, only those who are sick.

Now the parable has thir[2] parts in it, shortly: (1) We have the foolish resolution and journey of the younger son, and this is from ver. 11 to the 17th. (2) We have his coming home again, and the grounds and causes thereof, from the 17th verse to the midst of the 20th. And then (3) from the 20th verse, how his father received him when he comes home. O, how heartsome a welcome is there between our Lord and a home-coming sinner. Now this home-coming the Spirit of God sets it down in the rest of the verses. And, first, it is set down how his father received him when he comes home; and, second, how his older brother received him, who should have been blith[3] at his home-coming.

For *the father of* this forlorn son he sees him afar off, and knows him. Who has a warm heart to a home-coming sinner if Christ have it not? And, seeing him, he ran to meet him, and fell upon his neck and kissed him. There is never a word of quarrelling[4] at all on Christ's part when the forlorn child comes to Him, but causes bring the best robe and put upon him, and put shoes on his feet, and a ring upon his hand, and there

---

[1] Always.   [2] These.   [3] Glad.
[4] Finding fault, reproving.

is feasting and dancing for his recovery and restoring safe. The fatted calf is killed for him.

And then the *carriage of the elder brother*. He was in the field, and when he comes home he hears meikle [1] mirth in his father's house, and he calls for one of the servants to see what these things meant; and the servant tells the elder son that his younger brother was come home, and his father had killed the fat calf, because he had received him safe and sound. When he hears that his brother was come home, who had spent all his patrimony, and that his father had so received him, he was angry, and would not come in to the house where his repenting brother was, but was angry at him and his father both, and made a quarrel of it to his father. His father came out, and entreated him to come in. "But he, answering, said to his father, Lo, these many years have I served you, neither at any time transgressed I thy commandment, and yet thou never gavest me a kid that I might make merry with my friends. But as soon as this thy son was come which hath devoured thy living with harlots, thou hast killed for him the fatted calf." And the Lord is brought in mercifully choosing the elder brother also, for [2] all his hard quarrelling [3] his father for what he did, and saying, "Son, thou art ever with me, and all that I have is thine. It was meet that we should make merry and be glad; for this thy brother was dead and is alive again, and was lost and is found." The father calls him not to the elder son "my son," but "thy brother," telling he is as sib [4] to him as he is to

---

[1] Much.   [2] Notwithstanding.   [3] Finding fault with.
[4] Nearly related.

him. "And thou hast reason to be as glad as I at his coming home." Indeed, it sets¹ our Lord very well to be blyth² and glad, and the company of those who are glorious in heaven when a repenting sinner comes home. O, that is the matter of heaven's mirth, albeit others be angry that they are received in the house. This is the sum of the parable.

Now in the eleventh verse there is set down: (1) The occasion of the parable. (2) We have the suit of the forlorn³ son to his father. And (3) We have the father granting the suit of his forlorn son. (1) For the occasion of the parable, "A certain man had two sons." (2) The suit of the forlorn son to his father. "And the younger said to his father, Father, give me the portion of goods that falleth to me," as meikle⁴ as if he had said: "Father, I am tired of your company, and I would now have my own will, and therefore give me that that is due to me." Woe! to that sinner that gets that which falls [to] him and is his due, for that is hell!

And then we have the father yielding to his request: "And he divided to him his living." He yields to let the sinner fall upon his own weight, who will not be upholden by Him; that he may know what bottom he is on when he is not upon God. His father says to him, "If ye be tired of me and of my guiding, and will have your portion that falls [to] you, ye shall have your portion, and try what ye will do with your own strength, and with your own wit, and your own guiding;" and he divides his goods, and gives him his portion. And having done, he turns his back upon his father,

¹ Becomes. ² Happy. ³ The request of the prodigal. ⁴ Much.

and his father turns his back upon him, that he may see the odds between his father's house and the forlorn country he gaed [1] to, having left it.

Now for the first:

"*A certain man had two sons.*" You see that both thir [2] sons are not of one kind. The one of them is a repenting forlorn son, and the other is a professing son within the house, and no more.

The *doctrine* then that rises from this is clear: that the Kirk of God is not a clean house here upon earth, but our Lord has in it the elect and reprobate, gold and dross, vessels of honour and vessels of dishonour. And there is a bed spoken of Luke xvii. 34: Two lying in a bed, the one is rejected and the other is chosen; two grinding at the mill, the one taken and the other shall be lost; two walking in the field, the one shall be taken and the other shall be lost. The Kirk hereaway [3] is made up of thir [2] two sorts of persons, elect and reprobate. The Kirk is the Lord's barn floor whereon there is both caff [4] and corn. There are some in the Kirk that are believers and sons indeed; others that are only bastards and servants. Two lying in one womb together and one of them chosen and loved, to wit, Jacob, and another of them hated and rejected, namely, Esau. "Before the children were born, or ever they could do good or ill, I loved Jacob, but I hated Esau." Two sons in a family together—and one of them the son of a handmaid who may not be the heir, Ishmael; and the other the son of the promise, Isaac. "In Isaac shall thy seed be called." Wherefore is it that the Lord compared

---

[1] Went.   [2] These.   [3] In this world. See "Letters."   [4] Chaff.

His Kirk to a draw-net that is cast into the sea, and draws out of it all manner of fishes? All are not chosen who are in the family of the Kirk here; all are not one father's bairns.[1] Indeed though they be in profession, all are not in the right way to heaven who profess to be walking to it. This speaks reproof to two sorts of persons.

And, first, to those who defile the house of God. Bearest thou up rowme[2] in the house of God and walk not as it becomes the son of such a father, then the Lord He will soup[3] you to the door. The servant abides not in the house, but the son abides therein. There is a day coming when there shall be a separation of those that are now within the visible Kirk here, when those who are indeed and truly sons, and those who are bastards shall sunder. The professor who counts that holiness enough to hear the word, and to take His sacrament as it comes about, they shall be put out of the house; but those who follow the practice and power of religion, who follow Christ in everything shall be kept in as sons, and shall be sons indeed for ever. Second, this speaks also against them who will have a clean Kirk hereaway,[4] against them who separate from a Kirk because there are hypocrites within the same, who will have the visible Kirk here to be made up only of regenerate persons, and will join with no other Kirk to be members thereof. They will have a Kirk here that is all white paper. That is a man in the moon; that is not to be found here till we come to the triumphant Kirk in heaven. It shall indeed [yet] be made up of such only as are clean and

[1] Children.   [2] Takest thou up a place.   [3] Sweep.   [4] In this world.

white and pure. But the Kirk hereaway maun¹ have sons and servants in it. The Kirk here must have good corn and popple,² and the dike of God's providence must be going about both those. And so we are not to look that that barn floor shall be free of caff³ and popple.² Till the Judge come with His last fan in His hand, we are not to look for that here, to see a Kirk free of all errors. That is the Kirk that is spoken of Eph. v. 25, for which Christ gave Himself that He might sanctify and cleanse it by the washing of water and the word. But until we be landed in glory there will be within the walls of the visible Kirk, there will be heresies and errors in it, and sinful and wicked persons, there will be Judases in the Kirk whose God is their gain, there will be Diotrepheses in it who love the pre-eminence, and Hermogenes who deny the resurrection from the dead. There must be in the visible Kirk hereaway Scribes and Pharisees, who are heart enemies to the Son of God, and yet the Kirk is not to be separated from because of that.

Now the second part of the text is: The younger son his desire⁴ to his father. "And the younger son said, Father, give me the portion of goods that falleth me." There are no tint⁵ words here, but every word is to good purpose.

Why is it that he gives him who leaves his father the style of the younger son? It is even to tell us this, that it is a trick of youth for any to leave Christ, that it is an ordinary thing for young ones to tire of God's company, and to long to be at their own tutoring. It

---

¹ Must.   ² Cockle.   ³ Chaff.   ⁴ His request.   ⁵ Lost or useless.

lets us see this. I grant neither youth nor old age will bring folks to Christ till He Himself do it. Yet of all the glassy ways that can be wherein we are most ready to fall, that is youth. And the Word of God gives three reasons wherefore it is so.

First: Because those who are young they have no experience. They are like strangers who are new come to a country; they know not the fashions of the country. He knows not how to behave himself. He knows not the cross of Christ who is young and new begun, and therefore he starts at it. It is no marvel that our Lord make a question of this in Psalm cxix. 9, "Wherewith shall a young man cleanse his way?" Wherefore is it not said, "Wherewith shall a *man*, or an *old man*, cleanse his way?" but only [1] telling us this, that it is a question, and hard, for a young man to hold his feet and hear what God says to him.

A second reason is, the soul, while it is in the body, it works by organs, and while the organs are young the soul then it is light; while the lusting youth is strong, it is hard to serve God; while witlessness is bound unto the heart, as ordinarily it is in youth, and the affections are following the temper of the body, and it is strong and vigorous, it is a greater matter to see a man seeking God at such time than afterwards. For fra [2] one begins once to settle himself, then ordinarily the Lord, in old age, He lets them see what they have been doing in their younger years, and they are humbled when they see it. And therefore David, a man according to God's heart, prays, "Lord, remember not the sins of my youth;"

[1] But just to tell. [2] From the time when one begins to take thought.

and Job says (xiii. 26), because of the bitterness that was upon him, " Thou makest me to possess the sins of my youth."

A third reason of this is, there is no time of our age that is meet for God in itself, but the most unmeet time of all is the time of our youth, and yet the Lord lets us see herein that He will refuse none, of whatever age they be, who seek to Him—as young Joseph the Lord accepts of him, and young Daniel the Lord regards his seeking Him, and young David in Saul's court seeking the Lord He is found of him, and young king Josiah, they set themselves to obey the Lord's directions. And it tells us this far, that old age has no lawburrows[1] against damnation more than youth, and temptation may prevail with the one sometimes as well as with the other. When young Joseph will not be tempted by lust, yet old wise Solomon is tempted and overcome thereby. David, when he was young, was not tempted to uncleanness, and yet, notwithstanding growing old and secure, he is tempted by Bathsheba : letting us see this far, that it is grace that holds us up that we fall not, and neither youth nor old age.

O! that young ones would start to in time to seek the Lord while they are young, that they would begin to make their acquaintance with the Lord and to drink in the knowledge of the Son of God, that they would study to know the sweetness of His love, that they would set to to get their young hearts married on Christ! If they will do so once, give Him their love, and their hearts' love, it shall not be in their power to follow another lover again.

[1] Legal security.

"*Father, give me the portion of goods that falleth unto me.*" There [is] a trim[1] style the prodigal child gives! He calls him "father," yet says he, "albeit thou be my father, let me be my own man."

That he gives this style unto Christ it teaches us this far, that there be many in the visible Church who pretend to have God for their Father, and yet would be away from Him; that there be many who say, "Lord, Lord," that shall not enter into the kingdom of heaven. Many, when they are upon an ill course, they will give God His own name, and profess that they are His sons, and yet for all that it is not so—as Herod, when he was upon the slaying of Christ; and Judas, who betrayed Christ with a kiss. And Absalom, when he is on that purpose to slay his own father, and so to usurp the kingdom, he says that he has a religious vow at Hebron, and he must go there to perform it, whereas he intended no such thing, albeit he pretended so. When Judas was to betray Christ, he gives Him a low back[2] and kisses Him.

Let us learn, then, to know upon what ground it is that we give our Lord His own styles. Try what it is that makes us come to hear His word, and make a profession that we are His, for they are not all Christ's friends who give Him here a laigh good day,[3] and fair words, and a white-like profession. Many shall say to Him, "Lord, Lord," that shall not enter into the kingdom of heaven. Many at the last day shall say that they wrought miracles in Christ's name, cast out devils, eat and drank at His table, and so professed, and did outwardly very much; and yet they shall get that answer

---

[1] In irony—a fine-sounding title this!   [2] Bow.   [3] A low bow.

from Christ, "Depart from me, ye cursed, into everlasting fire, prepared for the devil and his angels." Let us, then, strive to be honest and sincere to our Master, and let us indeed be that for Christ which we profess ourselves to be, and if we do so, then the truth shall make us free. But if we have a fair face to Christ, but are not back[1] friends also, but rather enemies that way, better that we had never given our name to Christ to be His, than having once given our name to prove false to Him. There are many in the world that, while religion seems to be holy,[2] and it is well spoken of to be religious, and religion has the Kirk stamp upon it, many are there will then follow religion and back[3] it, will profess fair, and so follow the Lord that way, and will be as religious as any. But when times change, they change. To swear a covenant with Christ and to pretend to do for Him, and yet to be doing against it secretly! Woe! for ever is thy case who callest thyself a friend of Christ, callest thyself His son, and Him thy Father, and yet despisest His directions and art a friend to the house of bondage! Great are the woes that attend such. It is religion to be religious in secret as well as to be religious in public, to take Christ into your families. See what ye think of this—to take Christ for well and for woe, to resolve if there were no moe[4] to back Christ but myself, yet I will avow Him. That is that proves any to be religious. A colour of religion will not please the Lord. It is but a scorning Him. Those who believe all that the Lord says of heaven or hell, and everything; that is honest-like. But for those who only put the fair cloak of religion

[1] Supporters.   [2] Safe.   [3] Support.   [4] More to support.

about them to be seen so by the world, that will not carry you over death, but the Lord will discover you one day to your shame.

Now for the matter of this young man's prayer. It is, *Father, give me the portion of goods that falleth me.* What ailed him at his father? Wise bairns think their father's house to be good company, especially if their father be a great man. What ailed this young man to weary of his father's company? Would ye trow[1] that a natural conscience will see a fault in God, for God is the Father that is here meant? In Jer. ii. 5 the Lord says: "What iniquity have your fathers found in Me, that they are gone far from Me, and have walked after vanity, and are become vain?" Was there ever a people that "found sin in God"? and yet the Lord says, "What wrong did I against them." There is such a complaint as this (Mic. vi. 3): "O my people, what have I done unto thee? and wherein have I wearied thee? testify against Me." Who is there that leaves God but they find some fault in Him? All sinners who continue in sin they find something in God that makes them to tire of Him. What gars[2] the drunkard, the whoremonger, the idolater, covetous person, tire of God? Is it possible that any reasonable appetite can desire to be free of that which is infinitely good; if so be they saw no ill in Him, at least, apprehended ill in Him? What is this that sinners see in Christ, and what ails them at Him? What gart[3] people call Him a Samaritan, and He the chosen of God and precious, and God Himself? Is it possible, think ye, that men can obtrude this upon

---

[1] Believe.   [2] Causes.   [3] Caused.

a conscience that is led with reason that they should think good ill, and to esteem that which is infinitely good to be ill, that they should account that which is happiness and good itself to be ill? Yes! certainly there is never a sinner, who follows his own ways, but he has his something in God that he loves not.

There are some grounds and reasons for this, that a sinner, looking wrong upon God, sees something in Him that makes him tire of His company.

First: There is old nature in man. Like fool Adam, following his footsteps, that would be his own tutor, not trusting in God but in himself. And it is easy to prove that to be Adam's first sin, that he trusted not in God, and hearkened not what He said, but hearkened to that which his wife said, and the devil said to her; for if Adam had trusted in God he would not [have] believed what the devil spake. We all love this, to have a world of our own making. God awes them, and the cords that He lays on, they bind, and we dow[1] not bide that—to be bound by religion. We dow[1] not bear the Lord's bands, and therefore we would be quit of God and of His yoke. The law of the Lord awes the natural man so that he would fain be fra[2] Him, and to quit Him and His law both.

A second reason: Sinners they see God and Christ afar off. They see Him not near hand. There is aye[3] something between them and Christ when they see Him. And, you know, when anything is seen with any medium intervening, it cannot be well seen. Those who look to Christ through their gain or lust, they see Him not

[1] Can. [2] From. [3] Always.

right, they see Him not to be all glorious as indeed He is.

A third reason that makes them not to see Christ right, but with faults in Him, is, because they and their lusts and their conscience are all sib [1] together; and so all is seen wrong where the light whereby we see is wrong. Our conscience should control us in that which is wrong; but our lust and our conscience under corruption are like two thieves meeting together. Ilk [2] one of them tempts another to steal. And so they agree together in that which is spoken Prov. i. 13 : "We shall find all precious substance, we shall fill our houses with spoil." The blinded will and affections, they see always some fault in God, and ilk [2] one of them helps another to sin. Like those two inclined to lust meeting together (Prov. vii.), and saying : " Come, let us take our fill of love until the morning : let us solace ourselves with loves. For the goodman is not at home, he has taken a long journey ;" and the other party is allured, and goeth straightway after her, as an ox goeth to the slaughter, not knowing that it is for his life. Just so is it here. The natural light it is led away by the affections, that great witch. And ilk [2] one of them helping another to go wrong, never considering it is so till they be fanged [3] in the net.

Again, as a fourth reason, consider the way how men are led on to sin. Who in the world will not say that God is happiness, and who will not acknowledge but Christ is better nor [4] gain, or court,[5] or the world, or

---

[1] Related.   [2] Each.   [3] Caught.   [4] Than.
[5] Influence. See " Letters."

pleasure? But when it comes to that, Is Christ better nor¹ this gain? In the assumption there, the poor soul is led away, and the miserable will and affections they lead away the mind there, and ilk² one of them bewitches another to sin. There is this meikle³ power into the soul as some kings have in some parts to call together and dissolve Parliaments by their royal prerogative. So the will it is king, and calls all together as it pleases, and dissolves them again when it sees meet. It were good for us if we could learn to compare God and eternity, and all things that are here under the sun together. But that is the misery, the will has that meikle³ power in us as to draw all away from comparative judging of things, and lets only the one part be judged, but not the other. It is blind light that leads on a sinner to commit sin. The drunkard, when he is led to drunkenness, he sees only the present pleasure; he sees not that time coming when he will not get a drop of cold water to cool the tip of his tongue, and so cannot compare them rightly. Esau, in selling his birthright, he only saw the pottage, and found his present hunger. But he saw not that he was selling his birthright, which was to him a type of heaven.

O! but it concerns us very meikle³ to have rectified judgments, to have all things in us in their own right order, and minding heaven and the things that are above! There is a word spoken by the apostle, Rom. viii. 5, which clears this point: "They that are of the flesh savour the things of the flesh; but they that are of the Spirit, they mind the things of the Spirit." Unre-

¹ Than.   ² Each.   ³ Much.

newed men, there is nothing that smells well to them even in matters of religion; but what they see has honour, gain, lust, ease following upon it. But those who are spiritual, they will smell Christ another way; they will see in Him forgiveness of sins to be gotten, and that they shall be reckoned freemen of the Lord in that day when heaven and earth go together, and the earth shall all be burned in a fair low.[1] O! that will draw them to seek after Christ. But woe! to them who find fault with God and with Christ, and see something in Him that makes them to tire of Him.

But is there any who finds fault with God? Yes. Any who find fault with His ordinances and laws, they find fault with Himself. They who hear that He commands such a thing to be done or forbids such a thing, and will not obey the same, they indeed find a fault in Him. O! for the light of heaven to let us see whereaway we are going! And to this light, to Christ's Father and our Father, to Himself and the Holy Spirit, we ascribe all glory, praise, honour for ever and ever. —Amen.

[1] Flame.

The Forlorn Son seeks away from His Father.

" *And he said, A certain man had two sons: and the younger of them said to his father, Father, give me the portion of goods that falleth to me. And he divided unto them his living. And not many days after the younger son gathered all together, and took his journey into a far country, and there wasted his substance with riotous living.*"—LUKE xv. 11-13.

IT is a wonder, beloved in the Lord, to see a sinner tire of God and weary of His company. There is no ill in God nor anything that is worthy hatred. John says, "God is love;" and all things in God they are love also. Yet an ill eye sees colours wrong, and the sinner sees something in God which is not in Him. In Jer. ii. 5, the Lord there complains by His prophet: "What iniquity have your fathers found in Me, that they have gone far from Me?" What sin or what ill can a sinner see in God? And yet if they saw no ill in Him, impossible that they would leave Him, impossible it is that the reasonable appetite can flee from anything but that wherein it sees the notion of ill. But to see any ill in God, it is ill seen when all is done; for He is the excellency of all the creatures. We have [need] therefore for us to pray to the Lord that our

judgment and our light may be rectified, that so we make not a prayer to God to be away from Him, as this young fool did. There is none that leaves God who sees things rightly. All that look so upon other things as to embrace them and leave God, they have a wrong and unsound judgment. Esau looked not well, and compared not between his birthright and the mess of pottage that he sold his birthright for. He looked not to the end of it. The drunkard, he looks not well upon his lawless lust and desire after drink, and the anger of God that is hot as fire; and the dishonourer of God's name compares not his present satisfaction and the roasting his tongue in hell for ever and ever. Sinners see something in sin that none can see but themselves. But it is but the first sight they get; in the second sight it is like Eve's sight, to see the Godhead growing upon a tree!—if she would eat, and sin against God, she should be like God in knowing good and ill. So do we fools. We think if we will commit such a sin we will be happy. But it is but a mistake. We are beguiled in the end, and this is the case of many who go away from God.

But learn to keep your judgment and understanding clear, learn to know God and to know the creature, to compare them rightly together; learn to know the vanity of sin and the excellence of God, and then ye cannot go wrong. The soul that sees Christ, and considers what is in Him, it must love Him. And there is none out of love with Christ but such as see Him not.

Ye heard the substance of the young man's prayer, "*Father, give me the portion of goods that falleth me.*"

Never a word that[1] "he seeks of his father that he would bless him, or that he seeks his father's favour and goodwill to the purpose that he is upon;" but "give him the portion of goods that falleth him." The meaning is, "Give me my own will to follow my own way with something of this life," and there is the sinner's heart-wish morning and evening. All that the sinner seeks here is something divided from God, that he may get some created perishing thing out of his Father's hand. That is all that a sinner can seek who is left and forsaken of God, either the world, or the glory thereof, or the pleasure, or ease, or gain thereof, or something to satisfy the lawless desire of his heart and lusts. That is all the divinity the natural man has.

In a word, it is only this life that the natural man seeks, even that which our Lord reproves, John vi. 26: "Verily, verily, I say unto you, Ye seek Me not because ye saw the miracles, but because ye did eat of the loaves and were filled," and tells them what to seek, and what not to seek: "Labour not for that meat which perisheth, but for that which endureth to life everlasting which the Son of man shall give unto you." That is only reason from our misted[2] judgments that see not things rightly, and from this that the sinner would always be at something that he trows[3] to be heaven and happiness, when indeed it is not so, for there is nothing in the creature can do so.

But is there nothing at all in the creature that is good or can make a man good and happy? Yes. All

---

[1] About his asking.   [2] Darkened. See "Rutherford's Letters" cxviii.
[3] Believes.

the creatures of God in their own kind they are good. But when we make any of the creatures an idol, and make them a god, when we trust in the creature and place our heaven and happiness in them, then all the creatures are nothing else but vanity and vexation of spirit. When we do so then there is nothing good at all that is under the sun. When the creature is any ways divided from God, then it is not good. Whatever thou would rest upon without God or beside Him, that is ill. The creature as a creature is good; but the creature as an idol and a god is ill.

May we not, then, seek after the creature? Yes. But if thou seek it right it must be sought in God, the Creator. Seek ourselves in God, and we shall certainly find ourselves there. Seek yourselves, and seek the creature for God, and then ye shall find both God and the creature and yourselves. But if ye seek God out of God, and seek the creature out of God, then thou art seeking fire under you. And all natural men they are thus seeking fire under them. They seek their good things out of God, and so never get satisfaction to the soul. They seek a good thing that is like themselves. As it is in Psa. iv. 6: "Many say, Who will show us any good thing?" That is a well-fard[1] prayer to say, "Who will show us any good thing?" But the next verse tells us what the natural man's good things are, to have his corn, wine, and oil to abound. Their thought is how their house may be built up, and yet they may leave enough to their children behind them, as it is Psa. xlix. 11. And when they have gotten that

[1] Well dressed up.

their hearts are after, they are no [1] a whit the more happy, but rather further from happiness than before.

Again, third, How comes this that men desire to be away from God, and that they are set to seek something without God to place their happiness in, when they may be persuaded they will not get the thing that they would be at?

The answer is, Ignorance can never make a right comparison of things whereof it is ignorant. He that never saw Spain cannot compare Spain and Scotland together. If one know not both the members of the comparison they cannot compare. The natural man he knows something of the creature, of lust, of gain, of reputation in the world, and court,[2] &c., but he knows nothing of God; and therefore it is impossible that ever a natural man can make a right comparison between the Creator and the creature. And so the natural man is aye [3] wrong in his comparing.

The natural man makes a comparison as bairns [4] do sitting about their father's fireside, thinking there is not a fairer town in the world nor [5] they are in; for they never saw Rome. That is the best that ever they saw. They think there is no more pleasant garden or fields than where they live, because they never saw better, and so conclude there can be no better. All natural folks, they have bairns' [6] wits in this point; for they know something of this present world, but they know nothing of God, and therefore they make the comparison as they do. I grant, indeed, this world is a fair apple, and is

---

[1] Not. [2] Influence. [3] Always. [4] Children. [5] Than.
[6] No more intelligence than children.

good to have, it being rightly used; but alas! that we should be such fools as to prefer the world or anything in it to God! Alas! where is the wit of the Scribe and the scholar, when they go to seek their happiness in the creature, or anything beside God! When we do so it is even as we would go to mend an egg-shell or a lame vessel.[1] For any to go build themselves up in a coutch [2] of this world that time will take away, what folly is it! That night that the Lord shall take thy soul from you, and that good thing that thou sought beside the Lord, it shall take its leave of you, and thou of it. Thou shalt be forced to say then, "Oh, I made an ill comparison, for I looked not well upon things as they were, indeed, but with my blinded eyes." They see the creature and the Creator rightly who see anything in the creature to be dry and lifeless without God himself be to be found there.

"*And his father divided unto them his living.*" Why should his father [have] done this, given him such a suit.[3]

The *doctrine* it is this: They that love an ill end and have a wrong eye toward the creature that they must have, there is a Providence individually disposing that means shall be furnished to such for attaining their ill end, and for gaining their unlawful conquersh.[4] They that have an ill end before them and their intentions are poisoned in looking unto the last end beside God, the Lord in His providence disposes so that such shall

[1] An earthen vessel. See Rutherford's "Letters," clxxxii.
[2] A compact portion of land as distinguished from that which is broken up into parts separated from each other.   [3] Granted such a request.
[4] Acquisition. See Rutherford's "Letters," ii.

be blinded, and means shall be furnished unto such to lead them on into the blind way they have set before them. There are some spoken of by the apostle (2 Thess. ii. 11) that are pleased in unrighteousness, because they received not the love of the truth, that they might walk therein, and therefore " God shall send them strong delusion that they should believe a lie, that they all might be damned who believed not the truth, but had pleasure in unrighteousness." God sends means unto such proportionable unto their wicked end, and that they may accomplish the same.

Eve she fell in love with those words, "Ye shall be as Gods knowing good and ill;" and because she fell in love with them, and had that wrong end before her, therefore the Lord left her, and then she gaed¹ on in a course of defection as a boul² goes down a brae without stay, till she brought ruin upon herself, and all her posterity. Fra³ Ahab was once set for Naboth's vineyard that he would die if he gat it not, the Lord finds out a way for that; and Jezebel, that wicked instrument, she is employed to hatch that plot, and promises to get him the vineyard of Naboth the Jezreelite. And the Lord disposes of matters so that he shall get it. Scribes and Pharisees they were thristy⁴ for the blood of Christ, and the Lord's providence lets them see a way how they may be satisfied. A man comes to them and says: "What will ye give me and I will betray him unto you," and he and they make a market. They promise him threttie⁵ pieces of silver to betray the Lord of

---

¹ Went.   ² Ball.   ³ From the time that.
            ⁴ Thirsty.   ⁵ Thirty.

glory, and he receives them, and from that time he sought the opportunity to betray Him. The man that made profit and gain his end in following Christ, the Lord gives him an office like unto Himself. He is made Christ's purse master, and then at last he makes a market of Christ for his gain. It is said of some (Mic. ii. 2) they coveted a field, and the Lord answered them in means to fulfil their coveting desire. They " take it away by violence ;" if they get their end they care not by what means they come to it, and the Lord answers them in means according to the end. Now, there are two reasons wherefore the Lord does this especially.

First : It is an ordinary gate [1] in God to punish sin by sin. If thou will be at a wrong end, then the Lord will let you go out of His hand, and thou shall find wrong ways to follow that end. If thou would be at the world God says, " Take it to you, and thou shalt get means cast in thy way for acquiring the same ; " to teach us to beware of unlawful desires to be away from God, and after any other thing, and to beware of our lawless and idolatrous desires.

A second reason for this : The making the creature your end is idolatry, and the highest degree of idolatry, because the Lord He is the first author of all things and of our happiness. And if anything be made the first author except God that is idolatry. And [2] ye make that to be your God, whether it be a king, or court, or pleasure, or profit, that is idolatry. And Romans i. 21 says that the Lord punishes that by other sinful sins: " Because when they knew God they glorified Him not as

[1] Way.   [2] And if.

God, neither were thankful; but became vain in their imaginations, wherefore God also gave them up to uncleanness." And verse 28 says, " And even as they did not like to retain God in their knowledge, God gave them over to a reprobate mind, and to do those things which were not convenient." The Lord gave them over to that plague that they cannot repent, but follow after sin greedily. And therefore let us beware of such desires as we set upon the creature without warrant or beside the Lord, for [1] fear the Lord say to you, " Thou shalt get it, and an ill end with it."

Now, secondly, *that his father gave unto him the portion of goods that fell to him.* Wherefore does God answer an ill desire to any? This is a question that flesh and blood are inclined to make. Wherefore should the Lord so easily [have] given this forlorn child his will, and not told him the ill of the course he was taking himself to; and that he was in a happy case presently [2] if he would make good use of it? But his father gave him his portion, and he is content. He fell on his own weight, and that he may try whether it be better to be with him in his house or to feed upon the swine's husks of sin, and cannot find them, it may be, when he would have them.

The *doctrine* arising from this is, that it is not against the wisdom of God or the goodness of Christ to permit sinners to fall in [to] sin. It is not against the goodness of the Creator to permit Adam to fall, albeit at first he was made according to the image of God perfectly holy and happy. Natural wit and reason and the enemies of God's grace, they will not suffer any permis-

---

[1] Lest that. [2] At that present time.

sion of sin to be in God because sin comes from our will, and make all the cause of sin to come only from our nature and will; and when we have willed such a thing, then the Lord joins His concourse [1] to the committing thereof. This is indeed a devised justice in God, for this would prove the first sin to be before ever the first sin was committed. For why should the Lord [have] permitted Adam's will to look wrong, seeing He might [have] hindered the same? But we must go higher to see the cause why the Lord permits sin to be. He does it because it is the good pleasure of His will. It is the objection of that old heretic Marcion to say that the Lord envied man's estate and so permitted him to fall, or that He knew not of it, or that He was negligent and so permitted his fall.

Consider three things in God, and ye will then get the cause of this wherefore the Lord permits sin and permitted Adam to fall. The Lord has the nature of the creature to plead for him in this, a creature having free-will is unstable, and the Lord will make that to plead for him in this point. And they have well said who disputed this point, "Whether or not the creature could be created that it could not sin, that a creature shall be created unmovable and completely happy that way." That cannot be to create a creature after such a manner. Indeed, I grant the Lord may change the second act and so may hinder the creature to sin. But there is no reasonable creature but there is a power in it to fall, if God take away His hand from upholding him. Why, then, will some object, should the Lord make man

[1] Concurrence

such a creature to be under a possibility of sinning? That is even as to speir [1] wherefore did the potter make all the vessels of clay that they may be broken, and not that they cannot be broken?

The Lord at the beginning made man a creature, and a reasonable creature, and a reasonable creature endowed with free-will, and so had in him a possibility to stand or to fall, and it became the Lord very well to let him try his own strength, seeing He had given him free-will to stand or fall; and that is the second reason wherefore the Lord permitteth sin—even to let him know there is a great difference between his own will and the grace of the Mediator. And therefore it is that the Lord suffers men, and suffers His own children to fall in sin, that they may know that in themselves they are but frail creatures when God leaves them to themselves; that we may learn to put a difference between that which is ours concredited [2] to us of God, and that which is of free grace; that we may see when our will and the creature is left unto itself, that it is but a creature.

A third reason wherefore the Lord permits sin is because He made all things for Himself, and He has decreed that all He has made should be for two proposed ends to Himself—to wit, the glory of His justice, and the glory of His mercy. And fra [3] the Lord has "made all things for Himself, even the wicked for the ill day" (Prov. xvi. 4), why but the Lord may make man with a possibility to sin, and to fall, even for that end that we may see what it is to be holden in God's hand, and not to be left unto ourselves; that we may tremble and stand in awe

---

[1] Ask. [2] Entrusted. [3] Since.

to sin against God, and provoke Him to forsake us; that we may always put up the prayer unto the Lord, "Lord, lead us not into temptation;" and that all may know if the Lord leave them there is no sin but they would be ready to fall in it if occasion offer, even the sin of Judas, to betray the Lord of glory. Being left and forsaken of the Lord, thou wilt be ready to fall in that unnatural sin of murdering thy own brother, as Cain did.

And therefore this serves to teach all of us this lesson, to count meikle[1] of grace, for God has our heaven and our hell in His hand this way as He is pleased to hold or to let go. Thou standest by grace, and therefore take heed and beware [not] to provoke the Lord by sinning against Him who may loose His fingers from upholding you, and He doing so thou wilt not miss to fall.

Now the text says: "*Not many days after, the younger son gathered all together, and took his journey to a far country, and there wasted his substance with riotous living.*"

The *doctrine* is clear, and it is this: As soon as God leaves us, then there is no longer standing for us; as soon as [He] gives a sinner leave to sin, he must then sin necessarily. When his father had given him his portion, not many days after he took his journey to a far country, and spent all there with riotous living. When he is away he proved the man he was, for he was no more but a man, a perverse son, that could stand no longer fra[2] he was made his own tutor, and left his father's guiding. There is no longer standing fra[2] once God takes away His hand—especially, for a sinner.

[1] Much.   [2] From the time that.

There are three things that bring a necessity of a fall upon such—I mean upon such an one as stands with liberty having guiltiness with his liberty.

First: There is something in us that brings on a necessity of this falling. A misted [1] understanding, aye,[2] looking wrong. If there were no devil to tempt us to sin, there is in us a will going aye [2] downward to tempt us to wickedness. Christ tells us what it is that destroys a man, Matt. xv. 19: "Out of the heart proceed evil thoughts, murders, adulteries, fornications, thefts, false witness, blasphemies. These are the things which defile a man." The devil has little ado [3] to make us fall in sin. He needs neither bring fire nor timber to kindle up that fire, for there is enough of that within us; and the devil's tempting to sin is nothing else but to bring [4] [the person and the sin] together, to present an object to the understanding, the will, and the affections. And if that once be, and the Lord go away and desert, then the sinner cannot stand, because his props whereby he stood are tane [5] away; so the rotten house must down.

A second reason of this is: The thing that is most natural unto us now since the fall of Adam, is to sin. It is natural to us. And ye know there [is] no need to tempt the fire to burn timber. It is natural to it. And a stone being lift[ed] up, and loosed from any grip, there [is] no need to tempt it to go down; it must do it, because it is the nature thereof so to do. Our nature inclines to sin. The Word of God has said this of us, Eph. ii. 3. Our nature has an inclination toward sin

---

[1] Beclouded.   [2] Always.   [3] Trouble.
[4] There is a gap here in the MS.   [5] Taken.

as a stone has to go downwards. There [is] a man inclined to wickedness and to sin, and therefore when the Lord lays the bridle on his neck, and upholds not nature by his strength, he must fall. And then—

Thirdly: What is it that holds all the sons of Adam in that estate they are in now? There is an upholding power in God, which, if he had, he could not fall. God made them according to His own image, for He had habitual grace that He might have stood in the state of innocency. But the Lord took his actual working from him, and therefore he behoved to fall. And since it was so with Adam in the state of innocence, far more must it be with us, if God take away His upholding power, and leave us to the guiding of our own will, down must we go. If He take away the working in us to will and to do of His good pleasure, we can do nothing but that which is ill. And the question is here between us and the enemies of the Lord's grace. Whether man's will or the grace of God be strongest; or, if the creature can stand when the Lord takes away His grace, or, if he must fall, He taking away His efficacious grace? This text says it must be so. And this also answers another false position of those who are enemies of the Lord's grace. They say when the Lord has permitted the creature to sin, it is in the power of the creature to sin or not, to sin as well as before the permission came. No. There is a place in Isa. lvii. 17, that says the contrary: "For the iniquity of his covetousness was I wroth, and smote him. I hid me and was wroth, he went on frowardly in the way of his heart," and if that be a judicial hiding, all the world will not answer it. In Psa. lxxxi. 12, it is said, "The Lord gave the people at that time to their lust," and what followed upon that? "They walked in the way of their own heart." If the Lord once loose His hand from Adam, then Adam must fall. If the Lord but permit Pharaoh to keep the people of Israel in bondage, leave it to his free will to let them go or not go, then Pharaoh's heart is hardened, and he will not let them go.

The *use* of this point is, first, to condemn those who say they can keep a moderation in sinning, who think they will only take this meikle [1] of sin, and no more, even like the fool who says, "A little sleep, a little slumber, a little folding of the hands to sleep," and he is aye [2] the more ready for a new slumber. One will say I will do this little sin, but I will do no more; I will take this meikle [1] ill conquersh,[3] but no more. I will give it over when I have gotten that. I will only permit this looseness of my thoughts, but I will go no further on in sin. But remember that it is not in thy power to hold thy feet when the Lord looses His grip of you; and therefore hold fast thy grip of the Lord, and pray to Him to hold His grip fast of you, and that the Lord would not lead you into temptation. Thou knowest not when thy fire and the devil's timber are cast together, how soon they will make up a blaze; and therefore the hand of the Lord's grace is needful to be employed for upholding us; and, above all things, we would [4] employ the Mediator, Christ, and be thankful to Him, who has made the estate of His ransomed ones in Himself so sure and immovable.

Can we give thanks great enough to free grace, and to

[1] Much.   [2] Always.   [3] Acquisition, possession.   [4] Should.

the Mediator, Jesus, who keeps us that we fall not into the sin of Sodom, in Judas' sin, or Cain's sin? Make meikle[1] then of this grace of God, and employ it frequently. Well[2] is the heart that has gotten that grace to depend only upon the Lord, to father thy standing upon Christ only, and so to put thy trust in Him. This was Peter's fault that he lippened[3] not his standing only to Christ's strength, and it moved the Lord to let him know something of his own strength. For out of a conceit of himself he said, "Master, though all should forsake, yet will not I forsake Thee." But stay till death be presented before him, and he sees his Master bound and ill-used by men, and he be in fear of his life, and till his blood grow cold (for he spake that in hot blood). When it comes to that, he is made to see that man is nothing but man, and when God leaves him, he will prove but a brickle[4] reed that will fall with the least opposition. Well[5] to them who are upholden by the hand of the Lord, and are not lippening[6] to their own strength. Made meikle of Christ and of His free grace, and employ Him and His strength as ye would be kept safe to the second coming of our Lord. To this Lord, who is able to keep us and to present us blameless to His Father at His coming; to Christ Himself, to His Father and our Father, and the Spirit of grace, be all praise, and dominion, and glory for ever.—Amen.[7]

[1] Much. [2] Good is it for the. [3] Trusted.
[4] Brittle. [5] Good for. [6] Trusting.
[7] The MS. has the following note at the close of the foregoing sermon—"A sermon missed here through absence."

The Forlorn Son—the Grounds why he came Home, and his Prayer.

"*And when he had spent all, there arose a mighty famine in that land; and he began to be in want. And he went and joined himself to a citizen of that country; and he sent him into his fields to feed swine. And he would fain have filled his belly with the husks that the swine did eat: and no man gave unto him. And when he came to himself, he said, How many hired servants of my father's have bread enough and to spare, and I perish with hunger! I will arise and go to my father, and will say unto him, Father, I have sinned against heaven, and before thee, and am no more worthy to be called thy son: make me as one of thy hired servants.*"—LUKE xv. 14-19.

ECAUSE, beloved in the Lord, to believe that we have such a father as honours us to be His sons, and [because] if the state of adoption and of the adopted children of God were well known, it would be more thought of nor [1] by the most part it is, we would [2] think more upon it than we do. It is no small matter of a bastard of hell to be made a heir and a son of heaven; of one who has no claim to Christ to be made one who has free right to Him. And if it be not so, it is our own fault, for our Lord excludes none from Him who are within the visible Kirk. His offer of mercy and reconciliation is so broad

[1] Than. [2] Should.

and large, that they are in a woful and miserable case, who live in a land, or country, or congregation, or city, where Christ shines in the gospel, and yet they are not the better of Him. What a condemnation will it be that when the parable of the lost and forlorn son is preached to a lost world and a lost people, his going away and his returning again, and his father's receiving him, and yet they will not return!

Consider what is in God, and what is in the creature; and this is indeed the main lesson that we should set to to learn, to know our Creator, and what is in Him, that He has made all things and all things subsist by Him. And then, upon the other hand, to know sin and misery, to know ourselves, to know the bentness of our wicked hearts unto sin, [hearts] which run away from the Lord days without number. And if so be that we could rightly acquaint ourselves with these, then we would be made to acknowledge our own wanderings, and we would be made to come unto a liking of God; if we could win [1] to that, all were done that should be done. And then our preaching, and praying, and praising, and reading, and conference, exhortation, &c., would have a blessed effect with it, and we would still be seeking to know more till we came to the enjoying of the Lord Himself. And when thou hast gotten Christ Himself, and thou art in Him, O then, sinner, thou art at home; but never till then.

Now we have to consider: (1) upon what ground it is that the forlorn son came home; (2) what is his prayer when he comes to his father.

[1] Attain to.

THE FORLORN SON.

Now, for the ground whereupon he is stirred up to come home. It is clear enough in the words going before. He is in want, and at the point of tyning[1] for hunger. He thought himself to be in a miserable estate, and that made him to take up a new resolution, and then when he comes home, he seeks not to be in the rowme[2] that he should be in, that his father would make him a son in the house, but that he would make him as one of his hired servants. The motive that the Lord used to bring home this forlorn son is his want and his affliction, as we read in Hos. v. 15: "I will go and return unto My place till they acknowledge their offence and seek My face; in their affliction they will seek Me early." That is one of the Lord's ordinary means of wooing His own children. He woos them in the furnace of affliction when they may neither fend nor fee[3] as it were. Even when it is with him as it was with Manasseh, 2 Chron. xxxiii. 11, 12: "The Lord brought upon them the captains of the host of the king of Assyria, which took Manasseh among the thorns, and bound him in fetters, and carried him to Babylon. And when he was in affliction, he besought the Lord his God, and humbled himself greatly." He and the people sinned against the Lord, and therefore the Lord sent enemies against them, and he is taken and carried away captive to Babylon. And when he was so fettered there that he could not win away, then, in his affliction, he humbled himself, and sought the Lord. Deut. xxx. 1–3: "And it shall come to pass, when all these things are come upon thee, the blessing and the curse, which I

[1] Perishing. [2] Place. [3] Support nor hire themselves.

have set before thee, and thou shalt call them to mind among all the nations, whither the Lord thy God hath driven thee, and shalt return unto the Lord thy God, and shalt obey His voice according to all that I command thee this day, with all thine heart, and with all thy soul; then the Lord thy God will turn thy captivity, and have compassion upon thee, and will return and gather thee from all nations, whither the Lord thy God hath scattered thee." Hos. ii. 14, 15: "Therefore, behold, I will allure her, and bring her into the wilderness, and speak comfortably unto her. And I will give her vineyards from thence, and the valley of Achor for a door of hope;" that is, in the midst of great affliction I will speak unto her heart, and that ordinarily is the time when the Lord uses to do so. And there is a reason given for this, Prov. xxix. 15: "The rod and reproof," says the Spirit of God there, "give wisdom." If ever men do well at all, they will do well when the hand of God is upon them. Those that are not humbled by the Lord's visitations, what will humble them? It is true the Word of God uses this form of speaking, that "His word humbles" the heart; and sometimes it will do so. But such is the crookedness of our nature, that the most part they are not brought in to the Lord till the iron sinews that are in their neck be broken, and [He] souple [1] our stiff-neckedness.

Use. In all our afflictions let us speer [2] home to our Lord and husband, and say with the prophet: "It was better with me when I was under his guiding nor [3] ever

---

[1] French *souple*; S. English supple, make flexible.
[2] Ask the way home.   [3] Than.

it has been since." Let us strive to make that use of all the Lord's visitations, to acknowledge that it is God's messenger seeking you to turn home to Him again, because thou hast been a runaway. But do all that the Lord strikes, turn to Him by the straikes[1] that come upon them? No, certainly; there are many that fall further away from the Lord after they have been stricken. The Lord says of His people, Isa. i. 5 : "Why should ye be stricken any more? ye will revolt more and more." That is one of the ills that lie upon our nature, that many, when the hand of God lights on them to strike, it strikes them dead, and they wot not what He either says or does, but they are further from God nor[2] before, and when it is so, the Lord will tire of visiting such, and will seek them no more.

A second ill that comes of visitations to some is: Holiness in seeking God in the day of their visitation; and yet it is not holiness from the heart, but only from the teeth, forward. And therefore all the holiness and humiliation that we have under a cross, it should be well examined, because there are many while the hand of the Lord is upon them any way, they carry themselves humble like, and hing[3] their head as a bulrush; they will speak words humbly to God, and yet for all that they have but a lying heart; for their purpose in seeking the Lord and in humbling, is only that they may get the cross removed. We should beware with that, for it will beguile us when the cross is away.

How many are there in the world who will say in their sickness, "If the Lord will restore them again to

---

[1] Strokes.   [2] Than.   [3] Hang.

their health, they shall be sure not to be the old man." They will vow to forsake their ill ways, and to take up a new course of life, an[1] they are delivered from their disease, and yet afterwards they become as wicked and profane as ever they were before; and some worse. The ground of this comes from a false heart that gives God fair words while they are under His hand, and yet as soon as the rod is removed they, Pharaoh-like, harden their heart, and turn to their old bias again. And so blinded are they, who thus seem to turn to God when His hand is on them, that when it is off they turn away again.

And there is a third sort also in whom God wastes many crosses, and they are nothing the better; but they remain as proud as ever they were. Such are iron that no fire will soften, such as will neither wash nor wring; for all the pains can be taken, they will neither bow nor break. The Lord loses all the pains He wares[2] upon such. The dross is not taken from them for all that the Lord does to them. Albeit He cast them into the furnace, they remain still as they were at the first.

And then, lastly, there are some who take a wrong course under their affliction to be rid of it. They take not such a course as this son does to come home to his father that he may help him, but they use indirect and sinful means to win out of the fang[3] thereof. And such are in all their crosses like a stranger going to ride[4] a water, he takes the wrong ford, and falls in a weel,[5] and drowns there. The right gate[6] under any cross, if it be of taking anything from you, is, with Job, to say, "The

---

[1] If. [2] Expends. [3] Grip. [4] Go through.
[5] Eddy, whirlpool. [6] Way.

Lord has given, the Lord has taken. Blessed be the name of the Lord."

The right way to win[1] through the fuird[2] of that water and be safe, is to humble ourselves under the mighty hand of God, and He will lift us up, to see the world's vanity and the sovereignty of the Lord, the Creator, to consider that man is but flesh, but God is a Spirit, and if His straikes[3] be so heavy even in this life, O! what must the pains and torments that He inflicts on soul and body in hell be? If it be so great a pain to be four and twenty hours pained under the disease of gout or gravel, O! what torment must it be to be tormented in hell both in soul and body for ever in hell both night and day, no rest there; and to have that to close all with, never to be delivered out of that pain and torment. If we were wise we might learn meikle[4] of God in our crosses, if we would come to Himself by them and acknowledge that it is our Father that strikes us, and not an enemy, halflings[5] against His will, remembering always that He "delights not in the death of a sinner;" that He is not shooting[6] them away whom He strikes, but, by the contrary, makes them welcome who come to Him, and to consider, as it is, Lam. iii. 33, that He punishes or afflicts not willingly.

The first part of this forlorn son's prayer is: "*Make me as one of thy hired servants.*"

Look now where a converted sinner desires to sit. God needs to put him no lower than he puts himself. That is the vantage[7] of humiliation where it comes

---

[1] Get.   [2] Ford.   [3] Strokes.   [4] Much.
[5] Partly.   [6] Thrusting.   [7] Advantage.

truly. It lays him upon the ground, the Lord working with this visitation to let him see himself. He acknowledges that he is the most unworthy in all his father's house, acknowledges that he is unworthy of his father's company or of his presence; acknowledges it is much more than he deserves if he be handled by his father as a servant, let be [1] to be used as a son. Always this is a mark of a converted sinner when he is brought to think little of himself. As soon as the Lord began to show Himself to Peter, he became humble in his own eyes, and says: "Lord, depart from me, for I am a sinful man." The centurion's word to Christ: "It is a shame to see such a Lord under my roof who am so unworthy. Lord, I am not worthy that Thou shouldest come under my roof; but speak the word only, and my servant shall be whole." A truly converted sinner knows not how laigh [2] to set himself. If there were a pain and torment greater nor [3] the pain and torment of hell, he would acknowledge it to be his deserving, and that it is procured by him at the Lord's hands. How great a word speaks the Apostle of himself, Eph. iii. 8: "To me, who am less than the least of all saints, is this grace given, that I should preach among the Gentiles the unsearchable riches of Christ." When he considers that God had made him an apostle and a preacher of the gospel, and applies that to himself. "To me who am less than the least of all saints," &c.: great Paul that calls himself little, and not only so but less, not only less than apostles, but less than saints, than any who are begun to be sanctified, ay, less than

---

[1] Far less.   [2] Low.   [3] Than.

all saints, and less than the least of all saints. O! how low is that soul that sees itself well who has gotten a sight of its own vileness and so of its deserving.

Let us learn, then, to know that this is a mark of such as are in love with Christ. They think less of themselves than they can do of any other. Pride is not a mark of the children of God. There is a staff of pride in every one of us by nature as the Prophet Ezekiel speaks. And whoever they be who will be higher nor[1] God will have them (as there be many in the world), they are far from the strain this son is at. Humiliation: O! but it be a great grace, and pride is a sin of great parents, but it is a miserable ill. Pride was born in heaven, and it fell out of heaven; but it could never win there sinsyne.[2] The Lord "resists the proud, but He gives grace to the humble." The Lord says of him who is proud that He is his enemy. Woe! to that man whom God knows far off as an enemy.

And therefore learn this lesson to strike sail to Christ, and, for that effect, to know what sinful dust and ashes are. Consider if the Lord would turn thy outside out thou would be forced to say: "I am no more worthy to be called Thy son, make me as one of Thy hired servants," and acknowledge this of thyself.

Was this a good petition of his? Every way. See upon what ground he says this: "I have sinned *against heaven and before Thee.*" And upon that he brings in that conclusion.

It is a great matter if our humiliation be not a hindrance both to faith and prayer. Because thou hast

---

[1] Than.   [2] Since that time.

sinned against heaven and earth, should thou therefore conclude, that thou wilt not seek to be one of God's sons, nor to be one of the children of God. Many times we are so low in our own eyes, that we pray to the Lord for that which we deserve, but not for that which we desire. But let us acknowledge our wrong in this, and seek as meikle [1] from the Lord as we would be at, and not which we desire. He declines indeed to be esteemed a servant, or to be thought the basest of the servants, and yet he dare not seek to be in the room of a son. But when ye pray to the Lord this way seek for that which it becomes Him to give, and not for that it becomes your baseness and guiltiness to receive. Know to whom it is that ye are speaking. Ye are speaking to one who can make a son of a slave of hell, as well and as easily, as He can make a servant of him.

It is a great matter to be humbled, and yet to believe, both at one time. Ofttimes the one of these hinders the other, as Peter being humbled in his own eyes, says: "Lord, depart from me, for I am a sinful man." It had not been telling [2] him that the Lord had gone from him according to his prayer. But being humbled, follow not his example in this, but pray rather: "Lord, let me stay with Thee, for I am a sinful man," for no company is so good for him that has that disease as to be with Him who is the physician. And that woman who had the bloody issue being thus humbled in her own eyes, she seeks only to touch the hem of His garment. Had it been a sin for her to have sought to kiss His feet or His face? No, certainly. But her humble faith thought it very meikle [1]

---

[1] Much.   [2] Been for his good

if she should get leave to come that¹ near such a Lord as to touch the hem of His garment. But the humbled soul may come nearer Christ nor² she. It will be welcome to come nearer even to kiss His sweet mouth; for the best chair in heaven is prepared for such as are humble. O, what our Lord esteemed of that woman, who esteemed herself but a dog, and was content to feed with the dogs upon the crumbs that fell from the children's table! He says of her, "I have not found such faith, no, not in Israel."

A humble faith it is certainly, a high and a great faith, and a soul that thinks little of itself, O! what the Lord thinks of it. And therefore let us not be [led] that way to measure God's goodness by our wickedness. That is a false compass to measure our Lord with. Whatever thou be, wert thou never so sinful and wicked, yet the Lord is the Lord. That woman that is spoken of, Luke vii. 38, who did wash Christ's feet with her tears, and wipe them with the hairs of her head, she would [have] been welcome to come hither to embrace Him, and kiss His mouth. Ay, the more humble thou art, so much nearer art thou to thy Lord. Once learn this lesson, to think little of thyself; and when it comes to that, thou art within sight of Christ. When thou art humble, thou art within Christ's breath, and it shall blow upon you. Go not over³ far away from the Lord in thy humility. Learn to seek more of Him nor² thy deserving dytes⁴ thee to seek. It is an ill-dyted prayer that is dyted according to our deservings. But let us learn to dyte⁵ our prayers according to the Lord's

---

¹ So.   ² Than.   ³ Too.   ⁴ Directs.   ⁵ Direct.

mercy, and the riches of His free grace. To seek a drop of grace at the Lord's hands, because it is no more that we deserve? No, we deserve not that; and therefore seek a sea of grace from the Lord. Albeit, according to our deservings, it sets [1] us to get little. Yet it sets Him well to give meikle.[2]

Seek no less than Christ Himself, and heaven, and the remission of sins, joy of the Holy Ghost, peace of conscience, &c. Seek that which is given only to the sons of God and the heirs of heaven, and be not satisfied with that which is given to servants. Ay, the greedier thy prayers be, thou art the more welcome to the Lord, for He cannot endure pinched, narrow prayers. He is not content that thou should seek less than He minds to give, and is willing to give you. He is not like that king who said, "Ask of me what thou wilt unto the half of my kingdom, and I will give it unto you." Seek no half a kingdom of the Lord, but seek a whole kingdom. And therefore learn this lesson: Not to make your prayers over [3] narrow, but seek great things from the Lord contrary to that which Jeremiah (chap. xlv. 5) says to his servant Baruch; seek great things, even the greatest things that are in the Lord's coffers, for He is as able to give heaven as He is to give an acre of land or a drink of water. He is as able to give glory as He is to give grace. He is able to give the Spirit which He promises, by the prophet Joel ii. 28, to pour out, the spirit of prophecy that your young men shall see visions and your old men shall dream dreams. Be not narrow in seeking from the Lord, to seek over [3] little

[1] Is becoming us.   [2] Much.   [3] Too.

of Him. We are ofttimes too straitened in seeking from the Lord. The Lord is not troubled night and day with our prayers in seeking great things. And because we seek but little of the Lord therefore it is that many times we receive but little at His hands. But learn continually to seek more and more from the Lord, and tempt the Lord's liberality, as it were, in asking great things of Him, and then thou shalt get thy desire. And wite [1] thyself if thou receive little at His hands, for it is only because thou art narrow in thy seeking.

Now, howbeit he put himself out of his own room,[2] yet still he keeps God into his room,[2] for he calls Him "Father." That is good and right humiliation indeed, that holds the Lord always where He should be, as ye may see Dan. ix. 8-9, Daniel confesses, "To us belong confusion of face as at this day, to our kings, our princes, and our fathers. But to the Lord our God belong mercies and forgiveness, though we have rebelled against Him." That is right work. Let the Lord always be righteous and glorious, albeit shame and confusion should be written in great letters upon our faces. Let the Lord always be high and magnified, and all others put low that He may be high, as the Kirk acknowledges, Isa. lxiii. 16, "Doubtless thou art our Father though Abraham be ignorant of us, and Israel acknowledge us not. Thou, O Lord, art our Father, our Redeemer; Thy name is from everlasting." Albeit we be named apostates, and are not worthy to be called the sons of Abraham; yet Thou art worthy to be called our Father, for Thy name is called upon by us. So it is said also

---

[1] Blame.   [2] Place.

Jer. xiv. 7-9, "O Lord, though our iniquities testify against us, do Thou it for Thy name's sake: for our backslidings are many; we have sinned against Thee, for they put themselves very low," and then in the eighth verse, they say, "O the hope of Israel, the Saviour thereof in the time of trouble, why shouldest Thou be as a stranger in the land?" Their God is made the hope of Israel and the Saviour thereof in time of trouble. But for themselves they acknowledge, "Our backslidings are many, and we have sinned against Thee." This is the way that the Lord would have His children to carry themselves, always to put God in His room,[1] to make Him a Father, albeit I should be no son.

Now, is not this contradiction? If one call Him a Father to him, then he must be a son? Yes, it is true. But happy they who can set God on high, and can set themselves low, that He may be high. Happy they who can give the Lord that which is His due, if it were with the loss of all that they have in the world. Ware[2] upon God and give out for Him, albeit it were to tyne[3] all that thou hast in the world, and thou shalt be no tyner[4] when all is done. Thy husband, albeit he were dead in another country, yet let this content you that it is God who has done it, and acknowledge He is worthy of all that thou hast if it were meikle more. And this is the reasoning of a humbled soul, to exalt God as high as heaven; and if thou could get Him far up above the heavens to set Him there, and thou thyself to sit as low as hell.

[1] Place. [2] Lay out. [3] Lose. [4] Loser.

This must answer a doubt that many of the children of God have, and it is this, say they: "Whatever God be in Himself, yet I wot not if I have any claim to Him to call Him my Lord and my Father. If ye have no better reason for that, "that ye wot not if He be your Lord or your Father," but that because ye are sinful, then it is but the forlorn son's logic, and it holds not in all. But rather say this: "If I were a slave of the devil, a child of wrath and perdition, yet I know He is in heaven and is a Father, and I will look unto Him as to a Father, notwithstanding of all my transgressions, for this is a part of His glory to make them welcome, and to forgive them their iniquities and transgressions who have run away and misspent all, played the harlot with many lovers, when they return unto Him again. It is not possible that our narrow thoughts can comprehend this Lord. And this indeed is the very ground of our sinning, because we measure our Lord by ourselves. Because thou hast a false heart therefore thou thinkest so of the Lord also. Because we are varying and changeable, we expone our Lord to be of that same kind. Because we cannot forgive great wrongs that are done against us, therefore we expone[1] so of Him also. Never any shall have a solid and constant faith who look not over themselves and over their deservings to God, who considers not whatever our provocations and undeservings be, yet He is near unto all those who seek unto Him in truth.

O that we may learn to have right thoughts of Christ our Lord, not to measure Him by our short ell-wand, but

[1] Consider.

by His large measure that He is in Himself. And to this Lord, to Christ's Father and our Father in Him, to Himself and the Holy Spirit, one incomprehensible Godhead be praise for ever.—Amen.

The Forlorn Son—the Father's Welcome.

"*And he arose, and came to his father. But when he was yet a great way off, his father saw him, and had compassion, and ran, and fell on his neck, and kissed him. And the son said unto him, Father, I have sinned against heaven, and in thy sight, and am no more worthy to be called thy son.*"—LUKE xv. 20-21.

E have heard, beloved in our Lord, of the conclusion and logic of the first part of this parable, and of the behaviour of the forlorn son, when he came first home to his father. Now follows the second part thereof, which is the Lord's acceptation of His forlorn son, His welcoming him home again, and this is expressed in three particulars in the text. (1) The Lord's own behaviour towards: "*When he saw him afar off, he had compassion upon him, and ran, and fell upon his neck, and kissed him.*" (2) We have set down the preparation the father makes for him, and the direction that he gives unto his servants for welcoming him home again. He gives direction to make him a new man, and to adorn him with other ornaments than these he had in the days of his vanity. There is a change upon him, for he gets the best robe put upon him, a ring put upon his hand, and shoes upon his feet, and to kill the fat calf. And then (3) there is

the welcoming of both the father and all the house towards this prodigal son. There is a feast made, and the fat calf is killed, and great mirth and joy among all as it sets [1] our Lord well, and all the angels and glorified in heaven well to rejoice at the home-coming of a runaway sinner.

There is none who comes to our Lord in spirit, truth, and sincerity, who shall get a worse welcome than this, or shall be put away, because they have been running away from Him, John vi. 37: "Him that cometh unto Me I will in no ways cast out." No, in no sort He will send such away again. No, there is here not so meikle [2] as a sign of the Lord's anger for his former misspending of time and means and all; but a loving intimation of his Father's love towards him, and such sweet expressions as you will find in no other father welcoming home such a child. There is no quarrelling [3] of bygones now, but all these are laid aside. There is not a word of finding fault, that before he tired of his father's company; no rebuking him for his looseness, nor misspending that which he got. Fra [4] this forlorn son breaks his own heart, the Lord will not break it. When he is sad and mourning for his provocations, the Lord has nothing to say to him; but He will give him the garments of joy and gladness for the spirit of sorrow and sadness.

If we humble ourselves under the mighty hand of God, the Lord will lift us up. If we judge ourselves we shall not be judged of Him. If we had a casten down heart for sin, then should we get from our Lord the garment of righteousness and rejoicing. It were good

[1] Becomes.   [2] Much.   [3] No finding fault for.   [4] Since.

for us to come with such preparation as this to God and Christ, with a heart humbled and cast down for sin. But this is not a thing that we have of our own. This is not a flower that grows in our garden. All dispositions and preparations to make a soul meet for Christ, the King Himself sends before He come to lodge in that inns: "Every good gift and every perfect donation come down from Him who is the Father of lights." There is no man who can come out to meet Christ till first He come to him. No man can love Christ till He love him first, because our love of Christ is nothing else but an effect of this love to us. There would be no light in the earth, nor any glancing [1] in a transparent if there were not light without. We would not have light here, if the sun were not in the firmament. Even so if any let out a love look towards Christ, it is because He has loved us first. So we may learn for ever to sing a song of free grace shown in our conversion, that we may know on whom we should father it, that we make it not a bastard, that our home-coming to our Lord may only be put upon Him who is spoken, James i. 18: "Of His own will He begat us with the word of truth, that He should be a kind of firstfruits of His creatures;" and 2 Tim. i. 9: "Who hath saved us, and called us with an holy calling, not according to our works, but according to His grace and His own purpose, which was given us in Christ Jesus before the world began;" Tit. iii. 4: "But after that the kindness and love of God toward man appeared, not by works of righteousness which we have done, but according to His mercy He saved us."

[1] Shining through.

What is the ground of our salvation? The love that God carried toward man applied unto us. His free love is allenarly[1] the cause that moves Him to make a market to buy us; John iii. 16: "God so loved the world, that He gave His only begotten Son, that whosoever believeth in Him should not perish, but have everlasting life." It were good for us to seek all that we stand in need of for our salvation in Him; and happy they who get grace to know to whom they owe thanks for the work of their conversion, and know to whom their eyes should be lifted for the same, even to Him who has that draught in His hand (John vi. 44) to draw all men unto Him.

A word, now, of the Lord's behaviour towards His forlorn son. His kissing him and falling upon his neck tell us this far: when a sinner comes to the Lord truly humbled for sin, there is nothing then but free love and kindness and expressions of love upon the Lord's part: Rev. iii. 20: To him who knocks, the Lord says that He will open to him, and will come in, and they shall sup together. At the Lord's first meeting with a sinner, the Lord opens his heart by grace to let Him in, and there they sup together. There is a feast of love between them. And it sets[2] our Lord well to do so at the first conversion of a sinner. I mean not that the sinner has no sorrow before Christ and he meet. Ay! he has meikle[3] grief and sadness. But at the first meeting, I say, it sets[2] our Lord to give the humbled sinner joy and consolation, and a feast of His presence. And there are three good reasons for this. The

[1] Solely.   [2] Becomes.   [3] Much.

First is taken from the disposition that the poor soul has been under before, for our Lord has promised that such shall be comforted, and the reason is clear thus: there are none who are converted but those who are once [1] humbled, for our Lord has good news unto none but them that mourn; Isa. lxi. 1: He is sent to bind up the broken-hearted, to proclaim liberty to the captives, and the opening of the prison to them that are bound; and to them who are not humbled and mourn not, He has a day of vengeance to preach unto them. So those who are humbled and mourn, and meet with the Lord, must be comforted.

Second: It is also agreeable to the Lord's love that humbled sinners, at their first meeting with Christ, should get such arles [2] as they may never forget again all their days. Now I mean not by this that all the children of God can tell the very first mathematical point of the time of their conversion, for there be some with whom the Lord has dealt from their youth, and, with some, the Lord deals more smoothly in their conversion than He does with others. But for the most part I say this is His dealing, that when sinners have been going on into a course of rebellion, running away from Him, after their humiliation ordinarily He fills them with a feast of the sense of His love, that all their days they cannot forget it. And this answers a point that troubles very many of the children of God, "That they had once a hearty desire after the Lord and a rejoicing in His presence, they were earnest in seeking Him long syne,[3] and found Him

[1] One time or another.   [2] An earnest or a pledge.   [3] Long ago.

very kind to them, but now they find it not so with them." This answers the doubt. This is Christ's manner of dealing with His own, that at the first starting to the race He will give them a sight of the gold¹ and garland, but afterwards He will only give them blinks of it now and then. At the first He will give them such a sight and sense of His kindness as that they may mark the very day and hour of their meeting and His, and that we may cry forth to His praise, O the excellence of that day wherein the Lord began first to shine in upon a poor soul by the blinks of His loving-kindness, who had no mind of Him to make them seek after more of it. A

Third reason of this is taken from the case of weak beginners. For to scare weak beginners at the first with glowming,² they would then be discouraged. The first day that bairns go to the school it is no wisdom to strike or to boast³ them, but to make of them rather. When the Lord gets a new scholar to His school, the first seat He sets them in He puts them into His bosom, that so they may be forced to say, He is a Lord worthy to be served, and that they may be made to condemn themselves for biding so long away from such a Lord, who is love and kindness itself.

The *use* we are to make of this is: O, if we could get natural people persuaded but to take a trial of Christ's love! if we could make them but to kepp⁴ one of Christ's kisses! But O! it be a hard matter to persuade nature what grace is. Ay, it is the hardest task in the world to gar⁵ natural men believe themselves to be in such a

¹ Prize. ² Frowning. ³ Threaten. ⁴ Catch, or intercept. ⁵ Cause.

case as indeed they are in. If we could but come to this, to make the world believe the ill of drinking, swearing, whoring, covetousness, &c.; and, upon the other hand, to believe the superexcellency of Christ's love, then the field were won. But it is a hard matter to persuade two sorts of people of this, that there are thousands who believe they are in Christ who, notwithstanding, are deceived, and are not in Him.

The *first* [sort are] secure sinners, who know not what God is, or what heaven and hell are, and are going on in sin and will not be convinced thereof, nor rise out of the state they are in. No; were Christ in the flesh preaching to them they would not rise out of their secure estate.

A *second* sort of people hard to believe this are natural[1] civilians, who go under the name of honest men in the world. They are not adulterers, thieves, ordinary drunkards, or blasphemers, &c., they have a civil white life in their own eyes and the eyes of the world. O! but it be a great matter to persuade such to fall in love with Christ, because they think they have already as meikle[2] as to take them to heaven; and it is but a mistake when all is done. It is only nature that they take for true grace. And there are thousands in the world who are beguiled with this. I wish that ye would labour to know indeed what it is to have a conscience purified from dead works; to have many waking nights for sin; that ye were put to this, "Lord, if I had Christ I should quit all the world for Him, for He is more worth than it all." O! to be acquainted with the Son of God and His excellency. If men had such thoughts as these, and

[1] In the state of nature.   [2] Much.

knew what need they stand in of Christ, O! what a high price would they put on such an excellent Saviour as Christ is!

Now there is cast in here a word, by the way, of the prayer of the forlorn son and of his father's welcome to him. If ye will compare his prayer with the prayer he resolved upon while he was in a strange country, there is something left out of his last prayer, and he gets not all said that he would say. Ay, he gets it but half said. There can be no other reason for it but this. The forlorn son was struck with confusion and sorrow and grief for offending his father, and with astonishment and wondering that his Lord and Father met him, and that at their meeting there is nothing but words of love, whereas he deserved no such thing.

And there is none but when they come to seek God, at their first meeting with Him they shall find confusion and shall have broken prayers to God, like that we read in the Psalm vi. 3: "O Lord, how long! Return, O Lord, deliver my soul! O save me!" Sorrow and desire fighting together—and so the poor soul is overwhelmed. So was it with the forlorn son at this time: his heart was so tane [1] up with the consideration of his father's love, and with the sense of his own unworthiness, that it is no wonder that he forgot the half of his prayer.

We may learn here, that the prayers of the children of God when they come to pray to Him are not aye [2] so logical and so methodic, that there is nothing left out of them, that they should say that all their prayers are set down in rhetorical and logical terms; neither are we to think

[1] Taken.   [2] Always.

that God answers no other prayers but those that are formed that way. No; you will ofttimes find the prayers of the children of God to be imperfect this way; and yet the Lord for all that makes them and their prayers welcome to Him. For in prayer He looks not so meikle [1] to words as He does to the meaning of his own spirit. Ye will find in the Word of God there are seven sorts of expressions that are called prayer; and yet in our form of speaking we only call that prayer when a sinner pours out his heart to the Lord, and vocally utters his mind to Him.

First: The Lord He acknowledges crying to be prayer, even crying where there is no distinct voice, as in Psa. xxii. 1; and in Psa. lxix: "Why art Thou so far from helping me, and from the words of my roaring, O my God. I cry in the day-time, and Thou hearest not; and in the night season, and am not silent." And David is brought, in Psalm lxix., crying until his throat be dry, and till he be weary, and, indeed, crying to the Lord's majesty, albeit it be not joined with words. When the heart is going with the cry, it is prayer. When David makes a noise that way the Lord acknowledges that for prayer, and esteems it to be no less than prayer. Again—

Second: The Lord counts the very breathing, and that is less, to be prayer. The afflicted Kirk says (Lam. iii. 56): "Thou hast heard my voice, hide not Thine ear at my breathing, at my cry." When the Kirk of God is under distress they are but sending up their very breathing to the Lord, and beseech Him to accept of it.

[1] Much.

And David panting to the Lord, it is accepted. The speech is borrowed from them who cannot speak being out of breath, and so they pant. "I have panted for Thee all the day long," and the Lord welcomes that as praying.

Third : The lifting up of the eyes is exponed as prayer, and therefore in Psalm lxix. that is a part of David's complaint that his eyes failed with looking up, and he gat no answer of the Lord ; Psa. v. 3 : "O Lord, in the morning will I direct my prayer unto Thee and look up," says David. Looking up, with the eyes towards the Lord, is one of these gestures that He esteems. All these are sacrifices of the heart which the Lord makes welcome, albeit words be not joined with them.

Fourth : Making moans in prayer the Lord accounts it as prayer. Jer. xxxi. 18 : "I have surely heard Ephraim bemoaning himself." The like is spoken of King Hezekiah (Isa. xxxviii. 14), that he chattered like a crane, or a swallow, and mourned as a dove ; and Ezek. vii. 16 : "They that escape of them shall escape, and shall be on the mountains as doves of the valleys, all of them mourning, every one for his iniquity." The Spirit of God is speaking there of a repenting people that they shall mourn for their iniquities as doves of the valleys.

Fifth : Prayer is expressed by sighing and sobbing. The Lord is said (Psa. cii. 20) to look down from heaven, to hear the groaning of the prisoner ; and Rom. viii. 26 it is said, we ourselves know not what to pray, but the Spirit maketh intercession for us with groanings that cannot be expressed. Even dumb sighs that want auricular words and verbal expressions the Lord accepts them as prayer.

Sixth: Stretching out the hands is put for prayer; also as in Psa. lxxxviii. 9: "Lord, I have stretched out my hands unto Thee;" and in Psa. cxliii. 6, David says, "I stretch forth my hands unto Thee." The Lord accounts that to be prayer in His estimation.

Seventh: Even tears, where the children of God dow[1] not pray, they have a voice unto the Lord, as we may see Psa. vi. 8: "Depart from me all ye workers of iniquity, for the Lord hath heard the voice of my weeping."

Any of these expressions in prayer, whether it be crying, breathing, or panting, lifting up the eyes, making a moan, stretching out the hands, sighing and sobbing, or if it be but a tear, or some few tears where words are not, but the mind is confused with sorrow and grief, the Lord makes all these or any of them welcome, and counts them prayer. This answers many doubts that trouble the children of God.

Some will say, "Alas! I cannot get words in prayer, and so can look for nothing at the Lord's hand."

Answer: God is that[2] kind, that dumb beggars get alms from Him as well as speaking beggars. Alas! if we would learn to tell God in the morning in our family, what ails us or them. And ye need not a book to do this to signify to Him what ails you, for the Lord will accept of a sigh, if thou cannot get a look to Him nor speak to Him. Make both a sign to the Lord, and lift up your eyes and your heart to Him, and acknowledge to Him

[1] Can.   [2] So.

what ye are. Speak to the Lord as ye can, and I will assure you He will not find fault with your prayers for want of order and method, and because ye want logic in them; for it is the heart the Lord looks to. It is the sighing of his spirit that he specially beholds.

There be some who complain they could never get a prayer put up to God all their life's time that they could count [to be] prayer. There may be reasons for this, I grant, for there be some who will pray earnestly to the Lord, who will not get fine terms in prayer, and this is no want in prayer when all is done. For sometimes the constitution of the natural parts will do this, as want of that measure of natural abilities that others have, and sometimes the grief of the mind will be greater than that the tongue can express the same; but the Lord esteems more of the sighings of the spirit nor of all the finest terms that can be uttered. [By] the poets it is said that some, being about great matters, they have been so much tane [1] up therewith that they could not speak, and so have gone away stricken in dumbness, and that has been accounted sufficient to represent the weightiness of the matter; and therefore the children of God should not be cast down for any of those things.

But what cares He for the bowing of the head, or spreading out the hand, or lifting of the eyes, or breathing, or crying? No; He cares for no sort of expression that can be used where the spirit is not humbled in His sight. But where the spirit is humbled before Him, O! but the least expression that such can make is very welcome to Him, if it were but a sigh, or a sob, or a lifted-

[1] Taken.

THE FORLORN SON.

up head, or hand, or eye; till more come, He will accept of that, and will not let it go without an answer. If ye would set up a kirk to God, every one that has a family, in your families, and learn to speak to Him there, it would be a welcome and acceptable sacrifice to Him. It is a sore matter that so many should say they cannot speak to God in their families. If any of you have a suit to present to any magistrate, ye will seek him out and present your suit to him yourselves. Ay, ye will take upon you to speak to a king if it be a matter that concerns life and death. Nature teaches you to do that. But it must be the spirit of adoption that maun[1] teach you to pray to God; and I assure you all the book prayers in the world will not teach you this lesson to pray to God. The Lord gives the spirit of prayer unto His children in a special manner, and therefore this should be sought of Him. And this proves you to be the sons of God, indeed, when ye can thus speak to Him in prayer. What says the first word of the Lord's prayer? Says it not, "Our Father which art in heaven," teaching us this far that none can pray right to God but those who can in faith say "Our Father," and apply Him to be their Father. Those who can only call the Lord their Creator, the Lord who provides for them, who keeps them in being, they cannot pray right to the Lord, but only those who can call Him "Our Father."

Another thing here in this confession, he says: "*I have sinned against heaven and against thee.*" He was far from God while he was riotously wasting all that his

[1] Must.

father gave him. To say, "I have sinned against heaven and against thee, and am no more worthy to be called thy son," comes from another heart than he had before. And to say this as this forlorn son said it, none can do it but one who is a new and converted man. We read that David said this when Nathan came to him and accused him of his sin. He says: "Against Thee, against Thee only have I sinned" (Psa. li. 3). It is a great matter to say this right—not to say the syllables thereof distinctly; that is easily done; but to say this from the heart, this is a work of the Lord's Spirit, and only the converted child of God can say it after this manner. Where was this prayer when he prayed to his father: "Father, give me the portion of goods of that which falleth unto me; I am tired of your company, and therefore give me what you will give me, and let me go my ways and be my own tutor"?

But we may learn here: There is no man, so long as he is in the estate of sin, that is sensible it is so. But fra [1] once we are converted and turn unto the Lord, then we feel our sores, and see that we have been sinning against the Lord. Now there are three reasons wherefore it is so.

First: You know people use to say, "A green wound is half whole." All have reason to say they have sinned against the Lord. But sin is not sensible of itself. Grace, indeed, knows grace to be grace; but sin knows not sin to be sin. Death knows not that death is death, but life knows life to be life. A man that is beastly drunk knows not that he is so, but when he is fresh and

[1] From the time when.

free of drink, he will know himself to be so; for drink, where it is, puts the senses out of the right place, and so they cannot discern. Now, while a man is in the state of sin, he is even like a man dead drunk. Therefore it is said, "They are drunk, but not with wine; they stagger, but not with strong drink" (Isa. xxix. 9). To persuade the natural man that drinking is a sin, and such a great sin as indeed it is, that we cannot get done. Can we make the blasphemer of the Lord's name believe that for that sin, if he repent not, his tongue shall be tormented in hell's fire for ever and ever? A man that is in the estate of nature he knows not what the ill of those sins is. But when some sense of the life of God is begun in the soul, when grace begins to grow, and the Lord begins to show His loving-kindness in some measure, then they begin to see their wanderings. And when that is so, Ephraim begins to say (Jer. xxxi. 18): "I am as a bullock unaccustomed to the yoke;" but not till then. And there are two reasons for this—

First: Because it is an infused light from heaven that lets man see sin and the breach of the law. A natural conscience, I grant, will say something to this, but it lets not the sinner see sin every way as it is, for it lets him not see the main object against whom sin is committed —lets us not see that glorious Majesty whom we provoke by our sins, before whom the glorious angels cover their face when they behold Him, and the heavens are not clean in His sight. There are two things to be seen in Christ if we look right unto Him. There is light and divinity; or rather there is in Him light and Divine light. There is a Divine power that comes from God to convince a sinner of the estate that he is in. The natural conscience will see and discern those sins to be sins that pagans, wild Americans, Turks, may also see, as killing of father or mother, adultery, oppression, &c. But to see spiritual sins to be sins, as to see and discern the pride of their nature to be a sin—that they cannot. Unbelief in the Son of God, no[t] making conscience to sanctify the Lord's day, to set up His worship in families, to keep correspondence with Him in heart, &c.—a natural conscience cannot see such to be sins; for as the natural conscience cannot believe in the Son of God, it being a supernatural work, so the natural conscience cannot see unbelief in the Son of God to be a sin, for it sees no form[1] or privation therein. Thus it is supernatural light that maun[2] let us see such sins as these to be sins. That which is called divinity in the conscience, if it be right and sound divinity, it is a plant which the Lord Himself plants there.

I observe this now for this cause, because I persuade myself of this, that the main cause wherefore multitudes in the world run on headlong into many ill courses without any awe or fear of the Lord's majesty and of His judgments, it is because they have no supernatural light in their conscience, for where this supernatural light is, it prevails against all temptations that can be cast into our way to draw to sin. But where all the light that one has is natural light that is soon overcome. There is no man that will abstain from sin as sin, but the man who has more than the light of nature. The main reason wherefore the world goes on in sin, and

---

[1] A scholastic term. [2] Must.

there are so many gods set up therein to be worshipped, and wherefore men live in drunkenness and in the breach of the Lord's day, wherefore they fear not an oath, as Solomon says; the reason wherefore men care not to live contentedly in the ignorance of God, it is because they want this supernatural light to awaken them. Never man shall go right to heaven who is pleased with the way he is in, as natural men are pleased with their way. This form of service to God contents them, and they will never speer [1] whether that form be right or not. They never question but they are on the way to heaven, and that they have the marks of the children of God.

This says that many believe themselves to be right when they are wrong, and in the end shall be deceived; or [2] then they would be after [3] speering what shall become of them in that day, when they shall appear before the Lord in judgment. "Lord! if we could but once persuade you of this, that we could bring men to acknowledge they are in a state of sin, to be convinced that they are undone if they find not salvation in Christ, and win not to heaven another way than by anything I can do myself." And while the world is thus blinded as the most part, what marvel that they say they have faith in Christ, that they believe as well as any, while in the meantime there is no such matter!

For Christ's sake be not beguiled, and deceive not yourselves as the most part do. There are hundreds of you who hear me that trow [4] you are going to heaven and will not be put off it. But it is so. But when it

---

[1] Ask.　[2] If they did.　[3] Engaged in asking.　[4] Believe.

comes to that part of it, "Give account of your stewardship," and the poor soul maun¹ be judged according to the works done in the flesh, whether they be good or bad, O! there will be wakening then, and ye will see that ye have been far wrong! But alas! it is out of time when a sinner is once wrong, and doubts not that it is so. He goes on, and so still goes further wrong, even like a traveller going in an unknown way. He goes wrong, and ay the further he goes that way he is the worse and the further from his lodging; and when night comes he is disappointed of lodging, and lies in the fields, because he never doubted that he was in a wrong way, and so speered² not for the right way.

It were good for us to speer and try in time, if we be in the way to heaven or not, and to be earnest to know what shall become of you when ye shall be called to give an account of your behaviour, what it has been, how ye have spent your life, and what you have profited by the hearing of the gospel. What wilt thou answer to God, who hast had twenty years' occasion of hearing the Word, receiving the sacrament of the Lord's Supper, and had many occasions of that kind, and yet are not the better of these, not a whit wiser to salvation than at the first? But alas! I see I was beguiled. I thought I had been right enough, and yet thou shalt see then thou wast close wrong. Such are those who shall come at the last day and say to Christ, "We have preached, wrought miracles in Thy name; we have eaten and drunken at Thy table, &c., and so thought all was well enough." But Christ tells them they were mistane,³

¹ Must.   ² Asked.   ³ Mistaken.

and He shall say to them, "Depart from Me, ye workers of iniquity." This will be a cold meeting with the Son of God, and yet thousands shall be met therewith who will not believe it now, and will not examine their case to see if they be right or not. Lord, make us wise to see and try our case in time, that so we be not deceived with many others, and to this Lord, to His Father and our Father, and the Spirit of grace, be all praise and dominion and glory for ever.—Amen.

The Forlorn Son—the Father's Expressed Welcome.

"*But the father said to his servants, Bring forth the best robe, and put it on him; and put a ring on his hand, and shoes on his feet: and bring hither the fatted calf, and kill it; and let us eat, and be merry.*"—LUKE xv. 22-23.

HO has such opportunity, beloved in our Lord, of our Lord's kindness to a soul running to a free Saviour as those who have once been rebels and are come home again to their Lord and Father. None can sing mercies' song so well as they who can do it out of sense and experience. None can do this so well as one who can say, "Once I was blind, but now I see. I was dead once, but now I live. Once I was a child of Satan and an heir of hell, but now I am made an adopted son of God, and an heir of heaven." Who can speak more to our Lord's commendation out of experience, nor[1] a home-coming sinner thus made welcome to his Lord and Father again? You heard in the first part of this parable how our Lord was pleased with this forlorn, and what welcome the father gave him, or ever he spake one word of apology for himself, or ever he made any

[1] Than.

prayer at all, his father fell upon his neck and kissed him, for he waited not upon our God to move Him to be merciful unto us. He will not wait till He gets a hire for His mercy. He waits not till we make some way on our part for any good He is to do to us. He may not look for anything from us that will down-weigh the weights of His free love. O! so weighty as that is there is meikle [1] telling there. Nothing in us to prevene [2] the same. But or ever this poor forlorn son speak a word he falls upon his neck and kisses him. And then when he makes his prayer to his Lord, leaving the half of that he resolved to say unspoken, God welcomes it. The Son of God, the same Lord who is here called Father, He passed by all the slips of his prayer, and commands that he be received by the servants of the house as a son and not as a servant. And truly they will be very feckless [3] and confused prayers that come from any spunk of faith that our Lord will not accept and make welcome. Yea, in Hosea xiv. 2, he learns [4] His Kirk what to say to Him when they come: "Take with you words, turn to the Lord and say to Him, Take away all iniquity, and save us graciously. So will we render the calves of our lips," &c. He will take half-prayers, or He want all, even prayers where words are missed, and the meaning they intended to be at. Ay, He will take sighing and sobbing for prayer, the lifting up of the hands, or of the eyes, &c., so content is He with what His Spirit says, however it be said, as it is Rom. viii. 26, He knows the meaning of the Spirit. He seeks no more for a prayer at some times but a believing sigh that is a work of His Spirit.

[1] Much.   [2] Prevent.   [3] Worthless.   [4] Teaches.

And when we know not what we are doing, He knows well enough the meaning of His own Spirit, and can put a perfect commentary upon that, albeit we know not what it will do, that no man should think the Lord will not hear their prayers, because they have not good oratory to speak to the Lord in prayer, because they cannot speak as a print book, and set all the words in order, and so leave off to pray to the Lord. No, the Lord He hears the very breathing of His Kirk, Lam. iii. 56. Ay, when His children cannot speak, and they have no words to say to Him for what they would be at, they may be confident to be heard, for many a dumb beggar has gotten almost at His door. They who cannot set their words in good method and order in prayer, if their heart look honestly toward the Lord, then He accepts of the sighs and good meaning of such, and takes that for prayer, and will answer it. So that all who come to Christ as they are bidden, and come in truth and sincerity, may be comforted in this, that their prayers shall not be cast away of Him.

Now, we have the expressed welcome of the Lord towards his forlorn son, and the direction and charge he gives unto his servants for getting ornaments for his body, and entertainment for cheering himself and all the house. For the ornaments that he gives direction to get, it stands in three particulars: First: That they get the best robe and put upon the home-coming sinner. Like enough he was ragged, or he came home, as all are ill clad when they come first to Christ. Second: He commands them to get a ring upon his finger, that is an ornament of honour; and then, Third: To put shoes upon his feet. And then for expression of the joy of the Lord's mind, and the joy of the whole soul, and that all that hear what the Lord has done may be allured thereby, the fat calf is slain that all may rejoice at the home-coming of a lost sinner.

O! the rejoicing that our Lord and all the angels make for the home-coming of a lost sinner. There is more joy in heaven for the recovery of one lost sinner than there is for ninety and nine righteous persons. The Lord He knows not how to express His joyfulness and His kindness to a sinner who acknowledges what he has been doing, and repents of his misdeeds! O! repentance, it is an unknown work. Repentance is not known to be so acceptable a sacrifice to the Lord, as indeed it is. A home-coming soul that can get a bleeding heart for sin, that can thrust out an honest tear before the Lord for sin committed against Him, it knows not that God has a bottle to kep[1] that in. They know not that God writes down all their sighs and their sobs, their tears and their sad looks. And because this is not known by the most part, therefore repentance is a slighted and neglected work. The world loves nothing worse than sorrow for sin. They think it a sad and melancholious thing; but there is no joy hereaway[2] comparable to that joy which proceeds from an honest tear shed for sin, and for offending such a majesty as we have to do with.

Now, the first ornament that our Lord commands to be put upon this prodigal is "*The best robe.*" He commands to put a robe upon him, and the best of the robes.

---

[1] Catch.   [2] In this world.

There is no necessity that we should strike largely upon every particular in a parable, if the main scope of the parable be looked unto. And yet there is little in this parable that looks not clearly to point out the state of a sinner in the state of sin, and to show the Lord's welcoming when they return to Him, and to let us see what ornaments He puts upon them when they come to Him.

First: Ye see he is to be clothed with a "*robe,*" and with "*the best robe.*" While a sinner is in the state of sin he is a ragged creature, and so has need of a robe, if ye will consider him two ways. If ye will consider him as he is, a man in nature, or if ye will consider him as he is, a civil [1] righteous man; for man of himself as he is a natural man has no righteousness at all, or if he have any righteousness if he will say, it is as the phrase is, "A clout with many a hole in it," like that garment spoken of Job viii. 14; it is like the spider's web, that garment of man's righteousness—it holds no wind away. All our righteousness is like a menstruous clout (Isa. lxiv. 6). And you will find that all the garments that the natural man, while he is in the state of nature, they are so indeed. For while he has them he is not honest; nor marriage like to be married upon such a bridegroom as Christ. So long as we have no other garment but only our own natural righteousness, it is nothing else but sin, defiled further with sin. Isa. lix. 6: "Their webs shall not become garments, neither shall they cover themselves with their works; their works are works of iniquity, and the act of violence is in their

[1] Respectable character.

hands." The works of the natural man are compared there to webs, but their webs will not cover them, for the best things they do there are violence in them and unrighteousness. All those who would be married upon Christ, and would be handseled [1] new with Him for evermore, they must have another covering upon them than their own works, or their civil righteousness. There are two things in all natural garments that make them faulty.

First: That no natural garment we can have is able to hold away the cold from us. All those who stand to be Pharisees in the act of justification by the works of the law, or by their own righteousness, they shall be forced at last to say that it will not be able to hold out the rain of the Lord's indignation. And therefore David says, "Lord, enter not into judgment with Thy servant, for in Thy sight no flesh living shall be justified" (Psa. cxliii. 2). "If Thou, Lord, should mark iniquities, O Lord, who shall stand." All thir [2] and many moe [3] places. They are shamed both with the lining and the outer half of their garments, which are only covered with nature and civil honesty, and with a seeming righteousness that the natural man counts so meikle [4] of.

Another fault in a natural garment is that it is not honest before the Lord. It will be long or [5] God give that commendation to a natural and civil [6] righteous man, that He gives to His spouse in the Song of Solomon: "Thou art all fair, my beloved, thou art all fair : there is no spot in thee." Long or thou smell in his nosethirls [7]

[1] Gifted. [2] These. [3] More. [4] Much.
[5] Ere ever. [6] Outward. [7] Nostrils.

of myrrh, aloes, cassia, and cinnamon. The natural and civil righteous man has no smell of heaven, or of glory. But Isa. lxiv. 6, says, "They smell like a menstruous woman." All their "righteousnesses"—in the plural number—are like filthy rags that will never make a creature beautiful in the sight of God, and therefore there must be such a niffer [1] as that which is spoken of 2 Cor. v. 21: "He must be made sin for us who knew no sin; that we may be made the righteousness of God in Him." These two must be done or [2] we can be clean in the sight of God. Christ must be clothed with our sins, and we, again, must be clothed with His righteousness, and that is the fairest and the closest garment that any can be.

Now this garment is called "the best garment;" and it is the king's best garment, for it is the righteousness of our Lord. There may be good garments and better garments, but this is the best of all garments. Ay, this garment of Christ's righteousness is better in respect of the event, and for us, than if Adam had stood in the state he was in, and so we to have been clothed with Adam's righteousness. This is the best robe of all —the righteousness of God made ours, Phil. iii. 9 ; the apostle says, "He counted all things but dung that he might win Christ; and be found in Him, not having mine own righteousness, which is of the law, but that which is through the faith of Christ, the righteousness which is of God by faith," clothed with that righteousness, that is, the righteousness of Him who is both God and man. And look what wisdom of God is to be found here ! and what goodness and loving-kindness ! and

[1] Exchange. [2] Ere ever.

such a supernatural providence that whereas the devil, that old serpent, had a mind by Adam's fall to bring Adam and all his posterity in the compass of eternal damnation; yet the Lord has turned about the wheel, so that so many as belong to Him in His election shall get better nor¹ they lost in Adam, a more sure and permanent and glorious estate.

This reproves those who would have the death of our Lord Jesus for sinners to come by hazard; who say that the Lord at first intended not the incarnation of Christ and His death and sufferings of itself, but at the first He principally intended Adam's obedience, creating him in the state of innocence; and that he was able to stand, but that Adam fell, and then there was a necessity of a Saviour; that He intended no[t] principally, but it came upon our Lord by hazard. This is a wrong unto our Lord, who, from the beginning, intended the glory of His mercy and free grace, and also the glory of His justice. No; the Lord was not deprived of His first intention, as they say, and so behoved to take Him to a second thought. No; for from the beginning the Lord He intended the glory of His mercy to be manifested towards some, and to manifest the glory of His justice upon others, to the glory of His name. And we owe Him hearty thanks for this, that we should be made welcome to get the borrowed righteousness of Jesus; and if we get that, we shall be marriage-like, and our Lord will marry us. Alas! what will the civil² living of many do to them without this? No; such are in the way to be lost for ever, and to be naked, so that the

¹ Than.   ² Outward.

cold shall seize upon them, and Christ will not marry them to Him because they live and die and never see themselves to be sinners, and so cannot inherit the kingdom of God. Our Saviour says, "Unless a man be born again he cannot enter into the kingdom of heaven." The civil natural man he knows not what that is to be born again, and so lives and dies without seeing himself to stand in need of Christ. He contents himself with the outward calsay [1] godliness, and thinks that enough to take him to heaven. But certainly if thy natural pride be not subdued, and thy worldly-mindedness, thou cannot come there. If thou only seek to be approven in the eyes of the present world, that will fail you, for it is not the best robe; it is not the main thing the Lord gives His elect ones to live a civil [2] life. But those who are clothed with the robe of Christ's righteousness it shall not fail them, but cover them from the cold.

The second ornament his father appoints for him it is a "*ring upon his finger.*" This is a simple ornament.

We may learn from this that the laigher [3] a sinner set himself, the Lord will set him up higher. Albeit he set himself very low, the Lord will not do so also. The forlorn son would not believe when he sought a rowme [4] among the servants that his father would [have] advanced him to be a son; he thought it much if he gat that. But now his father makes him a son, and will have him no lower, and he is adorned with the best robe, and gets a ring put upon his finger. Thus we may see, let a humbled sinner set himself very low, God will not do so

---

[1] Causeway, street. civil state. [2] *I.e.*, a commonplace life as a member of the [3] Lower. [4] Place.

to him. Also Eph. iii. 8: "To me who am less than the least of all saints is this grace given to be a preacher of the gospel." Paul there is little in his own conceit, but God counts not so of him also. And when Ananias makes a question, Acts ix. 13, if he shall go to Paul shortly after his conversion the Lord says, "Go" to him, "for he is a chosen vessel to carry My name through the world." The Lord gives unto the humbled sinner a high rowme[1] and seat in heaven. The believer is never a whit the worse esteemed in God's books that he counts little of himself. That thou count'st thyself very base and low, shall not blot thy name out of the Lamb's book of life. High shalt thou be in the Lord's books if thou humble thyself very low. Better that the Lord lout,[2] and take thee out of the dust than that thou shalt build thy nest among the stars with Edom, and the Lord to pull you down out of thy nest.

This speaks against many of the dear children of God that put themselves far beneath themselves, and will not let it light[3] that God has thoughts of peace towards them while indeed He has great and large thoughts towards them for their good. But if believers knew what thoughts God has of them, and what a royal and stately throne He has prepared for them, they would then be over[4] fain, and would set their sails over high, and would not not be so much tane[5] up with the sense of the Lord's loving-kindness. But He will let His children mourn and walk humbly under the sense of their own unworthiness, that they may be the better fitted to make a high preaching of the Lord's goodness and

---

[1] Place. [2] Stoop down. [3] Let it appear. [4] Too glad. [5] Taken up.

free mercy, who louts[1] Himself to take up those who are so low, and respects them who are little in their own eyes and the eyes of the world about them.

The third ornament is "*shoes upon his feet.*" Albeit, it is true, we need not, neither will we, stand upon every particular, yet there is good ground for this in Scripture, that a home-coming sinner he is ordained for a journey after he is come home. In Cant vii. 1, shoes are spoken of: "How beautiful are thy feet with shoes, O prince's daughter." And Eph. vi. 15, among the rest of the pieces of the spiritual [armour], we are commanded to have our "feet shod with the preparation of the gospel of peace." Why would the Lord speak this to His Kirk and children, but to let sinners know when they are come to Him, they may not be barefooted. For there are thorns and sharp rocks in the way to heaven, and therefore we have now to take heed to that exhortation set down Heb. xii. 13 : "Make straight paths for your feet, lest that which is lame be turned out of the way." What a sweet word is that which we have in Psa. cxix. 104: "I have refrained my feet from every evil way, that I may keep Thy word." The righteous sinner must take heed where he sets his feet, and not set down his feet in every place, nor be barefooted, for there are moe[2] snares and rough passages in the way to heaven nor[3] ye trow[4] there be. How many are there who go to heaven and sink not in some myres[5] by the way? We have heard of none of these. It is well said that the way to heaven is like a mossy way, some wet their feet as they go through it, and yet win[6] through at last.

[1] Bends down.   [2] More.   [3] Than.   [4] Believe.   [5] Moss or bog.   [6] Get.

But some going on unawares they drown in a myre [1] by the way, and never win [2] through. The Lord's children in the way towards heaven must not be barefooted, but have shoes upon their feet, for there are many thorns in the way, as the examples of the servants of God that have gone before us declare. David's adultery and murder was a thorn strake up in his foot, and made him to halt all his days. Noah's drunkenness, and the Lord's chief disciple Peter, [who] in denying his Lord and Master, gets a thorn in his foot, tell us that we had great need to take heed to our feet, and to walk in Christ's way that He has gone before us, to have our feet shod against those rough ways. And how many are there in the world who live and die in adultery and harlotry, living a profane and godless life, not making conscience of swearing, drinking, breaking the Lord's day, and so tyne [3] the right gate [4] to heaven, only because they are not shod with the shoes of the gospel of peace, and see not the right way where they should walk?

There is yet a particular to be marked which is very worthy our observation, and it is also a part of the scope and drift of the parable, and it is this: That our Lord He makes more of the forlorn son coming home again to Him nor [5] he does of the other son who had stayed at home, not departing from the house. For ye see there are no ornaments put upon the eldest son, nor any melody for his biding in the house. Where we may learn this, that repentance and rising by the grace of God out of the state of sin, is better nor [5] all the civility [6] and Pharisaical righteousness in the world.

[1] Moss or bog. [2] Get. [3] Lose. [4] Way. [5] Than. [6] Outwardly moral life.

And in some respects this repentance and rising by grace out of the state of sin having fallen, is better nor [1] no sinning at all.

There are great questions about this, Whether it had been better for man not to sin, or to sin and get mercy for sin. It is true, I grant, there is danger in the one which is not in the other, and in reference and respect towards us, it were better not to sin than to sin. It were better not to be sick, and so not to need the physician, than to be sick and need his cures. But if we will look unto Christ's feasts and offers that He makes unto us, having sinned, and to the Lord's comforts and refreshments He has prepared for His own, we may say that it is best. And in respect of the Lord and what He gave for repentance; He gave a dear price for repentance, a greater price than was given for Adam's not sinning; for if [he] had continued there needed no repentance, and it was free; but the other cost a very dear price (Acts v. 31). Christ coft [2] repentance. He died and rose again to purchase repentance; and therefore it must be of more worth than Adam's not sinning, seeing it cost our Lord such a price. Ye will grant that a jewel that has cost ten hundred thousand thousand pounds must be better nor [1] that which cost but twenty pounds if he have any skill that coft [2] it. Repentance cost very dear. Ay, it is dearer nor [1] if Adam had stood in the state of innocence to this day, and all His seed with him. It cost no less price than the blessed blood of the Son of God. The Lord in His blessed wisdom foresaw this, for it is not without His providence that our Lord

[1] Than.   [2] Purchased.

He would suffer man to drown himself in the debt of sin, that he might get a royal and kingly cautioner to relieve him of his debt. He would suffer him to be under the hazard of hell that he might get a lovely Redeemer. He would suffer him to be sin-sick for that end, that he might get a drink of the blood of the Son of God. He would suffer him to do that which procured him to be shot[1] out of Paradise, and from the trees of the garden, that he might have right to the Tree of Life that grows in the midst of the Paradise of God, that bears twelve manner of fruits every month, and to the River of the water of life. And that certainly is better than his first estate was.

The Fathers said to this purpose, that the fall of Adam it was *felix culpa*,[2] not that it was happy in itself, but happy in regard to the consequents of it; to have such a disease as will have the Lord of life Himself to come from heaven for the curing thereof, and take our sickness and infirmities upon Him in our nature, and make us partakers of His Divine nature, and clothe us with the robe of His righteousness!

And if ye will look unto us also, this is better to sin and repent of sin, than to live in a Pharisaical righteousness, or[3] we had stood in our first estate; for there is no man who has such experimental knowledge of the goodness of God as that man has who has been over head and ears in sin. And our Lord gives not a fairer commendation to any as[3] that woman, who wash Christ's feet with her tears, and wiped them with the hairs of her head. Christ says she loved much because much

---

[1] Thrust.   [2] A happy sin.   [3] Than.

was forgiven her, for He had cast seven devils out of her.[1] And Paul was a blasphemer, a persecutor of the Church, thirsting for the blood of the saints, an injurious person, &c., yet being forgiven, and the Lord taking him into His service, he does more glorious works than all the rest of the apostles did. Now this teaches us two things shortly.

First: That we beware of turning the grace of God into wantonness. For whatever I have said of the excellence of repentance, and rising from the state of sin beyond standing in the first estate of Adam, and not sinning, comes all by accident of the grace of God, and no thanks to the sinner for it. And therefore let no man say because Jesus Christ is come into the world to die for sinners, and to purchase repentance and remission of sins, therefore we will live as we please, and go on in a course of sinning, for that is to tramp the blood of the covenant under foot. He who does so, whatever he be, he knows not the worth of the blood of the Son of God, and the excellence of Jesus our Lord. The dear blood of God that was shed for sin, it should teach us to beware of sin, that seeing our sins put Him to such pain, shame, to so many sore scourges and wounds, and many sad hearts, put Him to those words, "My soul is exceeding sorrowful even unto the death;" "My God, My God, why hast Thou forsaken me," should not this make us to beware to commit sin?

And another thing this teaches us, is to let us see what our Lord will do unto them who come home to

---

[1] Rutherford evidently held the opinion, now generally rejected, that the woman who was a sinner and Mary Magdalene were the same person.

Him, that He will receive them graciously and pardon them, that no man may despair, and think their sin to be such that mercy and forgiveness and a welcome are above anything they can look for at the Lord's hand. If thou wilt come home to God and Christ, repenting for thy sins, and seek to be into the kingdom He has purchased, there is more remedy for thy disease than can be spoken of, there is more sweetness in our Lord nor[1] the sinner believes to be in Him. The coming to the kingdom, let be to the kingdom of glory, is like the Queen of Sheba's coming to see the glory and order of Solomon's court, she confessed she saw much more than was reported to her. If the natural man know Christ's welcome He gives to a home-coming sinner, how He adorns, puts the robe of His righteousness on them to cover their nakedness, puts a ring on their finger to adorn them, and shoes upon their feet that they may walk the better in His ways, He gives them the joy of the Holy Ghost, and inward peace of conscience, gives them a feast of fat things, gives them to drink of the wines refined upon the lees; think you that they would love sin and the way thereof, as they do? Would they count so meikle of roses and lilies and windle-straes[2] that will presently fade, and there is no more of them. No, certainly. It is because the world knows not what it is to meet with Christ, whose breath is heaven itself, whose comforts transcend far the motions of all natural understanding, that they count so little of Him, and follow after other vanities. O, but there is meikle sweetness in meeting with Christ. Men know not what

---

[1] Than.   [2] Stalks of grass.

tranquillity and security under a pacified conscience are. O! but that is solid rejoicing under the hope of glory. Now for this hope's sake, and the hope of redemption laid up for the children of God, we render, to the Father of our Lord Jesus, and our Father, and to Jesus, and the Holy Spirit, all praise and glory for ever and ever.—Amen.

The Forlorn Son—he was Lost and is Found.

"*For this my son was dead, and is alive again; he was lost, and is found. And they began to be merry. Now his elder son was in the field: and as he came and drew nigh to the house, he heard music and dancing. And he called one of the servants, and asked what these things meant. And he said unto him, Thy brother is come; and thy father hath killed the fatted calf, because he hath received him safe and sound. And he was angry, and would not go in: therefore came his father out, and intreated him.*"—LUKE xv. 24-28.

THEY have no less nor [1] cause, beloved in our Lord, to be glad and to rejoice, whenever a wandering sinner comes home to Christ Jesus, who is so cheerful a receiver of them, who is so willing to receive them, and is so heartsome and kind to all His own who have any grace to claim kyndness [2] to Him. And we see there is good ground for rejoicing and mirth, at the home-coming of a wandering sinner here. And wherefore we should rejoice also, when our Lord He rejoices, and makes such mirth. When He is so glad at the home-coming of a sinner, the sinner himself whom this most concerns should much more rejoice, and be glad. And our Lord He gives a very good reason for this gladness and re-

[1] Than.   [2] Relationship.

joicing, "for this my son was dead, and is alive again; he was lost, and is found."

Now the last part of the parable is, How the elder brother—eldest or in possession, and so repute [d] eldest —took with the Lord's kind dealing towards his younger brother. The text says, "And when he drew near the house, he heard music and dancing," and knew not what it meant, as the natural man knows not what it is to come to Christ, and how welcome a sinner is to Jesus. They know not how sweet the Lord's breath is unto those who have been long away from the Lord and get grace to come home to Him again. And the elder son calling for one of the servants, he speers,[1] what meant that more than ordinary mirth that was among them? The servant answers, "Thy brother is come, and thy Father hath killed the fatted calf, because he hath received him safe and sound." And the son was angry, and would not go into the house. And the rest of the chapter is spent in a conference between the angry son and a kind and meek father. But we see the son that had an ill eye because his father's heart was good, and [was] the gentle and loving father; he was angry that his father had received the younger brother into his house again. There is nothing that makes a hypocrite's heart more sad than when God welcomes home a sinner to Himself. And the father again, as if he had done a fault, he speaks to his angry son in calm words, and gives a reason of his making mirth, and why he dealt so kindly with his younger son, and made so meikle[2] of him; "Son, thou art ever with me, and all that I have

[1] Asks.   [2] Much.

is thine. It was meet that we should make merry and be glad, for this thy brother was dead and is alive again, and was lost and is found." That is a matter of joy in heaven to the Lord and to the blessed angels, and the Lord avows that He is content at the home-coming of a sinner, howbeit the eyes of the wicked world dow[1] not endure it.

Now there be two excellent reasons given in the twenty-fourth verse, wherefore the Lord is glad and rejoices at the home-coming of the forlorn son. "This my son was dead, and is alive again; and was lost, and is found." There is a change made upon him. "My son is translated from death to life; he was lost, but now he is found." That is a matter of rejoicing to be avowed before the world when a sinner that was dead becomes living; when a sinner that was running away from the Lord turns home again to Him and is found of Him. And this is a cause of rejoicing to the Father and the whole house that the Lord has gotten home a lost bairn and a forlorn son that was running away from him formerly.

See now what is said of his estate before he come home to his father. Before he was dead and lost in an uncow[2] country; dead, and yet hungry, and would eat husks, and not long since he was coming home, and acknowledging to his father: "I have sinned against heaven, and in thy sight, and am no more worthy to be called thy son: make me as one of thy hired servants;" and was ragged, and naked, and bare, and you know the woful gate[3] that he was in. How then was he dead?

[1] Can.   [2] Strange.   [3] State.

for all these be actions of life. But, whatever a natural man does we may say he is dead, for all thir¹ actions of life he does are not the actions of the life of God; for he has not that life, and so he is spiritually dead and knows not the case he is in while it is so. And that is the estate of all those who are not within the kingdom of the Son of God, albeit they eat, drink, sleep, walk, laugh, &c., and go about all the businesses of this life, and work the works of sin as living men, yet in the Lord's estimation they are nothing else but dead men.

The best works of the unregenerate who are not born again by the water and the Spirit, they are but only works of dead men. And therefore never go to question if the heathen and those that never heard of Christ can do works good in the sight of God, as the patrons of nature have been careful to defend things done by them as good. All the actions of natural men are dead actions before the Lord, and the best thing they can be called is only to call them well-farded² sins. For actions are only good in God's estimation that can be called good from all the four causes. First, that are good in regard of the author of them; second, in regard of the matter; third, good in regard of the form or manner of doing them; and fourth, in regard of the end wherefore they are done. And if an action want any of these that it be not good in all these respects, then it is imperfect in the sight of God, and so ill. And therefore the Apostle says, Rom. xiv. 23, "Whatsoever is not of faith is sin." Now all the works of men, while they are in the state of nature, they are done without faith, and so

¹ There.   ² Painted.

they are sin. Look but to two things in the works of the natural man, and you will see all of them to be sin.

Works that come not from faith, if that the first motion of them comes not from the renewed man, these works are sin, as ye may see, Heb. xi. 6: "Without faith it is impossible to please God." Let all the world distinguish as they will, it is a thing impossible that a man can do works to please God and procure life eternal unless he have faith, and the works be done in faith; which cannot be said of the natural man. Let all the world distinguish in this as they will, the Word of God warrants us to say this. Make the works of the natural man as fair and as beautiful as ye will in your eyes, and never so life-like, yet the Lord esteems them to be no other but dead and sinful works.

And then look to the end of all that the natural man does, and in that they are wrong also. Nay, but, says one who takes their defence, they intend not always an ill end in all they do, who are not in Christ, for they do not all to the honour of an idol or a wicked god, or for the honour of the creature. But the Spirit of God says, 1 Cor. x. 31, "Whether ye eat or ye drink or whatsoever ye do, do all to the glory of God." Where a work wants this intention, and the doer of the work aims not at this, albeit he should give his body to be burnt in the fire, and bestow all his goods on the poor, yet the Lord says this of him, that he is no other but a sounding brass, and a tinkling cymbal. It is a work of sin and is not done in obedience to God, but He is therein disobeyed.

And for that they refer not the end of all that they do to the honour of an idol-god; albeit it were so, as they allege, there are none who profess to give religious worship to anything but virtually he refers the last end of all he does thereto. But be it so, that he does not refer it to an idol; yet because he refers not the last end of all his actions to God, and makes not Him his last end, it is certain he must have another last end to which he refers all he does; for all reasonable creatures, even devils and wicked men, they do all that they do out of a conceit to attain happiness, and therefore their wicked end must either be the Creator or the creature. But if it be confessed, as the adversaries themselves do confess, that the last end is not the Creator, because they understand him not in the Mediator Christ Jesus, then the creature must be their last end, and that certainly is idolatry. To make the creature, either the first author of anything, or to make it the last end of anything, it is to put the creature in the rowme[1] of God. For a man to do things for his credit, honour, his friend, &c., having no other end for what he does, is a work of a dead soul, and the Lord will not accept thereof as acceptable to Him.

One *use* of this is to see that the hearing of God's Word by the natural man, receiving the sacraments, reading, praying, &c., he will get no thanks for these, neither are they acceptable to God, so long as he is not in Christ. All these things that thou doest being out of Christ, will be but small bulk in the Lord's eyes in that day when thou shalt be judged of the Lord by thy works. And therefore careful should we be that we may be found in Christ, that our persons may be accepted in

[1] Place.

Him. And your persons being accepted in Christ, then the Lord will also accept of your works. But otherways all that the natural man does is wickedness; his prayer is sin and abomination before the Lord. When he is about prayer that is not in Christ, the smell of his sacrifice is unsavoury to the Lord. He cannot endure such prayers, and therefore great need have we to be assured that we are in Christ, that our works may not be dead but living works.

Observe while he says, "*This my son was dead,*" there is the estate of the natural man before he come to Christ. Eph. ii. 2, the apostle says: "And were by nature the children of wrath even as others." "But God for His rich mercy wherewith He loved us, even when we were dead in sins, hath quickened us together with Christ." Has not the natural man a soul, and can he not perform the works of nature? A man in nature is not naturally dead, but he is spiritually dead.

There are three things that a man in nature, touching his spiritual life, has not. And first, the natural man has not life itself; second, he has not reason; and, third, He has not sense or the use of his senses. These are all joined with life where it is; yet he wants them. And

First: I say he wants life itself, and all the natural motions thereof; and yet for all that he is hearing the Word and singing Psalms, and reading, &c. And yet these are not works of life in him. And he is praying. Now will a dead man do so? Yes; a man spiritually dead may do all these things so as he does them. All that the natural man does has nothing but an outside with it. The Lord sees the stinking bones of a dead corpse under all these. He sees seven abominations in such a man, and so He sees all abominations in him.

Second: The man in nature, he has no reason nor the reasonable presence of a living man. This may seem not to be very true-like. He is a governor of a city or a country side, and knows the laws very well, and he is a trim bookman. Can such a man be a dead man? Yes; all that such a man, who is in nature, does, is the work of a dead man; for there is never a word that he speaks, or a conclusion he makes, that is heaven-like, and therefore the work is dead. The very main end of all that he does is the world. It is that he may provide for him and his, that he may get honours, pleasure, court,[1] &c., and the things of the world. All his words, thoughts, actions, run upon this pin, the things of this present world. All his logic and strongest arguments for anything he does even in reforming the matters of the house of God are taken from this: "It will hazard my life and my office in the world, if I join not in such things." This is plainly the reasoning of a dead man.

Third: Those who are only natural they want the sense of life. They know not what that is, to have a soul wounded with sin, because of this, and so are just like the drunken man that Solomon speaks of (Prov. xxiii. 35)— when he is drunk with wine, every one goes by and beats him with rods, and he knows not that they do so till the wine be out of his head, and he wakes out of his dream; then the strokes he has gotten make him sore and crazed. Even so will it be with them who are in the

[1] Influence.

state of nature, when they are wakened out of their dream. O! the blasphemous oaths will lie heavy on him then, and the harlotry of the harlot will be a sore burden to him; and he who has loved the creature more than God, who is the Creator, such a man will never feel his wounds till he be brought to the Physician Christ, and the Lord once translate him out of darkness into the kingdom of His dear Son, that he be brought from death to life. But then he feels all the sore strokes he has gotten all his time by sin. The first fall Adam got by sin dang[1] him dead and all his posterity, and made him and his to want the life of God and His image wherewith they were endowed, from all mankind for ever in themselves.

Can this be, that one act of sin which works morally, can take away all the habitual justice and righteousness that are in man by nature? They who oppose the truth of God deny that man could lose by his transgression, but only by the decree of God that it should be so. But if sin be well looked to, it has two set of actions in it. The one is moral and the other is physical. Morally sin, even *reatus*,[2] deserves that, because of it, the sinner should be deprived of life; and then physically, the blot of sin puts out the image of God. And if any man will speer[3] how the first fall of Adam should put the life of God out of all mankind for all eternity? I answer, albeit we could give no natural reason, or any reason of logic or physic for this, yet this is sufficient for proof of it, that the Word of God says, the natural man cannot understand the things that are

---

[1] Struck.   [2] Guilt of it.   [3] Ask.

of God, for they are foolishness unto him, and Christ says (John vi. 44), "No man can come unto Me unless the Father which hath sent Me draw him." These and many other places say unto us clearly that, albeit we know no other reason, yet this is enough to tell us that man, in the state of nature, he is a corrupt creature, and sees not God, and is not for Him, that he loves not God in that estate, nor can love Him ; and this is the woful estate of every man so long as he remains in that case.

Now the *use* of this is : If so be that the natural man be so, how comes it to pass then that there be so many who will not be convinced that it is so with them ? how comes it that it is so hard a task for a minister to convince a natural man that he has a hard heart, and that he is in a state of sin, and that all by nature are ignorant of God ? This only is the cause, that all by nature are dead in sins and trespasses, and being dead cannot be brought to know they are so. No. Ye know all the art and logic in the world used to persuade or convince a dead man, that is in the grave, of the estate[1] of his body, that it is dead and under corruption, will not convince him to know that it is so, because he neither hears nor sees what they do or say to him. Even so is it here with the man remaining still in the state of nature ; he cannot be brought unto the faith of a hell to believe this, that "that day I came first into the world, I came in it an heir [of] hell." The natural man cannot be brought to believe this. The comparison holds well here between the natural man and the man that is buried in the grave ; there are lilies and flowers growing out of

[1] State or condition.

the grave, but it smells filthily within. Little knows the man that is in nature what an ill smell he would cast if he were tane [1] up and discovered. A man living in the state of nature, and so in the state of sin, he may be well busked,[2] and have a good smell outwardly, be an honest married man in his own house, not deceiving or wronging his neighbours, not a shedder of blood, and yet he is only a man buried in a grave when all is done, and some flowers growing above the grave. But when God takes him out of his grave, and lets him see the case that he is in, then all his sins begin to stink. When he is wakened, then he counts all these things that formerly the world and he himself esteemed much of to be but dung, as we may see example in the Apostle Paul, Phil. iii. 7 : He counted that to be a Pharisee, to be come of the royal tribe, &c., to be but loss and dung for Christ. So we may see a man shall never get a right sight of the miserable estate he is in till first the Lord opens his grave that by nature he lies in. And, that being done, he shall then be forced to say : "Once I was dead, but now I am alive ; once I was blind, but now I see ; I was once lost, but now I am found. Once I was a stranger and an enemy to God, but now, Lord be thanked, who has taken in a poor forlorn dyvour [3] to Christ, and has made me to know what is His will."

The other reason his father gives for his kind usage is, "*He was lost, and is found.*" That is the property of a man in the state of sin. He is a lost man, that is, he is such a thing as may be lost, or wander from the right owner without his knowledge, and may be torn of wild

---

[1] Taken.   [2] Adorned.   [3] Bankrupt.

beasts—a sinner in the state of nature. O! but there be many loose-handed devils to steal him away. In 1 John v. 18, the Apostle says, "He that is born of God sinneth not; but he that is begotten of God keepeth himself, and that wicked one toucheth him not." The man that is in the state of nature is not held up as he that is born of God is. The Apostle says of himself, "I know whom I have believed, and am persuaded that He is able to keep that which I have committed unto Him against that day" (2 Tim. i. 12). So that while a man is once in the state of grace God becomes his keeper, but so long as a man is in the state of nature he is a tint[1] creature, and he is ready to be turned away with any kind of religion; like unto those of whom the Apostle speaks (Heb. xiii. 9), who are carried about with divers and strange doctrines, and have not the heart established in grace, a comparison that is borrowed from ships, that every tide and every blast of wind that blows will blow and turn them as they come upon them, because she wants a rudder to keep her sure. So a man in the state of nature will receive any new gust in religion. Any wind or tide that comes from Satan and his instruments carries him away from his Lord. And the Apostle Peter (2 Pet. iii. 17) has a word to this purpose borrowed from beasts: "See that ye be not led away with the error of the wicked and fall from your own steadfastness." It is an easy thing for Satan to drive a man away from religion, who follows only that religion which a king loves best, and who places his happiness in court. Certainly it is easy to drive such from any point of faith. And therefore the

[1] Lost.

Word of God uses this comparison ordinarily to compare lost sinners to wandering sheep. David says, "I am gone astray like a lost sheep." And Matt. x. 5, 6, when Christ there is sending out His disciples to preach the gospel, and telling them what they shall first preach, He says: "Go not in the way of the Samaritans, but rather go to the lost sheep of the house of Israel." All these and many others say that a man in the state of nature is a man easily carried away with every wind of doctrine. Like the word Eliphas has to Job xv. 12: "Wherefore doth thine heart carry thee away, and what do thine eyes wink at?" To be like one in an uncou[1] country, or house.

Let us learn here to know how ill we are kept while we are in the state of nature, ready to be led away with court, honour, the love of the world, and to be stolen from the Lord. Has not the devil made sin to the natural man like new wine that is sweet in the down-going, that runs into his head who drinks it, and or he wit[2] it steals away his wit from him, and his feet, and deprives him of the use of all his senses? So while a man remains in the state of sin, he drinks his new wine till he be stolen off his feet.

But when is the sinner well kept? Never till he come into Christ's house and kingdom, for there he gets a new Lord, and there are new laws there; he gets a new tutor then that will answer for him. This is a sufficient reason, albeit there were no moe[3] to prove that fra[4] once we come in Christ's tutory,[5] that we are

---

[1] Strange. [2] Ere he knows. [3] More.
[4] From the time. [5] Under Christ's tutorage.

given over to Him, we cannot fall away again; for whoever they be that are given to Christ they are not their own, but they are bought with a price. We cannot keep ourselves well. We are always running away from our Lord. But when Christ our Lord comes and takes us home in His keeping, then are we sure; and never till then. For then we are our Lord's jewels, of whom our Lord says (Mal. iii. 17): "And they shall be Mine in that day when I make up My jewels." There is no man who commits himself unto Christ, who ventures his life and all for Christ's cause and for religion, [but] He will answer for all that are given to Him. And when He renders up the kingdom to His Father, He will make such compt[1] of them as that which we read, John xvii. 12, where He says: "Of all that Thou hast given Me have I lost none, but the child of perdition; that the Scripture might be fulfilled." There is no man lost by Christ but he who is a lost man in God's eternal decree.

Now when the older brother comes home to the house, he hears melody and joy and meikle[2] mirth in his father's house, and he knows not what it means. And therefore he calls one of the servants, and asks what these things meant.

The text it will clear this point unto us, that the father of the house—the Lord and His angels—they are glad at the home-coming of a sinner, for there was rejoicing and dancing at the home-coming of His forlorn son, and it must be a good spring[3] that gars[4] him dance. Indeed He is very blith[5] when a lost sinner

---

[1] Account. [2] Much. [4] Causes.
[3] A quick and lively tune upon an instrument. [5] Happy.

comes home to Him, and He makes a psalm of joy upon it. And this was the matter of Christ's joy at this time, that a forlorn sinner is come home. This is a matter of no small comfort to such as have a mind home toward Christ, that their home-coming will gar[1] the Lord rejoice. Is this modesty in Christ to dance? I am sure it is•love gars[2] Him to do it; and the apostle says love does nothing that is unseemly. The Word of God expresses to us in many pithy words the joy and rejoicing that the Lord our God has for the declaration both of mercy and justice upon mankind. As, first, for expression of God's affection when justice comes to seize upon the sinner who would have none of the Lord's counsel, nor hear none of His reproof, it is said, "The Lord laughs at his calamity, and mocks when his fear cometh" (Prov. i. 26). Laughter is not to the Lord an expression of affection as it is to man; but because this is one of the many ends that the Lord intends and aims at in the making of mankind, the declaration of the glory of His justice in so many as break their neck upon Christ, the Lord will "laugh at the calamity of such, and mock when their fears come." And then for the expression of the Lord's love and joy at the home-coming of a sinner, which is the declaration of the glory of the Lord's mercy in them who are appointed heirs of salvation, what expressions are these? Isa. lxii. 5: "As the bridegroom rejoiceth over the bride, so shall thy God rejoice over thee." Zeph. iii. 17: "The Lord thy God will rejoice over thee with joy, He will rest in His love, He will joy over thee with singing." And in

---

[1] Cause.   [2] Causes.

Solomon's Song viii. 6 there is an expression the Kirk has to this purpose, speaking to her beloved: "Set me as a seal upon thy hand, and as a signet upon thine arm." That which we wear between our breasts, because the breast is near the heart, and we love that well; and that which we make a chain and bracelet to our arm, we love it well. Now the Kirk prays that the Lord would make her so to Him, expressing this far unto us how excellent, how sweet, how lovely, all the Lord's elect and His lost ones, when they are found again, are to Him. And there is an expression not unlike unto this, Cant. iv. 9: "Thou hast ravished my heart, my sister, my spouse; thou hast ravished my heart with one of thine eyes, with one chain of thy neck."

All this says this much unto us, that whatever can be in the father to contribute for the good of the bairns [1] he has begotten, or what affection can be in the mother towards the fruit of her womb, all these are in the Lord towards His children, but in Him after an infinite manner, and are inimitable. They are in Him without any change or any imperfection at all; for the Lord needs no-wise to rejoice in this, for it adds nothing to Him, yet He expresses Himself this way to declare how greatly He rejoices in them who are saved when they come home to Him.

And also this serves to reprove that woful opinion of some who say that man's condemnation falls out against the will of God. No; certainly all that is in God is omnipotent, and so is His will omnipotent also. What He wills it comes to pass. The enemies of the grace of

[1] Children.

God bring¹ in God weeping, full of sorrow and natural affection towards men, because He is condemned not according to His will. But if it were so, they would make God to be far from that infinite perfection the Word of God ascribes to Him; Eph. i. 5: He does whatsoever He will in heaven and in earth that we should be to the praise of His glory.

If the Lord make so meikle of honouring a sinner, that He accounts it to be the matter of His joy and rejoicing, O! that we and these who are yet in the black estate of nature, could be induced to believe, what joy it would be to our Lord, that we would repent, and believe in Him and His gospel! The natural man he knows not that the Lord rejoices at his home-coming, and will not believe the Lord's oath for it: "As I live, says the Lord, I delight not in the death of a sinner, but rather that he should repent, and be saved" (Ezek. xviii. 33). He rejoices at the home-coming of a sinner. Make God blith,² and come home to Him and seek His face, repent of your ill-ways, and so make the Lord dance and sing that He has gotten home one who was running away from Him. Come home to the Lord and repent of sin that there may be a psalm over thy repentance in heaven. They are called a "destroyed" people (Hos. xiii. 9) to whom the Lord shows their sins, to make them mourn for them the more. O! that is the sweetest sight God can give to a sinner. When they been running to the devil and applauding themselves in their own ways, afterward to see them come greeting³ home to the Lord, touched in their conscience with rebukes

---

¹ Represent.   ² Happy.   ³ Weeping.

and challenges for sins; O, that is a matter of God's mirth, and a delicate [1] to Him. Learn to know this and have other thoughts of godliness than ever yet ye have had, to account them blessed who see their sins and by the discovery of them are driven to the Lord. And to this Lord who is the remedy of sin; to the Father of Christ and our Father; and the blessed Spirit who sanctifies and cleanses us from sin, we render all praise and glory for ever.—Amen.

[1] A delicious joy. "And with their delicates my taste let me not satisfy," Psa. cxli. 4, Scotch Metrical Version.

The Forlorn Son.

"*And he answering said to his father, Lo, these many years do I serve thee, neither transgressed I at any time thy commandment: and yet thou never gavest me a kid, that I might make merry with my friends: but as soon as this thy son was come, which hath devoured thy living with harlots, thou hast killed for him the fatted calf. And he said unto him, Son, thou art ever with me, and all that I have is thine. It was meet that we should make merry and be glad: for this thy brother was dead, and is alive again; and was lost, and is found.*"—LUKE xv. 29-32.

LET the world, beloved in our Lord, esteem of the children of God as they will, the Lord has aye [1] a good eye to them that repent and come home to Him. The Lord is kind to any without exception who will come and lay their sores upon Him and will give Him the weight of all that lies upon them. And the Lord seeks no more, in the matter of believing, of a humbled sinner, but that they lay the weight and burden of their salvation upon Him.

In thir [2] words there is (1) the reason the Lord gives why the forlorn sinner is so handled. (2) We have to consider how this elder brother that knows not God takes with this. At the first he knows not what it meant when he heard more than ordinary joy and

[1] Always.   [2] These.

melody in his father's house, and he calls for one of the servants, and asks what it means. There is no natural man that knows the sweet kisses and expressions of love that the Lord shows to a home-coming sinner. (3) We have the servant's answer to the elder son. "Thy brother is come; and thy father hath killed the fatted calf, because he hath received him safe and sound." (4) When the elder brother hears this, he is angry and refuses to go into the house. As the hypocrite he will not in any ways countenance the home-coming sinner. He will not welcome his brother when he is come home. Then his father comes and entreats the elder brother to come in. Then we have in the end, a conference between the loving father and the elder son, the father answering all the objections that the son could give against his kind and friendly dealing, and the son again accusing both his father for what he does and accusing his brother also.

First: He says, "*I have served thee so many years and served thee after such a kind that I never at any time brake any of thy commandments, and yet thou never gavest me a kid to make merry with my friends.*" And herein accuses his father of unjust dealing, accounting him as it were the transgressor.

Second: He finds fault also with his father's son; he calls him not his brother but "*thy son.*" "But as soon as this thy son was come which hath devoured thy living with harlots, thou hast killed for him the fatted calf." He calls him a drunken waster, and one who had spent all his father's goods with harlots. The children of God they will never get that praise from hypocrites that the Lord Himself gives them. And then we have the father's mild and gentle oration [1] to his son, yet entreating him and giving him fair words and giving a good reason wherefore this should be a time of mirth and rejoicing. "*It was meet,*" says he, "*that we should make merry and be glad: for this thy brother was dead, and is alive again; and was lost, and is found.*" Albeit he will not call him his brother, yet his father calls him his brother, and therefore, says he, this was a fit time to be glad and rejoice, namely, when a sinner comes home in penitence and mercy is shown to a penitent sinner. Now of thir [2] particulars shortly.

And first: We have to speak of this that the forlorn son gets such a welcome of his brother and that his brother thinks so of the joy that is at his home-coming, that he knows not what it means. Therefore we have to learn that—

The course of God's goodness to a home-coming sinner and of that rejoicing that the Lord and the blessed angels who are His servants, and the matter of the Lord's giving mercy to such a one, it is a hid mystery to the natural man. He that knows no better than mere nature thinks God's kindness that He shows to sinners the work of the gospel and the news thereof, inviting sinners to come to Christ telling them that they will be welcome, he thinks that to be an uncow [3] thing. That God should take a defiled sinner into His clean bosom, and give him mercy for all his sins, he knows not what that means; and therefore he offends [4] at it. The natural man knows not the things that are of God,.

[1] Entreaty.   [2] These.   [3] Strange.   [4] Is stumbled at it.

neither can he know them, because they are spiritually discerned. And he is carnally minded, he knows not the depth of the Lord's love; he knows not what that is for mercy and misery to meet together. He knows not, nor considers not, how kind and gracious the Lord is towards such, and what bowels of love and tender compassion the Lord has to a repenting home-coming sinner. No. There is no man that knows the greatness of the Lord's mercy, and how far His kindness is extended to home-coming sinners, but only he that will come and see, that will come and take a proof thereof himself. Sense is the best schoolmaster to teach us this lesson of God's goodness and His loving-kindness. By preaching, hearing, reading, contemplation of the cause and the theory of this, by all these we will only see this [goodness and loving-kindness] afar off. But once come and taste this goodness of the Lord, and come in within Christ's house, and hear heaven's music, and that will say more to you of these things than anything else can do, and more than ever ye would [have] believed.

A second reason for this is, This is a thing that is so contrary to nature that one who is a sinner, and withal a wicked sinner, that such should get mercy they cannot believe it. Scribes and Pharisees they wonder at this; and therefore Christ is challenged[1] for this by them, for going to Zacchæus's house, who was a publican; and He is challenged and sore accused, and calumnies raised upon Him for this matter, in that He ate and drank and kept company with publicans and sinners, who were a people most hated among the Jews, that none would

[1] Found fault with.

keep company with, but those that were like themselves, And Scribes and Pharisees and the Rabbis among the Jews break their neck upon Christ because of this, that He was so entire[1] and so warm-hearted to poor vile sinners. And this is one point of the gospel, and indeed a main point of it, that Christ in the gospel invites sinners to come, and receives repenting sinners be they never so vile in their own eyes and the eyes of others. So that repentance is a work of the gospel and not a work of the law. It is a thing altogether supernatural and not proceeding at all from nature. And then—

Third: That the Lord should extend more than ordinary mercy to sinners, who have been furthest and deepest in guiltiness, the natural man cannot away with it. And that slays all these who are opposers of God's mercy, and so come not to Christ for mercy, because they think the offers of the gospel are not so meikle[2] for them, seeing it is reached to them who transgress so highly in such a large manner. They cannot believe that, and foster themselves in that conceit, and take a wrong opinion of Christ. And thus they make hell to come upon themselves before the time, and the terrors of the second death before ever the Lord give out the sentence.

Now our *use* of this is to let us see what is the natural man's light, and what is his judgment of God's matters. That which is called free will in the understanding, believing God and Christ, the elder brother knows not what that means. This should be marked that the natural man who goes on into the ways of sin he has not

---

[1] So intimate with.   [2] Much.

right thoughts of God. All of them have false thoughts of God in their will and their affections. There is a hostility and enmity between their mind and the Lord, and His manner of dealing with poor sinners. He knows not what that means. What! has the natural man no light at all? Yes; he has some literal and natural light, but there are four faults in it shortly, and this is a clear difference between the light of the natural man and the believer's light.

First: There is no proportion between the light of the natural man and the things that are of God. Christ is little to the natural man, and so are mercy and repentance to a home-coming sinner little also. His heart is misted[1] and blinded, he sees not what wide bowels of mercy and love Christ has to a home-coming sinner. But the believer sees Christ and mercy and repentance all in one colour. He sees that Christ has open arms for receiving a repenting sinner. He sees there is a chamber of love to receive a lost and tint[2] sinner in Christ. He sees there is a door opened in Christ to receive those who come not into Him till the eleventh hour. Again —

Second: The light that the natural man has, it wants weight to draw the will and the affections and all the powers of the soul to love and embrace and follow after Christ. And therefore it may well be resembled to the light of the moon, especially in the winter season. The moon in winter has light, but it is not like the summer sun that has a melting and warming power with it. Whereas the light the believer has, it works upon his

---

[1] Obscured as with a mist.   [2] Lost, perishing.

heart to warm and refresh him with the love of Jesus, that as he knows Christ so he follows on to know Him. And these two are joined in Hos. vi. 3 by the spirit of God: "Then shall ye know Him if ye follow on to know Him." So that light and heat and refreshment follow the heat and sense of Christ's love that the natural man has. The natural man may see the gospel to be true, but he sees it not to be good, neither assents to the promises that are contained therein. Yet they are true promises but he assents not, or follows not in them as good, and so he goes no further on but to a bare light.

Thirdly and lastly: There is no liking, love, joy, desire, accompanying the light the natural man has, and because of this it is no wonder that those who have but little knowledge of Christ, it is no marvel albeit they misken [1] the Lord's dealing with His children, and call that which is the excellence of Christ and of the gospel, madness and daffin.[2] As certainly this will follow the not knowing Christ and His ordinances rightly, that so natural men may break their necks and stumble upon the works of God, as we may see in Psa. lxxxiii. 11.

Now the servant gives an answer to the elder brother, wherefore there should be mirth and rejoicing in his father's house. "*Thy brother is come: and he hath killed the fatted calf, because he hath received him safe and sound.*" The argument that the servant uses for that [which] the father did is: "Thy father hath received him a whole and living son who was once sick and dead, and therefore there is mirth and rejoicing." And the strength of the argument is tane fra [3] the hazard wherein

---

[1] Misunderstand.   [2] Folly.   [3] Taken from.

the forlorn son was once, and now, says he, he is escaped from that hazard and danger, and therefore it is most expedient and lawful, that there should be mirth and feasting and rejoicing in heaven. And so by this we may learn that this forlorn son he has once been in great hazard, he has once been over in the devil's camp, and so in great danger, but now he is returned safe and sound; and therefore the servant says to his brother: "He has received him safe and sound." The Lord would hereby teach us that we have been in a fearful and dangerous hazard while we remain in the state of nature. And indeed so it is. For being there we are under spiritual death, as it is Eph. ii. 2: "Called us from death to life." And being in nature, we are also under the state of condemnation: "And were by nature the children of wrath as well as others."

And therefore all those who are come to Christ, they have cause to be blyth,[1] and to rejoice and to praise Christ's rich and free grace, and to say with their hearts: "I thank God that whereas once I was a persecutor, and a blasphemer and an injurious person, one who hated Christ and the power of religion, &c.; but now I am not so, but, by free grace, I am become a new man." There is no man has such cause to sing a triumphant song of the Lord's praise as he who was once dead, and the Lord has given him mercy, and quickened him from that estate.

"*And he was angry, and would not go in.*" This was the older brother. There seems to be natural reason for this, that he would not go in, he being a civil[2] liver, and

---

[1] Happy.   [2] An outwardly correct.

an honest[1] man that way, one who had not at any time broken his father's command, as he himself says, that had not run away from his father, and tired of his company, and spent his goods with harlots and in debauchery, as his younger brother had done. This is a strange thing, thinks he, that he should make so meikle[2] of him. Because it is so, I will not go into the house. Reason would say that the elder brother has cause to stick here, and to be offended at what his father does. But this is one of the supernatural points of the gospel, and a very great one; that those who seem to be furthest from mercy, who have done most for stopping mercy to be extended towards them, the Lord He ordinarily gives mercy to such. And yet, on the other part, honest civilians and well-covered Scribes, Pharisees, that have a trim-like[3] outside, and seek for no more of religion, and seek not into Christ, the Lord hardens the heart of such, and gives them over to the spirit of error and delusion; and harlots and publicans, and very sinful persons, who are even seen to be great sinners, they get mercy and forgiveness, and are led into Christ to seek their life in Him.

We may learn here that it is God's way, and it is the way of the gospel, to ride upon the weakest, poorest, basest, and most contemptible things in the world, and to cause the glory of His mercy and goodness to shine upon them, and to cause the news of mercy to sound effectually to those who seem most lost in the world. Look wherever, at any time, God has shown mercy and the light and saving power of His truth, wherever the

[1] Honourable. [2] Much. [3] Fine.

Lord has shown the greatest works of mercy, whether it be upon nations, or congregations, or families, or particular persons, it has always been shown most clearly and effectually to such as the world thought least of. When Jacob is blessing his children, there is not a word spoken of any blessing to the tribe of Levi (Gen. xlix.); but when he is dying the Lord by him gives them a curse because "they slew a man in their anger, and in their self-will they digged down a wall. Cursed be their anger, for it was fierce; and their wrath, for it was cruel. I will divide them in Jacob and scatter them in Israel." And yet the Lord has chosen them for His portion, even the tribe come of him who gat his father's curse, the Lord chooses him out of all the tribes of Israel to be His portion. And a bastard Jephthah—the Jews abhorred any of that kind—yet the Lord will have him to be a judge in Israel, and the instrument by whom He will work a great deliverance for that people. And among the twelve Patriarchs, the odd and the castaway son Joseph, who was hated and sold of his brethren; the servant of God, Moses, at the direction of the Lord's spirit, says of him, " The blessing of the Lord upon him who was cast forth of his brethren."

And likeways when Christ is coming into Jerusalem in His triumph, as it was prophesied, riding upon an ass and a colt the foal of an ass, He will not have Scribes and Pharisees to sing His triumph, but bairns and little ones, cry out "Hosanna, blessed is the king that cometh in the name of the Lord." And where, when Christ was born, were all the Bible-men and the book-learned men that should have known so well, and observed the time and the place of His birth? And yet shepherds get leave to be the first preachers of His birth to the world? No; all the great rabbis and expouers of the law they had beguiled themselves with their light, and knew not that Christ was born, and the shepherds proclaim His birth that so the Lord he may triumph upon the weakest things, and these fardest [1] unlike heaven he will take them to heaven.

And this is, indeed, the sweetness of the mercy and love of our Lord, that even those who are furthest off from mercy in their own eyes, and in the eyes of the world, these shall get mercy rather than others who seem to be nearer within the reach thereof, that the Lord may make good that which is said by the apostle (1 Cor. i. 26-29): "For you see your calling, brethren, how that not many wise men after the flesh, not many mighty, not many noble, are called: but God hath chosen the foolish things of the world to confound the wise; and the weak things of the world to confound the strong; and base things in the world, and things which are despised, hath God chosen, yea, and things that are not, to bring to nought things that are: that no flesh should glory in His presence." He will choose the kinless [2] things of the world, and the nothings, to be his portion, that no flesh may glory before him, but that the glory of the salvation of all those who are saved may be to the Lord, and to the Lord allanerly.[3]

O happy and blessed is the case and condition of a sinner who is despised of all, yea, even of themselves, and thereby can come home to Christ. When thou

---

[1] Most. [2] Poorest, without relatives. [3] Alone.

comest to Him the Lord will not speer[1] at thee when thou comest, who was thy father, or thy mother, or what thy kindred is, neither will He speer[1] what thou hast been doing all the time till thou come to Him, if so be thou come to Him with a bleeding heart for sin. And therefore let never man speer[1] this question what they have been doing before who are come into Christ, for all thy harlotries and thy manifold sins and provocations be not bars away for those. And albeit Scribes and Pharisees hoot at you that thou should seek home to Christ, and be made welcome of Him; yet for all their ill will and their malice at Christ's dealings with His own poor ones, seeing He makes you welcome, make thou thyself welcome also.

What further says his elder brother to his father? "*Neither did I at any time break Thy commandments.*" The word in the first[2] language is, "I never went beyond thy commandment." Albeit this be the word of a proud Pharisee, yet it tells us what sort of obedience our God requires of us. That obedience he craves is not to go out of the straight line, not to decline to the right hand or to the left hand.

The doctrine is clear, and it is this: The law that God will have us to follow and to square ourselves unto as a line and rule, it is such a law as requires strict and precise obedience of us. The apostle says: "Walk circumspectly as in the day-time," that is, walk as those who count all their stops, and have light to see where they set their feet. God will either give such obedience as that, or He will account any obedience we give no

---

[1] Ask. [2] Original tongue.

obedience. And look to five things in the law of God, and that will tell us this is true.

First: The law of God it is a spiritual law, and it is not by hands, and feet, and tongue, and teeth, and obedience with the outward man that will satisfy God, but He must have the obedience of the heart and the inward man. And therefore the Lord lays charge upon our thoughts; Jer. iv. 14; Isa. lv. 7. In those places God will have the thoughts to be subject to Him: "O Jerusalem, wash thy heart from wickedness. How long shall vain thoughts lodge within thee?" "Let the wicked man forsake his ways, and the unrighteous man his thoughts: and let him return unto the Lord, for He will have mercy; and to our God, for He will abundantly pardon." And our Saviour Christ when He expones the the law (Matt. v. 22), ye will see exponing the sixth command, He not only forbids murder, but He says, "Whosoever miscalls his brother, and calls him 'Raca,' 'thou fool,' or is angry with him without a cause, he is a breaker of that command." And He not only condemns adultery for a sin and breach of the seventh command, but He says he that looks upon a woman and lusteth after her has committed adultery with her already in his heart; so that it will not be the outside of civility and of country holiness that will make a man accounted religious and holy in the sight of God, but the holiness of the heart.

Second: Look also to the universality of God's commandments, and that will tell us He requires such obedience, Psa. cxix. 6: "Then shall I not be ashamed, when I have respect to all Thy commandments." This says that shame follows upon that man who pretends to keep some of God's commands, and yet breaks other some wittingly. Not a drunkard and yet a harlot, shame will come upon such a man; not a cozener, and yet none may lippen [1] to his word, shame shall come upon such a man. And that it is the commendation given to Zacharias and Elizabeth, that they walked in all the commandments and ordinances of the Lord blameless. Again—

Third: If we will look to the universality of time, God requires such obedience of us, Psa. cvi. 3 : " Blessed are they that keep judgment, and he that doeth righteousness at all times." There are anew [2] who will keep the commandment of the Lord while the cross is lying upon them, or upon their house, or any of their bairns; but that place says: " Blessed is the man that doeth righteousness at all times." And then—

Fourth : In obedience to God's commands is to look to all the circumstances of our actions, to the end wherefore, to the manner how, and to the ground and principle from whence they flow. So the believer he must look to his intentions, what it is he sets before his eyes when he comes to hear the Word of God. If a man comes to the kirk to hear the Word for saving his honesty, because it will be a shame for him, he being a man of whom notice is taken, and in some place and reputation, if his place in the kirk shall be seen empty, or for any other by respect, then you obey not God after a right and acceptable manner. But if you can say, ye do what ye do in obedience to His commandments,

[1] Trust.   [2] Enough.

for that end that ye may win [1] a step nearer God, and may grow deep in His love, then that is right obedience. And then—

Lastly: In our obedience to God's commandments no man must make a pattern and rule of others in their obedience. What, albeit ye be as holy as that man, if ye be not holier than he, you and he may both go to hell together, as the Scribes and Pharisees ilk [2] one of them did imitate others. But made that them to be holy? No. Christ says, "If your righteousness exceed not the righteousness of the Scribes and Pharisees, ye shall not enter into the kingdom of God." It is a remarkable place that which we read 2 Kings xiv. 3, where King Amaziah is reproved of the Lord, that he did not as David had done before him. And may not a man be a good man, albeit he be not as holy as David was? Who can win [1] to that high pitch? Yes; I confess he may be a good man, and not win [1] so far on as he did. But this is to teach us that we make no man our copy in obeying the commandments of the Lord. But we must set that copy before us which Christ says of His Kirk, Cant. iv. 7: "Thou art all fair, my love; there is no spot in thee." You must see and strive by all means to be quit of spots in the world.

Now the *use* of this, that we have been speaking [of] is, to reprove them who mock godliness, and scorn those who fear an oath, as the Scripture speaks, and make conscience of their words and thoughts as if that were in needless preciseness. But the way to heaven is a straight and narrow way, and alas! the world knows it

[1] Get. [2] Each.

not. They scorn a strict and precise walking with God in everything. And alas! this is even now the sin that rings in Scotland, that any who would walk so as to approve themselves to God in everything, these get a new name to be "Puritans" and "Separatists." And I believe there be not many parts where the gospel is that have gone so far on in this sin as we have done, notwithstanding our light be clearer than the light of others; and therefore our judgment must be the greater, for we lie under the woe that is pronounced by the Lord against those who call evil good and good evil.

Now only a word [more] of two things in this parable that we may close it. And—

First: That albeit the forlorn son when he comes home be highly honoured and kindly entreated by his father, yet the elder brother will not go into the house where he is, but is angry at both his father and his brother, challenging them both.

Second: What is it that ails him at his brother and his father? Nothing, but only because God is good to him, he cannot digest that. Where we may learn:

First: That whenever a sinner comes home to Christ they shall then get the hatred and envy of the rest of the world. What fault had this younger brother done to him to be angry for? No fault at all. But because he came home to Christ, therefore he is angry. And what is the ground of the hatred, that is between the followers of Christ and the rest of the world? They have no other cause wherefore to be angry at them, but because they are come home to Christ, and because it is so, they cannot get the world's heart. That must be true which

Christ says and registers in His Testament: "Ye are not of the world, for if ye were of the world, the world would love his own: but because ye are not of the world, but I have chosen you out of the world, therefore the world hateth you. Ye shall get the world's malice, and all the quarrel that the world shall have against you shall be only because you are My disciples. The seed of the woman and the seed of the serpent cannot go together, but they must be at enmity." And how comes it to pass that there cannot be a kindly peace between Prelatists and Papists, and those who have bound themselves in a covenant with God? Even because we are not in one way. The Lord has said it, that their horns must be in our side.[1] And, therefore, let no man who comes to Christ look always for the wind fair in his sails, and that he shall lie always upon a soft bed, fra [2] thou hast tane [3] you to Christ. No; thou shalt be used hardly of the men of the world, who are not in the same course with you, and shall be forced to say as the prophet Jeremiah says (xv. 10): "Woe is me, my mother, that thou hast borne me a man of strife and a man of contention to the whole earth! I have neither lent on usury, nor men have lent to me on usury; and yet every one doth curse me." And the reason of all their envy is because the Word of God is his delight. That shall be enough for a quarrel to the world. Seek God, and ye shall get the world on your top.[4] Even thy father and mother and the wife that lies into thy bosom, if thou seek God, and they go not on into that

---

[1] *I.e.*, they will ever be pushing at us.   [2] From the time.
[3] Taken.   [4] Upon or against you.

way, also they shall be thy enemies. And, therefore, we must resolve to take the world's feid.[1] If we would have God's favour, whoever comes to Christ must make them[selves] for the scourge of the world's tongue.

Wherewith is it that he finds fault? "*As soon as this thy son came that hath devoured thy living with harlots, thou hast killed for him the fatted calf.*" The Pharisee has an ill eye towards the children of God, because God has a good heart to them. It is the natural man's ordinary to find fault with his neighbour's sins. It is ordinary for them to speak that word which we read, Isa. lxv. [5] : "Stand back by thyself, come not near me, I am holier than thou." A soul that is truly sanctified will be loathe to make a hole in his neighbour's conscience, that he may see what is there. No, he sees so many faults in himself that he sees not the faults of others well. He will say with the apostle, "I am the chief of sinners." The forlorn son speaks no ill of him, but he has much that he casts up to the forlorn son.

The last particular that we observe is: The Lord taking the forlorn son's part. "*It was meet* (says he) *that we should make merry, and be glad*," &c.—to teach us that God will for a while flatter a hypocrite, for you see the Lord reproves him not for his rough dealing. And woful is the case of that man under whose head God lays a cod[2] to let him sleep in his security, and wakens him not to whom he says, as it is in Hos. iv. 17: "Ephraim is joined to idols; let him alone." Now,

Lastly: That the Lord takes the defence of His forlorn son. "*It was meet that we should be glad and*

[1] Enmity.   [2] Pillow.

rejoice," teaches us this: Come home to Christ, who will, albeit all the world should speak ill of them, yet He will take their defence, and speak on their part. When that poor woman poured the ointment on Christ's feet, and the disciples began to murmur, and say, "It might [have] been sold for much money and given to the poor," Christ took her defence, and says, "Let her alone, she has wrought a good work on Me, for she did it for My burial; and wheresoever this gospel is preached throughout the world, this also that she has done shall be preached for a memorial of her." And Acts ix., when Ananias is bidden, "Go, preach to Saul," Ananias says: "This man has done much ill, and he has presently authority to bind all that call on Thy name, and carry them to Jerusalem;" but in ver. 15 Christ says, "Go thy way for he is a chosen vessel unto Me, to bear My name before the Gentiles, and kings, and the children of Israel." And—

O, but that is a sweet thing, that albeit all the world should say against you, yet if thou wilt come to Christ, He will take thy part. Let them call you what they will, never so ill, He will call you His love, His dove, His undefiled, &c. And well is the soul that has Christ's commendation and high song of praise. It is better nor[1] the commendation of all the world. What's the matter[2] what men speak of you if God commend you. What is the matter[2] albeit wicked men speak ill of you, if God speak good of you, for what He says all the world shall not get undone. Seek ye the Lord's commendation, and to be approven of Him, and

---

[1] Than.   [2] What matters it.

it makes¹ not then what men say against you. Lord teach us so to do for His name's sake. To this Lord, and our Lord, to His Father, and our Father, and to the Holy Spirit, be ascribed all glory, praise, and honour for ever and ever.—Amen.

¹ *I.e.*, does not signify.

The Worth and Excellence of the Gospel.

"For the weapons of our warfare are not carnal, but mighty through God to the pulling down of strongholds; casting down imaginations, and every high thing that exalteth itself against the knowledge of God, and bringing into captivity every thought to the obedience of Christ."—2 COR. X. 4, 5.[1]

HE most part of the world, beloved in our Lord, there are but few of them who put that price upon the gospel of Christ that is meet to be put upon it, and so did some of thir[2] false apostles. They called the gospel foolishness, daffing.[3] They thought it to be but baseness itself. But men's thoughts are not the measure whereby this gospel is to be measured, for the Word of God and the gospel of Christ, is not of the less worth in itself that men put a small price upon it. But our Lord He knows best what is the worth and excellence of this gospel of Christ. He who kens the vanity and daffing[3] of the vain thoughts of the heart of man, He kens[4] that albeit all the world should count light of His gospel, esteeming it but foolishness and daffing,[3] and a weak thing; yet He

[1] In MS. this sermon has no date, but simply "A sermon by M. S. R.," but from some of its allusions it seems to have been preached on Aug., 1640, see note page 1.
[2] These.   [3] Folly.   [4] Knows.

knows that the weapons of that warfare are not carnal and fleshly, but mighty through the power of God to the pulling down of strongholds. I say nothing now of what I spake before, but only I say this:

Be no party in the world. Make the gospel and Christ your party, and take not the gospel for your enemy; for resist the gospel who will, and, whoever they be that stand out against it, it shall aye at last overmaster them, and ding[1] them down, and tread them under foot, whether they will or no. How many have there been who have been setting their shoulders and their wits together to thrust this gospel out of the world. They thought it to be a cumbersome guest, and would fain [have] been quit of it, and so pressed to blow out Christ's candle. But they have been like drunken men, who in their drunken humour would run up to the top of a hill to blow out the light of the sun; but instead of blowing out the light thereof, they have only kythed[2] their own foolishness. Even so do men in the world, climb up, upon the top of their worldly pomp and ambition, to blow out this candle of the gospel. But the more they blow at it to get it out, they only kythe[3] their witlessness the more. It has evermore proved itself to be master, and more, against all who oppose it.

A second *use* that we are to make of this, that the weapons of the gospel are mighty, is: Wherever this gospel cometh, whether it be to a congregation, to a nation, or to a particular person, it will evermore be master. We may not think to make a servant thereof, because it is mighty through the power of God. It is

[1] Throw.   [2] Shown.   [3] Show.

the arm of the Lord, as it is in Isa. liii. 1; the prophet says there, "Who hath believed our report, or to whom hath the arm of the Lord been revealed?" And so never think to bruike [1] the gospel and make a servant of it; for ye can no more make the gospel a servant to serve you than ye are able to break the Lord's arm. And, indeed, he is a strong party who will make the Lord's arm either to bow or to break. And, therefore, wherever the message of the gospel comes, let it have its own proper place; make it master. Let it prove to be the power of God to lay down those high and strong turrets of pride, of self-love, of worldly-mindedness, &c., under the foot of Christ, that so He may be known thereby to be mighty. The gospel will not be a servant and drudge to any. It will not be a post-horse to run our errands for us. It will not be a servant to the greatest upon earth. If it be mighty, through the power of God it will keep its own place, who will, who will not.

Moreover, if the gospel be not the arm and power of God to bring us home to Christ and to salvation, it shall then be the blackest news that ever we heard in our time. It is not for nought that our Lord, who is mercy itself, pronounced such a woe against Chorazin and Bethsaida, even a more heavy woe than against Tyre and Sidon. Woe! to you for evermore to whom Christ and the gospel come, and yet mend ye not. And He also pronounces a woe and a curse against these who bring not out the fruits of the gospel where it comes. And, therefore, it were best for you to bring out the fruits of the gospel timeously; [2] for ye will not be quit

[1] Enjoy.   [2] Early.

of the gospel so easily and so lightly as ye trow[1] to be quit of it. It will either mend you or end you. If it do no more, it will leave a summons at your door declaring that mercy and salvation were offered to you, and ye would not accept of it.

If ministers cannot be means to save people's souls, they will yet leave a summons at the door of your souls, and will take the sun, the moon, stars, the stones, and timber of the kirk, in witness that we did our duty, and told our Master's message to you, but ye would not obey. And, therefore, for Christ's sake, seeing the gospel is come to you, take heed that ye despise it not, as ye will be answerable to Him who is the Master thereof. In Revelation xiv. 9, 10 there is a woe and an everlasting curse pronounced against these who receive not the gospel when it is sent to them. And, 2 Thess. i. 9, 10, the apostle says the Lord will come in flaming fire and take vengeance on them that know not God and obey not the gospel of Christ. There is no less doom pronounced against those who are disobedient to the gospel of Christ nor[2] the vengeance and the heavy curse of God. His word and gospel have not another word to say to the despiser of the gospel nor[2] the vengeance of Christ to light upon them. That is a heavy burden to light upon any. And therefore I beseech you, in God's name and in Christ's name, let the gospel have the one work, which is the proper work thereof. Let it be master, and think not to make a servant of it. Bow unto the gospel, least if ye bow not willingly unto it, it break you all in pieces.

[1] Believe.   [2] Than.

Our weapons of our warfare, they have might and power from heaven and from God to ding [1] down strongholds. Then it is so. It is but a daft [2] question and a foolish conceit of those who are enemies of the Lord's grace to say, that for all that might and power that is in the gospel, that yet, notwithstanding, the free-will of these to whom it is sent with that power, may say [3] or no to it, Take it, or reject the offer thereof, as your free-will pleases. This is nothing else but a conceit of those who never kent [4] the power of the gospel. And we may know the gospel to be mighty through the power of God if we will look either to Him who is the author of this gospel, or if we will look to the matter that is contained in the gospel, or if we will look into the manner of the working thereof.

For the author of this gospel, it is no other but God Himself. Indeed, if this gospel were the word of a man only, albeit it were spoken unto the soul of a man, then I think man's free-will might say or no to it,[3] as it pleased. But the gospel is not the word of man to man, but it is a love-letter that is written to us by our Lord Himself, and is dited [5] by His Spirit. And why may it not command our will to yield unto it, seeing the Lord Himself is the author thereof? It is a great indignity offered to our Lord to say, Let Him speak as He will, albeit it were never so pithily; and let Him work with His word as He pleases, that yet, notwithstanding, to say or no, to accept or not accept as He pleases, that albeit our Lord shoot His arrows at man, yet He may either resist or jouk,[6] and let the fire go by him. He that framed the

---

[1] Cast. [2] Unwise. [3] Say Yes or say No to it.
[4] Knew. [5] Dictated. [6] Evade.

arrow He has put might and power in it, He has put steel in the point thereof, that it may pierce where it lights. And, when He intends to bring in a soul to Himself, He shoots not as it were at the rivers and so to shoot at it begess,[1] but He shoots as it were at a mark; and He aims and sets right on before He shoots, and so cannot but light into the mark, and His arrow it will pierce where it lights.

Again, if we will look unto the matter that is contained in the gospel, we will see that it is mighty through the power of God, for all the world cannot frame and make up such logic as is contained in the gospel. All the wits in the world cannot pen such a glorious description of the New Jerusalem as is contained in the two last chapters of the Revelation. Nor can all the wits of men and angels make such a description of the Son as there is made of Him (Heb. i.) All the world cannot come out with such a description of the power of the gospel as that which is here. And, therefore, albeit hell and all the powers had said that the gospel shall not prevail, yet seeing He said that it shall prevail, they shall not be able to resist it, but it shall prove to be mighty through the power of God, who is the author thereof.

Third: if we will look unto the manner of the working of the gospel, we will also see it to be mighty to ding[2] down all our strongholds. If God were not omnipotent, there might be some show for this, to say that man's free-will might say aye or no to the gospel of Christ. But He who knows all the several parts and

---

[1] At random, by guess.   [2] Throw.

the turnings of the heart of man, shall not He know how to win in into it? How can He make any creature by His power but He maun [1] also know by His power how to move it as He thinks meet? He who when He backs His word with power can win into [the] heart where there are seven devils and speak to it, can He not win into any man's heart how backward soever it be? I am sure there was never a man who had more hurtful thoughts of the Son of man, Jesus Christ, than the Apostle Paul had, for he dought [2] not endure to hear of His name, nor to hear of any who professed His name, but persecuted them all most cruelly. And yet our Lord, He did no more but speak a word or two to him; and with these same few words He spake to him, He cast him off his high horse whereupon he rode so triumphantly, and lays him laigh [3] down upon his back and under His feet. And whereas he was going of purpose to persecute the members of Jesus Christ, he says to Him, "Lord, what wilt Thou have me to do?" To hear our Lord casting down, at an instant, such a strong and cruel opposer of the gospel of Christ, and presently to make him say, "Lord, what wilt Thou have me to do?" that is a cast of the power of our Lord's right arm. And so they are but fools to say that nature, or free-will, or man's heart is able to decline from the straik [4] of God's Word when He resolves to work upon them by it.

Now Lord be thanked that it is so, that we are not able to resist it but that it is mighty and powerful to overcome us. There is a trim [5] place for proving of this point,

[1] Must.   [2] Could.   [3] Low.   [4] Stroke.   [5] Fine.

Cant. ii., where the spouse, which is the Kirk, is telling the manner of her well-beloved's working. He worketh by love. Now love, it cannot be ravished or hindered any way, albeit the lover may be ravished, or tane[1] away, or kept away from the thing beloved; yet love cannot be so, for if it can be ravished or hindered, then it is not true love. In ver. 4, "He brought me to the banqueting house, and his banner over me was love." And when the banner of love is holden up by Christ over the Kirk, is she able to resist then, and to hold Him out, as she pleases? No; for the next verse says when this banner of love was holden over her she fell a sound[2] [Authorized Version, "sick of love"], and therefore she says in the next verse, " Stay me with flagons, and comfort me with apples : for I am sick of love." This is our Lord's gate[3] of working upon the hearts of those whom He is minded to turn to Himself, He casts a lump of love over them, and when He does that, He can gar[4] the rebel fall a sound of love.[2] When a soul is running fra[5] God and fra[5] the consolations of His Spirit; when Jesus once sets His love upon you, and speaks to thy soul, it shall not be in thy power to resist, or to win out of His hand again. Let men make a principle of free-will, or determine whereupon it is that the word sets first. But when the Lord speaks to any, and backs His word with power, it makes them to set their heart upon Jesus; and the soul that Christ loves, He looks upon it in love, and, when the Lord does so, the soul is far fra[5] indifferent then, whether it receive Christ and His word or not; but there is a necessity laid upon them that they must yield.

[1] Taken. [2] Into a swoon from love. [3] Way. [4] Cause. [5] From.

And the Lord also, He is far fra[1] that, that He counts whether these to whom He speaks give obedience to Him or not. He speaks not so. But whoever they be to whom He speaks, if they submit not willingly He treads them under foot, and makes them pliable, and so makes good that word spoken, Deut. xxx. 6 : " And the Lord thy God will circumcise thy heart, and the heart of thy seed, to love the Lord thy God with all thine heart, and with all thy soul, that thou mayest live." Take with [2] your rebellion to God all of you, not [only] with that natural power of resisting the grace of God, but take with that wickedness and sweirness[3] that is in the soul, and that opposition that nature makes to Christ till He subdue it by His power. And Ezek. xxxvi. 26, where a new heart is promised by the Lord, and He promises to take away the old and stony heart.

But say they there, " That new heart that is promised to us there, it is promised upon condition that we resist it not." But look to the text, and ye will see that it mentions no such thing as " I will give unto you a new heart *if you oppose it not ;* " but the text says absolutely, " A new heart also will I give you, and a new spirit will I put within you: and I will take away the stony heart out of your flesh, and I will give you a heart of flesh. And I will put My Spirit within you, and cause you to walk in My statutes to do them." There our Lord He meets with the wits of men and opposes Himself to all objections that they can make of this kind, while He promises to take away the stoniness of the old heart, and then to give a new heart also, and to cause those

---

[1] From.   [2] Acknowledge, own.   [3] Unwillingness.

whom He takes in hand to walk in His statutes. This in effect is our Christ's gospel. Even the power and the mighty arm of God to bring in the rebel soul to Christ and to make it Christ's own captive, and to make all of us say, "I find there is more life and power in His word than ever I could have believed there was to bring me into grace whether I will or not."

And, in effect, who are those who oppose this power of the grace of God? and it has been very well observed by learned men, that there was never any who opposed themselves unto it, but those who kent[1] nothing of the grace of God themselves. And thus the grace of God it revenges itself upon them. Because they resist and oppose the power of it they shall never get profit or benefit thereby. And, indeed, few—few whoever kent[1] what the power of the grace of God meant—durst take upon them to be an Arminian, or to speak against the power of the grace of God; but if any know rightly the power of the grace of God, it were the way to make souls fall in love with it, and to make them loath to say anything against it.

Now if this word and weapons of our warfare be mighty through the power of God, pulling down strongholds, &c., we have sweet *uses* arising unto us from this. And—

First: O, if we could get your hearts summoned to obey this, that ye would come in to Christ, and give over your hearts to Him to be wrought upon by His word. Alas! and[2] any of you have a bairn that is unlettered, ye will send it to the school that it may learn there. Others,

[1] Knew. [2] If.

through feeling of disease on their bodies, will have recourse to the physicians. If a man have a weak and troubled estate he will have recourse to the lawyer, and will concredit[1] his cause to him. And yet thou hast a rebellious soul, and yet thou wilt not give over that to Christ to take and order therewith, and to work upon all the powers thereof, and to change them by His word. If we could once win on this far, to let God's word work upon our hearts by our Lord's power, we would then find that we get a sweet niffer,[2] we would get a new heart for an old heart, we would get new spirits for old spirits. O! but that is a sweet and a happy change. And there is no way for us to become new men and women, but only this, by renouncing ourselves over to the power of God's word to be wrought upon by it, and, if we be not new men and new women, it had been better for us that we had never lived. Woe! is to that soul for evermore that has no more of Christ than nature gives unto it! We may get some learning by being at schools, wisdom may be acquired by pains, riches, &c., and the world may esteem of a man for these things; but yet, for all that, he is nothing else but Christ's painted tomb. For all these, he is all rotten and filthy within; for as beautiful-like as he looks without, yet within he is nothing else but the workhouse of the devil. Say of such a man what ye will, make him never so trim[3] a man for natural parts, wanting a spiritual work, yet he is no other in Christ's account, but a trim[3] limb of the devil. Will the world call him an honest[4] man, then he is an honest[4]

---

[1] Entrust. [2] Exchange. [3] Fine.
[4] Honourable or respectable.

heir of Satan. If ye will call him a civil[1] man, yet he is no other but a civil[1] heir for hell, whatever the world thinks of him or himself. Yet this is the account that God has of a man so long as he has not given himself over to be wrought upon by the word of God.

Second *use.* An[2] there be any here who are complaining of a rebellious heart, of a stony and hard heart, I say to such; "Look if ye cannot get faith to believe in this gospel of Christ, to lay hold upon thir[3] weapons that are mighty, through the power of God, to the pulling down of strongholds, and get faith to believe in it. Thou wilt not find the heart to be so backward. A soul which has such a hard, a rebellious, and a stony heart, it burdens them very sore. But here [is] a ground of comfort to such, if thou can get faith to believe it, that albeit thy heart were never so rebellious, hard, and stiff, yet there are weapons in Christ's armoury that are able to ding[4] it down, to humble and soften it. Thou wilt say, "I cannot get my haughty heart humbled, nor can I get it win off the love of the world, and I find many lusts prevailing there wherewith I am greatly borne down." But here is our comfort, if we have faith to believe. This word of the gospel, it is mighty through the power of God to bring all these in subjection. If ye can get but this far as to be chased into Christ, by reason of the sight of your sins, it is sweet and comfortable.

O, but I like these souls well who are ever mourning for sin, who are complaining of a hard, rebellious, uncircumcised, stony heart. But here is a ground of comfort for such, that God's word is mighty through His

[1] An outwardly correct.   [2] If.   [3] These.   [4] Cast.

power to bear down sin. If we could once win to this, to think that sin is a burden, it were good for us, it would drive us in to Christ. Thou art nearer to heaven when thou art bemoaning the estate of thy hard heart, and art putting it in Christ's hand to be healed, than when thou thinkest all well with you. Thou art meet then to receive of Christ's pity, for He is a Lord ready to forgive all such as come to Him in humility, He is a physician who will take sick folks in hand to heal them who have no money to give for their cure. He is indeed the poor man's physician. He seeks no more of us, but only to tell Him that we are sick. He has a hammer to beat down the hard heart. He has a sword to cut it in pieces. He can make whole the broken heart and afflicted spirit for sin; He can give a new heart and new spirit. Cast not down your heart, because ye find the hardness thereof; cast not away your confidence for all that, but believe in God's word, which is mighty through the power of God to bring it under these.

The Lord be thanked that there is this meikle [1] power in the gospel of Christ, as to make a soul that is sick for sin whole again, as to make a hard heart a soft heart; that there is virtue into it, as to pour down that Spirit upon us, promised to the house of David (Zech. xii. 10), the spirit of prayer and supplications, and the spirit of repentance and mourning for sin. And if we could attain to this, it were a sweet preparation for a solemn fast and humiliation when the Lord is glooming [2] upon the land for the sins thereof, and the Lord is calling to solemn fasting and humiliation for the sins of the land;

---

[1] Much.   [2] Frowning.

it were meet that every one of us should take to heart our own sins and the sins of the land wherein we live, and be humbled before God for them, that so the Lord might comfort us.

Now, where are the fruits and effects of thir [1] weapons of our warfare? To pull down strongholds, to cast down imaginations and every high thing that exalteth itself against the knowledge of God in bringing in subjection everything to the obedience of Christ. These be even all things that be either within or without a man that set themselves in any way against the gospel. It brings all of them in subjection. Especially it casts down all these fortifications that be inwardly in the soul against Christ and the gospel, even all these things that natural men lippen [2] to.

Now, whose is the house before this work be wrought? Matt. xii. 44, answers this question. Satan says, "I will return into my house whence I came out." So the goodman of that old house is no other but the devil; and Christ our Saviour says in another place, "How can a man enter into a strong man's house, unless he first bind the strong man and cast him out?" He means there that Satan is master of every man's house until Christ come into the soul and bind him and cast him out, and take possession there Himself. That may gar [3] all our feathers fall, albeit so oft we will say that we love Christ. For speer [4] at all men and women, they will say that they love Christ, and they are angry that any should think otherways, yet by nature all of us are keeping a castle against Christ, and were keeping it for

---

[1] These.   [2] Trust.   [3] Cause.   [4] Ask.

the devil's service. And of necessity before ever Christ come to dwell into the soul, all these high towers they must fall to the ground, and Christ must bring in a new work with Him, and make us new creatures. And this is one of the works of the gospel, even to lay all the heights that are in man's soul down even with the ground, to make sin and the devil and all these lusts that are keeping up the castle of the heart from him, fall flat to the ground together. And He soops[1] all that muddy house to the door, that so He may make a pleasant house of ashler work for Himself. It seeks to cast down all the old rotten barns that formerly have been built there by sin and the devil, and to exalt us, that so the king of glory may come in as it is, Psa. xxiv. 7 : " Exalt yourselves, ye gates; be ye lift up, ye everlasting doors : that so the King of glory may come in."

All this serves greatly to ding[2] down our proud natures, to let the natural and the civil[3] man see in what estate he is in God's sight, albeit he have a good report before the world, that yet notwithstanding he is not a man great in God's sight unless the gospel has gotten work in him to ding[4] the high towers that are in him. If thou hast never had a sick soul for sin it is a token that Christ and His word have never had any work in you; it is a token, if it be so, that as yet we are God's rebels; and woe is to them for evermore who are in that case, and will remain in it stubbornly. He has wisdom to call in rebels, and power to make them submit themselves to Him. But He has also a rod of iron to bruise them all to pieces, who proudly stand out

[1] Sweeps.   [2] Cast.   [3] Outwardly correct.   [4] Cast.

against Him. Well's[1] them who can give over the old house to Christ in time, who resolve that nature and their sins and their own old hearts will never take them to heaven. Aye, albeit they have some knowledge of God, and be acquainted with divinity that way liberally; yet [they] know that all these are no other but the keeping up of a castle against Christ, and building up forts against Him, and are made to acknowledge that we are ever in a woful estate until the gospel come in with the power thereof, and ding[2] down all these strongholds that are in us; and to account so of ourselves that we know nothing till we know that Christ has thus wrought in us. Mark the speech of a learned man who doubtless had a very great measure of learning, yet he says of himself: "I know nothing, neither do I desire to know anything but the Cross of Christ and Him crucified; whereby I am crucified to the world, and the world is crucified to me." All the natural and civil[3] honesty in the world will not do the turn to bring us to heaven, till we once see that by nature we are in a damnable case, and, in God's mercy that if He please He may cast us away from Him for ever to hell. If we be not made Christ's captives we shall be captives and bondmen in hell for ever. Except we become a fallen down building that Christ may build us up, we shall questionless be miserable for ever.

Now of this point a word or two of some things. First, concerning some ordinary faults that are in some, making them to hold by these towers. Next, we will show unto you some marks of these where these strongholds are casten down. Third, we will show unto you

[1] Good is it for them.   [2] Cast.   [3] External good name.

WORTH AND EXCELLENCE OF THE GOSPEL.

the way that the Lord keeps in casting down these strongholds.

Now for the ordinary faults that are in men in holding up these towers. They are:

First : And there is no man who is born without this : Thir[1] walls of sin and strongholds they are not altogether casten down so long as we are living here. If it had not been so, one who was a chosen vessel of mercy, the Apostle Paul, had never used that speech spoken, Rom. vii. 18 : " I know that in me, that is, in my flesh, dwelleth no good thing." This was spoken by him after his regeneration. And woes them! who acknowledge not that there is some of the old work of nature to the fore[2] in them so long as they are here. Why ? How can this be true ? Because there is nothing that altogether expels original corruption that is in all of us but only glory. I know indeed that true grace sneds[3] away the branches off that tree, and wins in upon the stock also. And grace casts down the walls and the roof of this house. But for the root of this tree, and the ground stones of that house, there is nothing gets that hoked up[4] and takes order with it but only glory. Aye, the children of God, when the house has been casten down by the grace of regeneration, they have been ready many times to build toofalls[5] for themselves again ; as we read of Noah, Lot, David, who fell in heinous sins after they were freely regenerate[d] of God, and the falling into these heinous sins, it was the building of toofalls[5] and little houses of sin and corruption again.

[1] These.   [2] Still remaining.   [3] Lops off.   [4] Dug up.
[5] Small buildings adjoining a large one.

But there be others again, against whom the Lord is shooting the arrows of His gospel, and yet there is not a hole made into their walls by them, nor a branch sned [1] off their tree for all that can be done to them. We may read of the like of these, Acts vii. 51, where the Apostle Stephen is preaching to some Jews, and in the end he says unto them : " Ye stiff-necked and uncircumcised in heart." He shoots strongly at them, but there is not a hole made into their wall for all his shots, but they fortify it so strongly that it shoots back again at himself, who preached to them, and they presently stone him to death for what he did. And so did they to Christ Himself. He shot at them by the preaching of His word and working of miracles among them, to batter down their old walls; but they shot out again at Him and crucified Him. This is a pitiful mark where the gospel is preached to people, and it convinces them of sin, and all that that produces in them is, it raises hatred in their heart against the preachers of the gospel. But there is not one hole made in their old work for all that they can do, but it stands upright unshaken.

But there be a third sort of people whose old walls and strong towers, preachers, by their preaching, make to totter and shake, but incontinently [2] when they find their walls begin to shake, they set to to put props to them to hold them up; such as we read of Cain and of Ahab, they did this—they returned to their former pleasures and their old sins again, albeit their consciences were challenged for the wrongs they had done. And, indeed, these persons are in a very miserable case, who get their sins

[1] Lopped off.   [2] Immediately.

discovered and laid open to them by the preaching of the word, and yet go home presently and away to the tavern, or, when they go out here, fall to their swearing, and so heap up their sins continually and obdures[1] their conscience. These are in a very fearful case if they were sensible of it.

But the best sort of the hearers of God's Word is these who fald[2] themselves willingly to Christ our Lord, when He speaks to them by His Word and preachers, who are content that the Lord ding[3] down their towers of pride, of worldly-mindedness, of filthiness, that He bring to the ground their high castles of self-love, lay under His feet their love to the world, ding[3] down their conceit and love they have to superstition and idolatry. And in the Word of God, ye will find six several marks of such hearers as these, and we shall point at them. For the—

First mark, look Acts ii. 37, where the Apostle Peter preaching to a number of souls who were converted to Christ, it is said, they were pricked at the heart by his preaching. The words he spake to them were such as if a serpent had stinged them, they were so sharp they pierced the heart. When the Word of God begins to batter at the hearts of such, and to discover unto them the great towers of atheism that are in them, the high walls of profanity, the deep waters of bloodshed, the strong desires of filthiness, when they see such a slavery to all sorts of sin, and are borne down under the sense thereof, then the heart of the child of God it is stinged, it is pricked, it is rent, and pierced, as it were by it.

[1] Hardens.   [2] Bow.   [3] Cast.

The *second mark* of such is set down to us Jer. xxxi. 18 : " I have surely heard Ephraim bemoaning himself thus ; Thou hast chastised me, and I was chastised." When once the soul is complaining of sin and is borne down under the sense thereof, and is sending up complaints both to God and to His servants against it, it is a token that these high towers are beginning to fall down, but as long as thou art continuing in thy guiltiness of sin, and are not complaining against it, that is not the gate [1] to heaven. Albeit thou hope for heaven, yet it is not well with thee, it is a token that there are high towers into thy soul, that the work of the old Adam is yet standing fast.

A *third mark* of these who fald [2] willingly to Christ, and stoop to His Word, is this : They begin presently when their sins are discovered to them, to make syllogisms of their own, even as the unjust steward, who was shot out of his service, for faults committed by him. When he was out he begins to think with himself : " What shall I do now ? I cannot beg for shame. None will pity me for work. I cannot work. And I have not of my own to keep me." And so he resolves he will back to his master again. Let him cast him in prison if he will, for then he kens [3] he maun [4] find [5] him. Happy is the soul when it comes to such an estate as that ; it sees it has nothing of its own to live upon, and so resolves it will go back to Christ. Let Him cast it in prison, if He will, it is in a better estate nor [6] it was then. Sich-like [7] [was] the forlorn son when he had

---

[1] Way.   [2] Bow.   [3] Knows.   [4] Must.
[5] Find him the means of living.   [6] Than.   [7] Suchlike.

spent all that he had, and had no more. He resolves that he could not die for hunger in a far country, and, at the first, he thought he could not for shame go home to his father, yet when he saw that no other could be, he resolves that he will do it, go home, and offer his service to his father, for he thought it better to be a living servant nor[1] a dead son.

A *fourth mark* of these who stoop willingly to the gospel is: It raises into them an earnest desire after a Saviour. I will not say but in some this desire of a Saviour is not so throughly[2] spiritual as it should be; yet there is some desire in him after Christ, and he sees that far, that he may not want Him, and he desires that Christ would come in into his soul and ding[3] down all his haughty lusts and imaginations, and wishes that he were in body and soul made captive to Jesus.

A *fifth mark* of these who are obedient to the gospel of Christ is: He looks, evermore looks, to the promises with a long look of love. He never hears such a promise as that Christ Jesus came into the world to save penitent sinners, but he thinks with himself, "O! if I were one of these whom He is come to save. And O! if I could have my heart steeped into these gracious promises."

A *sixth mark* of these who yield unto the gospel is: There is no man who prizes Christ so highly as such a man does. O! he would give heaven, if he had it, to have Christ. There is nothing he would think too dear to be sure of Christ. You know that woman who is spoken off by the Evangelist Luke, who washt Christ's feet with her tears, and wiped them with the hairs of

---

[1] Than.   [2] Thoroughly.   [3] Cast.

her head. If her hair had been heaven and her tears, she would have thought them over [1] ill to wash and to dicht [2] Christ's feet; she had such a high estimation of Him. When once the soul comes to this pass; "O! miserable man that I am, who shall deliver me from this body of death," and knows how far thou art oblist [3] to Christ for delivering you from it, it will make you to put a high price upon Christ, and make you to say, "O! that I could give anything for Him that I might get Him. If heaven and earth were mine I would give them for Him." There will be no pinching then, when the soul is once truly humbled by the word of God. There will be no pinching then what we give for Christ. It would not be then, "Wilt thou give thy sinful lusts for Christ? wilt thou quit thy pride for Him? wilt thou quit the world and the things thereof for Christ?" We will stand upon nothing then, but we will quit all willingly that we may gain Christ. And these are very lively and clear marks of a downcasten and humbled soul by the word of God.

Now for the way and order that the Lord keeps in casting down thir [4] strongholds. The text tells us that nature and the old man it is first cast down, it is all shot to the ground; and so the law it has work first to cast down before the gospel get anything ado to raise up. And this is to let all of us see what estate we are in by nature, even in the state of damnation. I know this casting down of the old work it is rather a preparation for working than any proper work.

But what is the first work that the gospel works upon

[1] Too ill, *i.e.*, not good enough.   [2] Wipe.   [3] Bound.   [4] These.

the soul? There is a question about this among some. Some say that repentance it is the first work; others say that believing it is the first work. But I think there can be no true repentance without some measure of faith preceding. But verily I think there is a work into the soul that goes before either faith or repentance. Our Saviour Christ has a word John vi. 45, 46: "They shall be all taught of God. Every man therefore that hath heard and hath learned of the Father cometh unto Me." So there is a sort of hearkening to the word of the Father, that is in some before it be in others; and while He speaketh of a resurrection in the former verse, it is likely to be meant that that is the first work. Then this is the first work that is wrought into the soul— howbeit the habit of all the rest be wrought then also— even a spiritual hearing and apprehending of Christ by the soul; and then in the next place follows believing. And Christ our Lord He puts a difference between this hearing and faith, for the soul it can never come to Christ to believe in Him until it have once some apprehension of the first work wrought into the soul, until it learn to make a difference between Christ and other men by a spiritual hearing of God's word, till they learn to know His tongue by[1] the tongue of all others. Where before they had but a light conceit of His word, now they esteem greatly of Him and of His word; and having attained to that, then follow believing in Christ and resting upon Him. And then follows the third work, a godly sorrow for sin, which indeed is formally the work of repentance, for whatever sorrow they had

[1] To be different from.

formerly, it was nothing else but a legal downcasting for sin, but no true repentance and godly sorrow till then.

Use. Then there must be a humiliation and downcasting in all who rightly know what Christ is. I would send all of you to this mark to see and try if ye have ever had this humiliation and downcasting, and consequently to try if ye have Christ. Alas! I trow,[1] examine the most part, and speer[2] at them how they gat Christ, and how He came to them, or when were their high castles dung[3] down. I trow[1] they maun[4] be forced to answer that they have either gotten Him in their cradle, while they were young, and kent[5] not of it, or they have gotten Him sometime while they were sleeping; but for grief and sorrow for sin, for one tear for offending God, they never kent[5] nothing of that kind. I would be loath now by saying this to bind sorrow for sin unto tears, for I know there is a true sorrow that is without tears, and I know there is a real sorrow that is beyond tears. But this far, I say, that there maun[6] be a true humiliation for sin one way or other before Christ come into the soul. But alas! I trow[1] all Jobs [Job vi. 4] be dead to have such sorrow, and find such grief for sin as he had. To have the arrows of the Almighty drinking up their spirits as he had, I trow[1] the most part kens[7] not what that means, as to have such a deep sort of offending at themselves for offending of such a good Lord, even, to be angry at the heart at themselves, for offending Him; and when this is, it will drink up the spirits.

[1] Believe. [2] Ask. [3] Cast. [4] Must.
[5] Knew. [6] Must. [7] Knows.

I pray you try whether or no this work be in you, for many will be beguiled at the last day, thinking that they have gotten these things, and when it is tried it will be found to be nothing else but a plain imagination. And God, at the first, sees all such to be but false and counterfeit work; their repentance, their believing, and all that they have; and so that they are not in Christ. And therefore we should never rest until we get sure wit[1] whether we be in Christ or not, if we be passed beyond nature as yet, if we be stepped from the kingdom of darkness to the kingdom of the Son of God. Lord, waken all of us to put ourselves to a trial in this point, and to see that we be not such who profess to be in Christ, and yet in the meantime remaining in nature. Now to this Lord, Father, Son, and Holy Spirit, be all praise and glory for ever. Amen.

[1] Knowledge.

The Apostle's Choice.

No. I.

"But what things were gain to me, those I counted loss for Christ. Yea, doubtless, and I count all things but loss for the excellency of the knowledge of Christ Jesus my Lord."—PHIL. iii. 7, 8.[1]

HERE is no man, Beloved, that has a reasonable soul, but his soul it has a choice, and something that he counts his good and happiness that fain he would be at; and as many as have reason with them, there is some good thing that fain they would have. And the apostle that speaks these words that now are read, he teaches us his choice.

This text it is the apostle's choice of all things that were in the bosom of the created world, of all things that heaven has, of all things that earth can afford. He tells what is the thing among them all he would fainest be at. Comparing himself with the false apostles who lived then, and being disputing against their ceremonies and service-book, and all such idle toys as these, he turns his back upon them; and after he

[1] In the MS. "at the communion at St. Andrews"—no date is given.

has bidden the Philippians beware of these snares, for they were not apostles of Christ's sending, he tells them in the next rowme [1] what it was that he loved best of all other things, when he had compared his choice and their choice together; for that which the false apostles would have been at was circumcision as under the law, albeit the blind people they saw not this—which was something like unto Christ, and an old ordinance of God—Christ before this time had adumbrate [2] these shadows. When the apostle compares the two ways together, and considers that he himself was once upon that course, he counts of himself as one that was a king yesterday, but is become a beggar for all these things the day; he counts himself like a drunken man who thinks, in the time of his drunkenness, that he is very rich, but when he comes to himself and is fresh, he counts all that he conceited of then not to be worth a drink of cold water. When he looks unto Jesus and saw His loveliness, the apostle would say no less to them, comparing himself to them, and his choice with the false apostles whom he is forbidding them to follow, than that they should not open the ear in the least thing to mix the law of Moses and Christ's ordinances together. And to induce them to this, he comes in with his own experience of Christ, what he thought of Him beyond all other things, and says this much in effect, that all the false apostles they tell you of ceremonies and of righteousness by Moses' law. And he tells of himself: "If I would be proud of these things, then I might boast with the best of them of as great privileges

[1] Place.   [2] Given a shadow of Himself.

as they have, whether religious, natural, or civil. But," says he, "when once I gat a sight of lovely Jesus, I abhorred them all, and could not abide them in comparison of the excellence of Christ Jesus my Lord." He says, "I am one who has as meikle [1] to boast of as any of them has. I was circumcised the eighth day as well as they, and so gat the outward seal of the covenant. I am a Jew as well as any of them, and more, I am come of the royal tribe of Benjamin, of whom came the first king that ever was in Israel; for the outward observation of the law I was a Pharisee, and for my zeal I was one who persecuted the gospel and Christ as sore as any did, and for the righteousness which is of the law I was blameless, a civil, honest [2] man. I carried myself so as no man could spit on my cloak." But that is a sweet turn that follows after the reckoning up of these things. He says, "When once I began to know Christ, fra [3] once I gat a sight of that lovely Saviour Christ, then all these things whereof I thought so highly before, and that they were my gain, I thought but basely of them, and counted them but loss. Fra [4] that time they had no rowme [5] in my count book, but I cast all of them away, having once fallen in love with Christ."

So will every soul do who has had another lover nor [6] Christ, and then gets Christ for his lord and love. This is the original work of a soul that has been meikle tane [7] up with civil privileges in the world, or any outward thing, that has thought meikle of court,[8] honour, riches, pleasure, &c. And then he comes to know what

---

[1] Much. [2] An outwardly respectable man. [3] Since. [4] From.
[5] Place. [6] Than. [7] Much taken. [8] Influence, station.

Christ is by experience. Such a one shall be forced to say, "I never knew what happiness and blessedness was till now. All those things wherein I placed happiness before were no other but empty appearances thereof until once I met with the Son of God." That is a real mark of a soul that has indeed met with Christ; it can put all other things down laigh,[1] and the Son of God up high in his own rowme.[2] And it must be so with them who have gotten a sight of Christ, and knows what He is. Bairns they cannot compare youth with old age, because they have never yet known what old age is. But those who are come to old age, they can compare the one with the other, and having tried both, and known what youth is —not other but daffing,[3] and hunting after nutshells, in respect of old age. There are none of those who are in glory but they know well enough what it was to be in the estate of sin, and what lying happiness it is that is promised to sinners here. They know well enough what is the ill of night drinking, and what ill is in that to deny a covenant and to quit Christ; they know what it is to sell an exceeding weight of great glory for this present world. Even so the children of God, who are fallen in love with the Son of God, they can speak more of the vanity of all things that are hereaway, and of the excellence of Jesus, than all the world beside can do.

Now for the particulars contained in the words. The apostle tells us here what it was that was the wail[4] of his wit, and ye know well enough what he did, and what he made his choice, for he was no fool; and he says that all the fair satins, and pasments,[5] and gold-lace, that he

---

[1] Low.   [2] Place.   [3] Folly.   [4] Choice.
[5] Strips of lace or silk sewed on clothes as ornaments.

had before he came to Christ, when he came to Christ he counted them all to be beggar's rags, and that is in the seventh verse, "*But what things were gain to me, these I counted loss for Christ;*" and then in the eighth verse he confirms this yet more, for it might [have] been objected: " What, Paul, count ye nothing of circumcision, esteem ye so little of that to be a Jew, to be of the royal tribe of Benjamin, for your profession to be a Pharisee, to have such zeal, to be blameless touching the outward righteousness of the law?" "No," says he, "I rue[1] nothing of what I have said, '*Yea, doubtless I count all things but loss for the excellency of the knowledge of Christ Jesus my Lord, for whom I have suffered the loss of all things, and do count them but dung that I may win Christ.*'" And then in the next verse follows his wish what it is that he desires. And first what it is that he would not have. He says that he would not for the world " be found in his own righteousness, which is by the law." In that righteousness whereof the false apostles teach, in that righteousness that nature has, for as glorious like as it seemed to them. And then he tells what it is that he would have. "*That he might have the righteousness which is by the faith of Christ,*" even to be found in that righteousness which is of God by faith. " That is," says he, "the main thing that I would be in hands with."

First : Look for the dependence of thir words.[2] How is it that the apostle compares himself with thir[3] false teachers, who follow the now dead ceremonies of Moses' law ? He says, " Let them who know no better follow these dead ceremonies and services, but for me, I have

---

[1] Repent. [2] Look at the connection of these words. [3] These.

changed all these things now. I have quit them all, and tane¹ me only to Christ."

Then we may see that there is a far difference between a minister who is fairly called of Christ under the New Testament, and those false teachers who have their face towards Rome, or any other false religion that leads away from Christ. All these who are false teachers, and lead away from Christ, they would evermore be at nignayes² and dead ceremonies in the service and worship they profess. But the apostle would say here, and all true pastors with him, "Let the Pharisees and those who know no better, go on with their dead ceremonies and their service-book, but for me, God send me Christ and His righteousness, and if I get Christ and His righteousness to be mine, then adieu to them and all their ceremonies, and to their righteousness by the law, and all these things."

This is a note of the false kirk and of the false apostles; they would evermore be at ceremonies. The religion they would be at is a religion that stands all in fair shows, a religion for Kirk and market. But the religion which is the way to heaven, and the true Kirk, and [which] Christ's ministers would be at, is a religion that is spirit and life, a religion that specially is inward more nor³ outward. [In] Isaiah i. 13 there is a number there who were for the new moons, holidays, multitudes of sacrifices, meikle⁴ fat of lambs and rams. But the Lord and His prophet they are for this (Isa. i. 16): "Wash you, make you clean; put away the ill of your doings from before mine eyes; cease to do evil, learn to do

¹ Taken.   ² Unnecessary ornament, gimcracks.   ³ Than.   ⁴ Much.

well." And Micah vi. 6, there are some there for offering thousands of rams and ten thousands of rivers of oil, for giving their firstborn for their transgression; but the Lord tells what it is that He seeks, "To do justice, to love mercy, and to walk humbly with thy God." And Matt. xv., there is the like dispute between the scribes and Pharisees and Christ. The scribes and Pharisees they were all for religious ceremonies, as they called them, such as eating of meat with unwashen hands, vessels, &c. But Christ and His disciples they were more for keeping the commandments of God than for observing the traditions of men.

Use: Learn to make a difference rightly of the two parts of the controversy that is between the prelates and the land. What is the quarrel that the prelates and their adherents have at Scotland this day? It is not because we will not follow the Bible and God's ordinances in His worship; but their quarrel at us is, because we will not follow a service-book and ceremonies, and because we will not have a creature of their upsetting, a prelate, to be head of the Church. And this is our comfort that the controversy stands thus, that they are not coming against us for not following the Bible and the revealed will of God in His Word, for we are willing that matters shall be judged thereby both in Assemblies and Parliaments. And, blessed be God! that the matter stands so, that it is not religion that they are pursuing us for, but something that is like religion, and we stand for the defence of the true religion. And this also serves to put a difference between an honest person and those who come with an honest and prepared heart to the communion, and those who have no other motive to induce them to it but for the fashion. Those who come to the communion because they would be illspoken of if they did otherways. O! but that be a naughty end, and such will not come speed. There is a far [1] difference between these and such as come here, and care for nothing else, if so be that they can meet with Christ Himself, and care not what all the men in the world say of them. O! that this were our end and errand this day. And I lay this upon your conscience to try yourself hereby whether your end in coming here this day be to get Christ or not.

The apostle goes on and says, "*What things were gain to me those I counted loss for Christ.*" Then this tells us that the apostle he had what was gain to him, as well as the false apostles had. He had whereof to boast as well as they. "Are they apostles? so am I. Are they circumcised? so am I." The apostle says by this, "I can ride up with the best of them and something more, if they come to a boasting for things of that kind." Compare the life of the believer and the life of the natural man together, and let the natural man lay counts and figures of his state here and multiply them until doomsday. We that are believers, we have all that the natural man has, and something more. And there be four things wherein believers are beyond all the natural men in the world.

First: The wicked have this world, and they have it as the men of this world. They bruick [2] it as "the men of this earth," as it is Psa. x. 18. And the world it is

---

[1] Great.   [2] Enjoy.

their patrimony and hire. The believers have the world also, but in another manner than they have, for we have it only as our inns, to stay in while we are here, and not as our patrimony and hire. There is none of us who lies out of the world more than they do, but the world is only our moveables, while it is their patrimony, and their portion that is ordained for them. That is the difference betwixt the heir and him who is only a servant, for the son has always the estate prepared for him, but the servant he gets no more than his penny fee,[1] and when all is done he is put to the door. Whatever the natural men in the world have we have it also, but we have it after a surer way than they have it. And this should teach us to use this present world as though we used it not, seeing it is not our heritage but only our moveables.

Second: For natural and worldly men, the sun it shines upon them by day and the moon by night, the rain it falls upon the just and unjust; but we have the Sun of Righteousness to shine upon us, which they have not, and that is better nor [2] all other things that are in the world. They have the sun and the moon and these other profits and pleasures in the world to laugh upon them; but we have Him who made all things and can undo them when He will, to laugh upon us, and that is much better.

Third: Natural men they have the toom,[3] empty, and frothy creature; but we have the blessing with these things. They have bread for their use; but we have the staff of bread, which is better. And—

[1] His wages paid in money.　　[2] Than.　　[3] Empty.

Lastly: and I make an objection of it—they have ofttimes a fairer wind in their sails nor [1] we have here; but yet they have not law-burrows [2] of it that it shall be always so. They have more of court and pleasure, profit and ease, more than we have while we are here—and it is true that we have the cross more than they ofttimes; but they are not sure that it shall continue so. But albeit they have these things, and we want them, yet we have that which is spoken of Rom. viii. 37 : " We are more than conquerors through Him that loved us." They have court and kings upon their side, and we have them not; yet this is enough against them all, that we have Him upon our side who to this hour never tint [3] a battle, whatever party He had against Him. They have Spain and antichrist and the powers of the world with them, yet God be thanked that we have Him for us who guides all these at His pleasure. We have Him on our side who gets that stately style ascribed to Him, Rev. i. 5: " The Prince of the kings of the earth," so that all others, were they never so great, all of them are under Him. And so we may see they have no reason to tire who have sided themselves in a covenant with the Son of God, for before all be said that is to be said, and before the field be done, we shall be forced to say that we have gotten the highest of the brae above our enemies, and that the shadow of the Sun of Righteousness has looked upon us.

" *These things that were gain to me I counted them loss for Christ.*" Here is a strange change, that these things that before were gain are now become loss to the apostle;

[1] Than. [2] Legal security. [3] Lost.

and yet it is a change incident to all those who are in Paul's case; and the reason of it is, because whoever they be who are not in Christ they see not things as they are indeed, but he looks upon them so as they seem to his sophistic reason; but when any comes to Christ and gets His light they will be forced to say, "The thing that before I thought as my very heart or the apple of my eye, whereof I thought quit me of the one as soon quit me of the other, yet when once I came to Christ and gat a sight of Him, I counted nothing at all of these."

The *doctrine* is clear. A man who once comes truly to Christ changes his mind, his estimative [1] faculty is altogether changed. Moses, he lived forty years at Pharaoh's court in Egypt, and there is no question but at that time he thought meikle [2] of it to be such a great courtier in such a great king's court. But when once he gat faith to behold Christ and the recompense of reward, he had another thought and estimation of things than before. He esteemed Christ's worst things better than the things that were in Egypt; and so do all those who are indeed converted unto Christ. You count meikle of gold now, but if once you knew what Christ is, you would count it nothing in comparison of Him. If you had once your cheek laid to His sweet cheek, and had one blink of that glorious and beautiful face of His, ye shall then change all your opinions and thoughts that now you have, and you shall cry shame upon all the painted idols in the world, in comparison with fair Jesus, when once you have gotten a sight of the Son of God; and indeed it must be so. This says that natural men

---

[1] Judicial. [2] Much.

they have false counters wherewith they lay their accompts [1]—the natural man has no good arithmetic. See you not what is counted of Christ by the world. Acts iv. 11: "This the stone which was set at nought by you builders." Men use to write ciphers for nothing, and so they put Christ for a cipher and counted Him nothing. But counted they so of themselves even in slaying of the Lord of glory? No. They counted themselves wise, for they say, "If we receive this man, the Romans will come upon us and take our nation from us." And the woman of Samaria when He came first to the well, and tells what He could do, she says, "Art Thou greater than our father Jacob who digged the well?" And where laid she Christ in the meantime? She thought Him not so much worth as a drink of cold water. This is the estimation the world has of Christ. And the Papists they have this estimation of Christ; they think themselves and the fathers are worth something, but for Christ and His truth they think it not worth a drink of water to them.

Now where fra [2] comes this, that men in the world count so little of Christ?

Answer: Because there is something broken in them that makes five seem to be seven; there is something wrong in them that makes gold seem to be God. That blind mind that thou hast naturally will never let you see Christ to be Christ. But once come to Christ Himself, and then ye will be put from such thoughts. He will give unto you another sight, that old sight will be put out of the office.

[1] Accounts.   [2] From.

And there is another reason for this. The apostle says of himself (1 Cor. xiii. 11): "While I was a child I spake as a child," &c. A man, while he is in nature, is no other but a plain bairn; but when once he comes to Christ he becomes an old man, and so his thoughts change. You know what a man of thritty[1] years will think of the nignayes[2] and the clay houses that he was wont to build when he was a bairn. The timber of them would be of loch-reeds, and the theiking[3] of it of leaves of trees, and all these things that they thought meikle of when they were bairns when they hear of them will laugh at themselves, and count nothing of them. Even so is it with a man that is come to Christ, when he is laying his counts he lays down the world and all that is in it for a cipher, and lays down counters for Christ.

A third reason is: A man who is come to Christ he is a man risen from the dead; and what thoughts think you will you have of all things that are here when you see all that is here set on fire together? What will you think of honours, riches, pleasures, &c., when you see the Son of God set down upon a white throne to judge the world, and with your eyes you see all these things consumed and wasted? Will not a man say then that he has been nothing but a fool that set set his heart upon these things that perish so suddenly?

Use First: This serves to let these see who are truly and indeed converted to Christ the first thing that ever they get. See and try if you would know this. If ever you have changed your minds as yet; for that is certain that these whose minds and estimatures are nothing

---

[1] Thirty. [2] Gimcracks. [3] Thatching.

changed, they are never come to Christ yet. Ephraim is brought in saying, "What have I to do any more with idols?" Fra[1] once Israel returns to the Lord, they will have no more to do with idols, nor anything that may provoke Him. If you love the world, your night drinking, your idols of profit, pleasure, ease as well as well as ever ye did, and be raxing[2] your arms after these things, until your sinews be like for to break to compass them about, say what you will, and profess what you will, you have gotten no new thing as yet, ye are not come in grips[3] with Christ, for you lay down Christ and heaven and glory for a cipher, and your court, favour, profit, pleasure, &c., for all things. O! but there be many false arithmeticians in the world, who in laying their compts[4] lay down the world for thousands, but when they come to lay Christ, they lay Him down for a cipher or for a penny. But stay till you begin to count over again, and then you shall be forced to say that you laid a fool's count, that thought so meikle of a clayey world that evanishes, and thought so little of Him that made the world and all things therein and endures for ever.

Use Second: We see that men they must either change their thoughts, or it will be very ill with them in the end. They must change. Their thoughts as well as their practices must be changed. We must be cast into a new mould, otherways we are lost and tint[5] souls. If thou be in Christ thou lookest to pleasant things in the world, as a stranger does to fair meadows, orchards, palaces, coaches, courts, and pleasant countries until he

[1] From. [2] Stretching out. [3] Close dealing. [4] Accounts. [5] Perishing.

is far afield. He looks to all these things with a sigh, if he love home well, and says: "He had rather be at home in his own country nor [1] have them all." Such is the estimation that those who are in Christ have of the things of the world. He can let out a hearty laughter at all things that are in it; and count nothing of them all, to be at home, in glory with Christ, and with His Father.

"*I count all things loss for Christ.*" Was that a loss to be circumcised, to be of the people of Israel, to be descended of the royal tribe of Benjamin, and to be blameless for [2] the outward things of the law? The apostle tells us by this, that whatever comes betwixt a man and Christ to keep him from a right estimation of Christ, albeit all the brave pasments [3] and gold fuilzie [4] in the world were upon it, it is no other but plain nothing, and we should count so of it. If anything come between me and Christ, whatever it be, away with it. The apostle would say, "The time was when I counted as meikle of these things as they did, but when once I met with Christ, and saw things with daylight"—for the sinner and the man who are in nature see all things with moonlight—then he says of all these things, "I counted them all loss that I might gain Christ" (Matt. xvi. 26). There is a man pre-supponed there to have gained the whole world; and who is there in the world that has gained, if that man has not gained that has gained the whole world? But it is said of such a man, albeit he should gain—as who yet ever gained it all—yet if in gaining

---

[1] Than. [2] With respect to. [3] Strips of lace or silk sewed on clothes. [4] Gold-leaf. French, *feuille*; Latin, *folium*.

thereof he lose his own soul, he is a loser when all is done (Rom. x. 3). It is said that the Jews which followed after the law of righteousness they attained not unto it, and so they lost by following thereof, for they tint¹ the righteousness of Christ. Whoever follows after something which seems to be theirs, and that they would be at, and then tines² Christ by following thereof, such men are losers, get they that which they follow, or get they it not. The works that Papists do to merit by them, they are their loss instead of profit, for they come between them and Christ. Whatever it be, court,³ honour, or pleasure, or anything else that thou followest, if it come between thee and Christ, thou art a loser in seeking of it. Aye, if it were in seeking that which is spoken of Prov. i. 13, "All precious substance," or seeking that which is spoken of Prov. vii. 18, "To fill thyself with love," yet if it come between you and Christ it is loss. And there is good reason it should be so. What is it which makes a man lose in the world? Is it that which is taken out of his rent for a year? Albeit, something be tane⁴ away that way, that is not meikle; but if anything be tane⁴ away from a man's stock that is it which makes loss. So whatever takes away any of Christ from us, who is our stock, that is loss indeed, and may be justly called loss. And God knows there be many who lose this way. There be many who for winning of court, honour, favour of kings, profit, pleasure, they care not to sell their covenant, and Christ, and His Kirk. And, alas! what winning is there when all is done. God knows there is just nothing. They use to

¹ Lost.   ² Loses.   ³ Influence.   ⁴ Taken.

say of merchants, they are rich. But another who knows better will say, Stay till all his counts be fitted,[1] and all his creditors paid, and then you will know whether he be rich or poor. It is even just so here. To get a higher style in the world, to quit thy covenant with God, what winning is there when sinners shall once become sin-sick, and their compts[2] begin to be laid, and they must pay again, all the pleasures that they have gotten that way, and he must vomit it all up again? As it is Job xx. 15, and they will see they are losers. You think you are well set up now, if you get riches and honours and pleasures; but stay till the Lord come, and say, "Pay me for all the court, honour, pleasure, &c., that ever you gat;" and there will be a great poverty soon then. Stay till Christ come to crave a count of men and women, how they have spent their talents, and they shall be seen to be very poor. I speak only of one place (Rev. vi. 15) for clearing of this point—Kings and great men, rich men, chief captains, and mighty men, they are cited there before the Son of God. And what are their great places and their great wages that they gat worth to them then? They cry out, "Mountains and rocks fall on us, and hide us from the face of the Lamb that sits on the throne, and from His wrath, for the day of His wrath is come, and who shall be able to lose [stand?]." So that there is no loss like unto this loss, for me to lose my country, wife, bairns, &c. So did David these things, and the children of God may lose them. But to lose the precious soul, woe to thee for evermore who does this, for thy loss is never kent[3] till

[1] Settled.   [2] Accounts.   [3] Known.

then. Of all the losses in the world that is the most fearful to lose Christ, and so to lose thy own soul.

What is the other part of the apostle's choice, or that which he would be in hands with? "*For the superexcellent knowledge of Christ Jesus my Lord.*"

Why says he not for Christ Himself rather than for the superexcellent knowledge of Christ? Christ is one thing, and the superexcellent knowledge of Christ another, and yet in substance both of them are one. There is a great question anent this. What it is that is the greatest happiness of the glorified in heaven, and what it is that is the main happiness of those who are journeyers towards this kingdom? But the happiness both of the one and the other stands in this superexcellent knowledge of Christ. There were very grave and learned men who lived at the time when Paul lived, for it is probable that there went letters between Paul and Seneca, who was a very learned man, and that they conversed one with another. But what counts the apostle to be his superlative knowledge? Even this, to trust and believe in a Saviour slain and despised by the world. There was no wisdom in his accompt[1] like the knowledge of this. And look to this superexcellent knowledge of Christ in three things, and you shall find it to be so.

First: All the wisdom natural men can speak with will never make the thing they speak of go into the heart. All that the moralists in the world can speak of heaven or of hell, all that they can speak of the deformity of vice, and of the beauty and comeliness of

[1] Account.

virtue, can never make it go into the hearts of men and women. But Christ, when He speaks in the gospel of these things, He can speak into the heart, and speaks daily to the hearts of many, and whoever gets a sight of Christ Himself in the gospel, O! so fair, so excellent as the knowledge of Him will be to them. All the knowledge of all the sovereigns in the world will be nothing to them.

Second: The gospel is superexcellent in the knowledge thereof. Is there no further knowledge of Christ to be had there as Mary's son, a carpenter's son? Yes, He is to be seen there as a plant of renown, as Ezekiel calls Him; as the branch of righteousness as Zachariah calls Him; and as Isaiah says, He is to be seen there as wonderful in His works. There He is miraculous. In His death He is to be seen as life, so that He is a wonder to all to think upon.

Third: Look into Christ's offer in the gospel, and that is also wonderful, and His knowledge is superexcellent in that: To offer a kingdom to all His followers. How long shall it endure? For an hundred thousand years? Aye. It endures for evermore. It lasts for all eternity. Let Christ make an offer of that when it is racked on God's wheel, it would give meikle at such a time to have an interpreter to repeat its own case to it, meikle more if Christ should make this offer to it. Ye shall find also that in this offer there is peace to a troubled conscience, ease to a troubled mind. To offer a kingdom, thus how great a matter is it? Who is there can offer an eternal kingdom but only He? A soul may dream of a kingdom, but none can speak it into the conscience but He who can say, "Come and see." Come therefore to this sacrament with disposed hearts, and set to your nose to the sweet smell of the Son of God, bend your ears to hearken to the offers, and ye shall see and hear super-excellent knowledge there.

The Apostle's Choice.

No. II.

" The knowledge of Christ Jesus my Lord: for whom I have suffered the loss of all things, and do count them but dung, that I may win Christ."—PHILIPPIANS iii. 8.[1]

OW like, beloved in our Lord, that the apostle is meeting with a doubt here, in the eighth verse of this chapter, which might seem to rise from that which he has said in the seventh verse thereof. And does the apostle count all his former gain to be loss for the excellency of the knowledge of Christ Jesus? even all these fair and great privileges that are in so great request among men, and the men who were of his profession they thought no little thing of thir[2] privileges, to be of the seed of Israel, an Hebrew of the Hebrews, come of the royal and kingly tribe, to be for profession a Pharisee, for zeal a persecutor of the Church, touching the righteousness that is of the law blameless. It might have been said to Paul, " Paul, think ye nothing of all these?" The apostle answers to these, ver. 8, and says, "I will eat nothing in of that which I have said, but confirms

[1] In MS., "Afternoon for thanksgiving."   [2] These.

it." "Yea, doubtless, and I count all things but loss for the excellency of the knowledge of Christ Jesus my Lord. Yea, also, I count them to be but dung. I count them not worthy the least of my love to take any of it from Him."

The *first* thing we learn here is, Labour once to win in a way of commendation of Christ, and then His praise shall grow among your hands. Speak once good of Christ into your heart, and ye will not win soon off that text again. The more that you think of Christ, the more will that matter grow among your hands. The more you enter upon thinking of Christ's fulness, the more will you love it. Paul, the longer he speaks of Christ, the higher he grows in estimation of Him, for he said before, "I count all things loss for Christ," but now, "I count them dung for Him, that I may gain Him." Learn to be content to lose all things that ye may get Christ, and if you do so, indeed, you may be sure you shall get Him. You will see this to be true also Cant. v. When there is a question moved to the Church, the spouse of Christ, "What is her beloved," say they, "more than another beloved?" Compare verse sixth with the sixteenth, and ye will see the answer to be clearly this way. In verse sixth, she answers: "My beloved is white and ruddy, the chiefest among ten thousand, His head is as the most fine gold, His locks are bushy and black like a raven, His eyes are as the eyes of doves, His cheeks are as a bed of spices," &c. And then, having described Him in all His parts in the sixteenth verse, she says of Him: "He is altogether lovely," and, "therefore wonder not," would she say,

25

"that I make so meikle¹ din for my beloved, for there is nothing in Him, but that which is most desired." And Psa. lxxiii. 24: "Thou wilt guide me with Thy counsel, and afterwards receive me to glory." But he goes higher in the next verse: "Whom have I in heaven but Thee, and I desire none in earth beside Thee;" and so still ascends. Isa. xl. 7, the prophet, speaking of the Lord's greatness and majesty, says, "All nations before Him are as nothing, and they are counted unto Him to be less than nothing and vanity." So that whoever they be who take themselves to speak of God, or of Christ, in their excellency and glory, if they think rightly of it, they will be dipped over head and ears in it. No created paper and ink are able to describe the Lord as He is. Aye, His word tells not all to us what He is. It is not possible for us to get a copy of Him. Set a thousand worlds of poets to make songs of Christ they could not say the thousandth part of the thing that is true of Him.

Use First: This serves to teach all the ministers of Christ this common place of preaching. Above all things learn this, to put our Lord Jesus high up above all, that so He may be a world's wonder to men and angels: for to speak rawly² and caldriffly³ of Christ, and not to grow continually in the praises of His excellence, is one of the faults of the friends of the Bridegroom.

Use Second: If there be so meikle¹ to be spoken of Him, while we are here, O then, when we come to our Father's house, and shall see Him as He is, face to face, what large thoughts shall there be of Him then, when

---

¹ Much.   ² Unpreparedly.   ³ Indifferently.

the thoughts that are of Him in the kingdom of grace are so great! What shall these thoughts be of Him that shall be in the kingdom of glory? What marvel is it that that song of His praises lasts for ever and ever, that they never weary who sing this song, for He will byde[1] all the songs of praise of the glorified. [Why] but we to whom Christ has given pawns[2] this day that He was slain for our sins, what should we do to Him again, but lift Him up high in our praises and put Christ high in His rowme[3], and everything under Him in their rowme?[3]

Third use: If it be so that our Lord is so high that He can never be enough praised, why is there so meikle din this day in Scotland for adhering to a covenant and for quitting of a covenant? No, the din[4] is not for a covenant or a ceremony, or such a thing is not the main thing that is in controversy in Scotland this day. But whether Christ should be only King and Priest unto His own Kirk to give out laws, or if men should rule there as they please. And this should put all Scotland and all the world to it to hazard for such a glorious Lord as Christ is.

Before the apostle go from this he has a word that is worthy to be observed before we leave it, "*Christ Jesus my Lord.*" When the apostle is speaking of Christ, he must have a kiss of Him to himself by the way, he must of necessity speak something to let his hearers know what he thought of Christ. To teach us this far that whenever we speak of Christ, whenever we preach of Him, or

---

[1] All their songs of praise will not surpass what He is.
[2] Pledges. [3] Place. [4] Noise of battle.

whenever we hear of Him, to strive evermore to apply Him, and to take Him home to ourselves. There be three good reasons of this, why both the apostle and all others with him, they should labour to apply Christ unto themselves when He comes near unto them any way.

First: Because to speak or hear of His name and not to smell of Him thereafter, it is a very great miss when Christ speaks to us and comes to offer Himself to you in the sacrament. When Christ goes away, and has not met with you and thou hast not gotten a kiss of Him, woe! to that person whoever they be, woe! to that soul to whom Christ offers Himself, and they notwithstanding get no good of Him. Christ comes to thy elbows, thy eyes, and thy ears, and all the parts of thy body, and soul; and yet, between you and God,[1] if thou can say, thou has met with Him to day, and woe to them that cannot say it. And this apostle he has reason to speak of Christ, for he knows His worth and excellency (Col. i.), he is speaking a word of Christ there, and having spoken a word for Him, he digresses a little from his text, that he may speak more of Christ (v. 15), "Who is the image of the invisible God, the first-born of every creature; for by Him were all things created that are in heaven, and that are in the earth, visible and invisible," &c. It is even with all of them that has a right estimation of Christ as with them that go unto their coffer and see gold lying there and stay a while tirling[2] it over, they have such pleasure in it. So is it with all those who get a glance of Christ in the Word or the sacraments.

[1] Would that. [2] Turning.

Second: Those who have gotten a sight of Him, they ought to stand still and look more upon Him, for He is well worth looking on. And we who are ministers, if we carry Christ to others, and be gathering in the Lord's bride to Him, should not we ourselves be the better and get our drink silver [1] at the least? Woe! to them that preach Christ to others, whatever they be, and cannot say, "My Lord Jesus Christ."

A Third reason for this is, because wherever Christ is rightly and kindly spoken of, He evermore leaves tokens that He has been there, He leaves some drops of myrrh behind Him, and that makes them speak more to His commendation.

Use: All these who have heard of Christ this day, and have been partaker of Him in the sacrament, let them take something of Christ home with them—sick folk, take home physic with you; blind folk, take home eyes with you; lame folk, take home feet and hands with you; ignorants, take home knowledge with you, for Christ is all in all, and this is indeed to eat and to drink worthily.

Another word. Let us mark of this that the apostle says, "*Christ Jesus my Lord.*" This is a homely word that He speaks, even as if there had been no moe [2] in heaven or in earth who had right to Him. It might have been said to Paul, Is Christ yours more than He is the world's? Yes; but He is common to all believers. Christ is like a ship that is divided among so many owners. The ship belongs to every one of them. Even so David, and Thomas, and His apostles, and all believers have their

---

[1] *I.e.*, our perquisites.   [2] More.

own property in Christ. And yet, albeit He be a common Saviour to all believers, yet every believer in particular may make Christ his treasure and his portion, and this should hearten[1] us to go in application of Christ to ourselves as ours, and never to rest till we come to that. There is no common thing in the world like unto Christ, for He is free to all believers, even all that are in Him. The saints they have a free heritage that no man has anything to say against it. Where was he that could ever say : " The sun, the moon, the earth were his property " ? These things are common to all, and every one is like to scart[2] out other's eyes for them ; but having once gotten Christ by faith in thy soul, thou may say of Him, " My Lord and my God ; " and O ! but thou art rich for evermore who can say this far indeed, and art sure of it.

The apostle he goes on and says : *"I have suffered the loss of all things, and do count them but dung, that I may win Christ."* The word in the original is, "I have made shipwreck of all things." He says, " I am content to cast away all the gold pasments, all the satins, all the velvets that I had being a Pharisee, and let them tine[3] for Christ. I am content to quit them all, and to let them all go to nothing, to that end that I may make Christ my gain." And the apostle he speaks not here of himself only as an apostle, but he speaks of himself as a believer, and speaks after that manner. Tine[4] what he will, he shall aye keep Christ to the fore.[5] And indeed He is well worthy of His rowme,[6] and

---

[1] Encourage.   [2] Scratch.   [3] Perish.   [4] Lose.
[5] Before him, or in his possession.   [6] Place.

woe! is [to] them, and they shall say it one day, Woe! is [to] them for evermore, who cast Christ overboard that they may keep Christ and honour and the world. And there are four sorts of persons who wrong Christ this way.

First: There are some who have even heavy a loadening[1] in already, and so cast Christ overboard, because Christ and that loadening[1] which they have already, cannot agree, and before they quit their other loadening they will quit Christ—1 Tim. vi. 9: "They who will be rich fall into divers temptations and snares, and into many hurtful and foolish lusts, which draw men into destruction and perdition." It is not said that they are rich, but they who will be rich. They resolve that they will take in a burden of the world and will sail to heaven with [it]. Nay two ills light upon such.

First: The world and Christ they will never agree together. Your gain, your ease, your credit, your riches, &c., they may well agree with Christ as long as the weather is fair and both go one gate.[2] But stay till the wind change, and it come to that whether you will quit your credit, your gain, your pleasures, &c., or Christ and religion, and it will be seen then, that such take them to the world, and to things thereof, and are content that Christ and religion and a covenant and conscience be all casten overboard. Let them sink or swim rather ere they quit their temporal peace, or ease, or gain. And O! but that be a miserable change.

Again: Where the love of the world and the things

[1] Load.   [2] Way.

thereof carry over [1] high a sail, and are proud of them, He denies to give them grace, for He resists the proud. They content themselves with the outside of religion, and labour not for the power thereof. Alas! Is this holiness enough? to come to the communion, to sit reverently in the kirk, and have no more but that? I grant it is not ill indeed. But if thou hast no more of religion but that, it will be a sail to blow full of wind and blow you into the midst of the sea and drown you. For the Lord He shall seek an account of you for all the occasions of the Word and Sacraments and other exercises of that kind that ye have been at albeit the most part see not this, and shall ask of them, how they have profited by every one of these occasions? and He shall try and search them whether they came in sincerity to seek the Lord in all these exercises, or if their errand was to seek any other thing.

There is a thrid [2] sort of persons that are sailing, but they are sailing close under the water; and these are they who know that they do wrong, and yet notwithstanding, they will go on in that same ill course; and, indeed, if there be a fearful case of impenitence in the world, this is most fearful, to add drunkenness to thrist,[3] and to walk on into the imaginations of their own heart, saying, they shall have peace in so doing. The Lord will not spare such, but the anger of the Lord and His jealousy shall smoke against them. And—

Lastly: There be some that this cancer and ill are into the spirit; they pre-suppone that they have faith, and yet it is but a rotten faith. Look to the faith of many,

[1] Too. [2] Third. [3] Thirst.

and it will be found to be thus with them. O woe! to you for evermore, who are beguiled in a matter of such consequence as this. Every man trows[1] that his profession and his grace are good enough, that there is neither crack nor flaw into it, and yet many are deceived. Never man suspected his own gold but it is good enough, and yet many have but brass instead of it. It were meikle[2] better for us in time to try whether we be in the faith or not, than thus to be deceived in a matter of so great importance, for woe! to them for evermore who beguile themselves in such a matter as this, that when they go at that last day to open up their profession, to find out their faith and their grace, and that they find nothing there, but only a show, and a fair glori-flenkun[3]—think you not but this will be a miserable mistake to many? Aye! that it will; and so learn to beware of it.

"*All things.*" What should Paul cast this away and make shipwreck of it, to be of Israel, to be come of the tribe of Benjamin, to be as touching the law a Pharisee, blameless before all men? *Answer:* Yes; the world and all that is in it is to be casten away, in three cases.

First: The world is to be casten away in so far as it is an idol, and when it will be in Christ's place. In that case cast overboard with it.

Second: If the world will have the yolk of your love, and the heart of it, then the world is not worth the keeping. When the apostle looked upon all other things into the world that he loved, and laid them into the

---

[1] Believes.　　[2] Much.
[3] Perhaps for *flichen*, anything very small—a snowflake.

balance, and laid Christ His alone [1] in the other balance, he found Him to be weightier than all, that He far overvalues them all, and sees that he has been no other but a befooled man in setting his heart upon them so long, and so is content to quit them all for gaining Christ.

Third: We must quit the world and the things thereof. If there come a competition between Christ and them, that we must either quit the one or the other, as sometimes there will come terms of competition this way,[2] *in foro contradictorio* as they say—the matter will be soon decided by one who looks to heaven and to glory that is to be had by adhering to the Son of God, and then looks to the hundreds of all other things. They will say, "To hell with all other things that would hinder me from bruicking[3] the Son of God." "Court, go thy way, and take thy leave, and all the pleasures thereof," Daniel says, "and welcome death, and to be all torn with wild beasts rather ere I quit to speak with God in prayer." "I here write a free resignation of the world and all things therein, rather ere I want a communion that way with heaven. This seems to be a fair spoken word, to quit all things in the world for a communion with Christ. And yet there be four things in Christ that will say that, without exception, all other things should be quit for Him.

First: Look what Christ Himself is—He is all love. He is all essential love, for if the creatures have any good thing in them to draw the heart after them, they have it only from Christ.

---

[1] By himself.
[2] In the market where there are competing sellers, or at the bar where there are opposing advocates.   [3] Enjoying.

Second: See what the Scripture says of the loss of heaven and the loss of other things. Matt. x. 39: "He that findeth his life shall lose it;" Matt. xiii. 46: "This is the pearl hid, which when a man had found, he went and sold all that he had and bought it." What will buy heaven? If all the angels in heaven were sold, what would they do to the buying of heaven? Ay! albeit there were as many of them as there have fallen drops of rain since the world began, and a thousand times more, they were not all able to buy it. So that there is no loss comparable to the loss of heaven. What reck [1] of the loss of gear, wife, children, country, &c., if thou keep heaven and keep Christ. Thou may then look over thy shoulder and laugh at them, and look to Him who can carry you through the sea dry shod, and will bear you through all difficulties, and at last set you in glory.

The third consideration to make us quit the world for Christ, is in consideration how the Scripture sets Christ above all things both as God and man. First as God (Isa. xl. 18) He is set alone: "To whom will ye liken God? or what likeness will ye compare with Him?" And then as man, He is always alone also both as king, priest, and prophet—Psa. lxxii.: Kings they are put beneath Christ, for they must all fall down before Him. All kings think it an honour to hold Christ's stirrup and acknowledge that to be true which is written of Him— Rev. xix. 16: "King of kings and Lord of lords." There was never another gat that style but Himself; and Heb. x. 12: All priests are put under Him and prophets also, for Moses is put down and Christ is put

---

[1] Care for.

up. And the angels, who are far above any creature, they are all of them put down and Christ is put up. And then, in His power, He passes all other kings. Who is there that has such a cloak to put about him as glory? and who has such chariots at their command as He has? who can say that word which He says, Isa. l.: "I, at My rebuke, dry up the sea; I make the rivers a wilderness: their fish stinketh; . . . I clothe the heavens with darkness, and I make sackcloth their covering?" Will ye tell me where dwells that king that can draw a web of darkness from the east to the west, so that at midday nothing shall be seen if he please? Where is that king that can dry up the Red Sea at his pleasure? Kings are only kings on land, but they cannot command the sea. They have not the chair which is spoken of Psa. xxix.: "The Lord has His chair in the seas." That is the Lord's royal chair that belongs to Him only. The Lord He is God of the sea and of the land also, and is another manner of monarch in battle nor [1] poor silly [2] bits of clay are.

And then the last consideration is that there is no benefit of God good unless we get Christ with it.

Let our *use* of all this be to stir up all these who spend their love, their confidence, their fear, upon the earth and the things thereof, to come here and to ware [3] all upon this one thing; poor bits of needy creatures that fall in love with the world and the things thereof, that are so toom [4] and empty, come here and fall in love with Christ who can furnish you all things whereof you stand in need. O! fools, that they are, who are tooming [4]

[1] Than.   [2] Weak, frail.   [3] Spend.   [4] Emptying; see note p. 17.

their purse, and yet, for all that, get no bread to stay their hunger. They are reproved for it, Isa. lv.: "Wherefore do ye spend your money for that which is not bread? and your labour for that which will not satisfy." O! that we could learn to set all our desires upon our lovely Jesus, and learn to find and see all that we desire in Him; as, indeed, all that we can think of is completely in Him. If this were known and believed, certainly we would not so much set our hearts and our affections upon other lovers as now we do.

"*And do count them all but dung that I may win Christ.*" The word that is before is not in the first language here, for the superexcellent knowledge of Christ, as some translate it, but it is for Christ Himself. It tells us this far, that there was no created thing beside Jesus that He was seeking, telling us this also, what it is that is the formal object whereunto the soul looks, and what it would be at. It is not the remission of their sins, or peace of conscience, sanctification, justification, or any of these things that are purchased to us by Christ, but it is Christ Himself they would be at. Look, then, if that be the proper thing whereunto your soul looks, to be in hands with Christ, John i. 12: "To as many as received Him, He gave them power to become the sons of God;" 1 John v. 12: "He that hath the Son hath life; and he that hath not the Son hath not life." That is the main thing the child of God desires to be in hands with, even with Christ Himself; to be seeking to have a full portion of joy in the Holy Ghost. But seek Christ before that. Conviction of sin may be sought for, but Christ Himself is more.

The losing of a hard heart may be sought from Christ, and yet Christ Himself is more, and therefore He should rather be sought. And look unto thir [1] two things, ye will see good reason for it.

First: See what the Lord's covenant says, "I will be thy God and God of thy seed." Abraham he gets that of God in place of all other things. Christ is the only treasure and the only storehouse that the weary traveller can look unto so long as they are on their journey.

Again, all these other things, beside Christ or without Him, they are nothing else but creatures. To seek forgiveness of sin, joy in the Holy Ghost, losing of a hard heart, &c., it is to seek the creature without the Creator. The learned call all these things *objectum quo*, but Christ is *objectum quod*. Christ is the only bolster whereon the wearied soul can rest itself. How little think ye would a soul sensible of Christ's presence, or His absence, be affected with anything that they could get, if so be they get not Christ Himself at a communion? It is good, indeed, to get the remission of sins, or strength to walk in His ways; but it is best of all to get Christ Himself. You know whoever marries a bridegroom they put a difference between himself and the rings, jewels, and other propines [2] that are sent by him to her. Now all these things are so, being contradistinguished from Christ Himself. They are the gifts wherewith He propined [3] His bride, and so should love Himself above all these things.

Look unto two or three examples of this preferring Christ to all things else, Cant. iii. See how many the

---

[1] These.   [2] Presents.   [3] Presented.

spouse of Christ had there to comfort her, and would not be comforted by any of them, but only by Himself. She was in her bed, and it would be thought her warm bed would comfort her, but it did not. Nor were there any in the streets that could comfort her, neither watchman nor virgins, but she says, "Saw ye Him whom my soul loves," so that she declares that Christ Himself is more to be desired than any other is. And Mary Magdalene (John xx.) had odd [1] company with her, five chief apostles. If she had been a Papist, she would have thought it better company to be at the holy grave. Beside these, she had the company of the angels and Christ Himself, but she took Him for the gardener. But all these could not comfort her. The angels and Christ ask her, "Woman, why weepest thou? What ails thee? Hadst thou not good company here, having the disciples, the angels, and the gardener?" But she says, "They have taken away my Lord, and I know not where they have laid Him, that I may take Him away." "A fig for them all!" would she say, "fra [2] I want Christ."

Use: If God would give unto you all created pleasures and big [3] you a Paradise of all created things, yet never be content until ye get Christ Himself. A soul that is sensible of Christ will be like one out of their own element without Christ. O! if thou kent [4] what Christ were would thou count thy cothouse, or some of thy world's goods, or a pint or quart of blood over meikle [5] to quit for Christ? Whoever does so knows not Christ rightly. O! to be in love with Christ and to love Him-

[1] Uncommon.   [2] Since.   [3] Build.   [4] Knew.   [5] Much.

self for Himself. That would put some moderation upon our sorrow when we go away from the communion, not having so meikle[1] faith, so meikle[1] love, so meikle[1] repentance, so meikle[1] joy, &c., as we would wish having gotten some sense of Christ Himself coming into the soul. O! sound may they sleep the night who have gotten this. Lord, send it to them who want it, and confirm it to them who have gotten any measure of it. And to this, Lord Jesus, to His Father, and to our Father, and the Holy Spirit, be glory and praise for ever and ever.—Amen.

[1] Much.

www.ingramcontent.com/pod-product-compliance
Lightning Source LLC
Chambersburg PA
CBHW032018220426
43664CB00006B/286